# BLOOD & BONE

# BLOOD &
# BONE

**JACK SHULER**

*Truth and Reconciliation
in a Southern Town*

The University of South Carolina Press

Published by the University of South Carolina Press
Columbia, South Carolina 29208

www.sc.edu/uscpress

Manufactured in the United States of America

21 20 19   10 9 8 7 6 5 4 3 2

*Library of Congress Cataloging-in-Publication Data*
Shuler, Jack.
   Blood and bone : truth and reconciliation in a Southern town /
Jack Shuler.
      p. cm.
   Includes bibliographical references and index.
   ISBN 978-1-61117-048-1 (cloth : alk. paper)
   1. Riots—South Carolina—Orangeburg. 2. African Americans—
Civil rights—South Carolina. 3. Orangeburg (S.C.)—Race relations.
4. Orangeburg (S.C.)—History. I. Title.
F279.O6S57 2012
323.1196'073075779—DC23                                    2011045349

This book was printed on Glatfelter Natures, a recycled paper with
30 percent postconsumer waste content.

*For Orangeburg*

# CONTENTS

## ILLUSTRATIONS

## ACKNOWLEDGMENTS

This book would not have been possible without the generous encouragement of the Department of English at Denison University, especially the glue that holds our pirate ship together, Anneliese Deimel Davis. Thank you to the Denison University Research Foundation and to Denison University for providing generous financial support for this project.

Many wonderful people read drafts and listened to me talk endlessly about this project, including Jim Davis, Gene Shaw, Maria Zeguers Shaw, Katharine Jager, Fred Porcheddu, Linda Krumholz, Bill Hine, Craig Keeney, and Michael Griffith—much respect to all of you. And to Dennis Read and Paul Thompson, my eleventh-hour team, I owe you both.

Noah Wood offered his excellent eye. Christopher Davis offered his excellent ear, transcribing many of the interviews.

Thank you to those people who helped turn a project into a book: Marcus Rediker (who connected me to a superb literary agency), the Sandra Dijkstra Literary Agency (Sandra Dijkstra and Elise Capron, have negotiated and cheered for me through all the ups and downs), and to my always awesome editor Alexander Moore, as well as Curtis Clark, Jonathan Haupt, Karen Rood, and everyone else at the University of South Carolina Press. Thank you.

Thank you to those who helped with the research, either in the archives or by connecting me to possible interviewees: Bill Hine, Ashley Till, Barbara Keitt, Erica Prioleau-Taylor, Buddy Pough, Clemmie Webber, all the Denison University librarians (especially Josh Finnell and Susan Rice), Craig Keeney, Ruthie McLeod, Ellen Shuler Hinrichs, Marion Shuler, Curt Campbell, Thomas Salley, First Presbyterian Church of Orangeburg, Jud Jordan, Ayesha Venkataraman, and Gail Martineau. A special thank you to Holly Burdorff for reading reels of microfilm and tracking down obscure newspaper references. Most important, thank you to Jack Bass and Jack Nelson (rest in peace), the better craftsmen.

I spent about six weeks crossing *t*'s and dotting *i*'s at the New York Public Library in the Allen Room—a wonderfully quiet place for researching and editing that is kept humming by Jay Barksdale. While I was in the city, my friends Katherine and Joe provided a roof over my head.

A special thank you to the students of my spring 2010 English Senior Seminar. Thank you for your open minds (and hearts) and thirty-two new eyeballs examining this event. It was a pleasure to spend time with y'all: Kristine Aman, Kevin Burdett, Joseph Butler, Hannah Daugherty, Eric Elligott, Lindsay Goudy, Mary Aurora Grandinetti, Angelica Guitierrez, Alex Hupertz, Christina Marino, Laura Masters, Tyra Owens, Christoffer Stromstedt, Leah Taub, Emily Taylor, and Eliza Williams.

Thank you to those who allowed me to interview them between spring 2009 and summer 2010:

Jerome Anderson ( January 6, 2010)
Three anonymous National Guard soldiers (March 19, 2009, and
    July 15, 2009)
Jack Bass (e-mail exchange May 15, 2009)
Dr. Oscar Butler (March 19, 2009)
Gilda Cobb-Hunter ( January 4, 2010)
Calhoun Cornwell ( January 6, 2010)
George Dean ( January 6, 2010)
Hannah Floyd ( July 16, 2010)
Don Frampton (December 16, 2009)
Henry Frierson (March 18, 2009)
Lee Harter ( January 6, 2010)
William Hine (March 20, 2009, and January 5, 2010)
Cathy Hughes (March 17, 2009)
Clyde Jeffcoat (February 6, 2010)
Charlie Jones ( January 6, 2010)
Judson Jordan (March 18, 2009)
Dean Livingston (February 6, 2010)
Bo McBratnie (February 6, 2010)
James McGee ( July 14, 2009)
Nate McMillan (March 20, 2009, and January 7, 2010)
Zachary Middleton ( July 16, 2009, January 6, 2010, and February 6, 2010)
Paul Miller (March 19, 2009)
Johnalee Nelson (March 18, 2009, and January 4, 2010)

J. C. Pace ( July 17, 2009)
Cleveland Sellers (February 5, 2010)
Ernest Shuler (March 18, 2009)
John F. Shuler Sr. (May 9, 2009)
Mike Smith (February 8, 2010)
Carl Stokes (February 27, 2010)
John Stroman ( July 15, 2009)
Ashley Till ( July 13, 2009)
Angie Floyd Vaughn ( July 16, 2010)
Mary Williams (March 19, 2009)
Geraldyne Zimmerman ( January 7, 2010).

Thank you for your honesty and your trust and for teaching me so many things about my hometown. I would also like to acknowledge the folks I interviewed at Kent State University on May 4 and 5, 2010: Carole Barbato, Timothy Moore, and Laura Davis.

I started writing as a teenager and was encouraged by many Sandlappers along the way, including several of my teachers from Orangeburg Prep. During the summer of 1994 I had the good fortune to attend the South Carolina Governor's School for the Arts (SCGSA), where amazing teachers such as George Singleton and fast friends such as Hayes Oakley taught me to accept criticism and to practice, practice, practice. SCGSA is one of South Carolina's treasures. Finally a well-known writer from the upstate named Dori Sanders gave a reading at the Orangeburg County Public Library when I was fifteen. I went to the reading and gave her some of my poems. A week later she wrote me a letter of encouragement, a simple act of kindness I've never forgotten.

I am inspired every morning by the constant motion and energy of my daughter, Amelie Jane. In many and important ways, AJ, this book is for you and your generation. Don't lose hope—another world is possible. Thank you to my dancing partner Ceciel Shaw—AJ's infinitely patient mother. Ceciel, your support and inspiration keep me going.

To my family and friends, especially John F. Shuler Sr. and Jane Clinge Shuler, I love you.

Finally I would like to express my gratitude to the people of Orangeburg to whom this book is dedicated. Y'all raised me, and for that I am eternally grateful. A portion of the proceeds from this book will go into a fund to help those young people who would like to play sports with the Orangeburg Parks and Recreation Department but can't afford to do so. When I was a kid growing up in Orangeburg, running track, playing football and soccer (and one season of basketball) introduced me to people young and old, black and white, whom I might not have met otherwise. For information on how you can contribute to this project and for updates on this book and the community behind it, go to www.jackshulerauthor.com

## CHRONOLOGY

1670
The colony of Carolina is settled and chattel slavery established.

1735
Orangeburg is settled by a group of Swiss Germans.

1739
*September 9*
The Stono Rebellion, one of the largest slave uprisings in colonial North America, takes place fifteen miles south of Charleston.

1822
*July 2*
Charleston resident Denmark Vesey is executed for planning the liberation of slaves in South Carolina.

1860
*December 20*
South Carolina is the first state to secede from the Union.

1865
*February 12*
Union soldiers under the command of General William T. Sherman sack Orangeburg.

1924
*April 20*
The lynching of Luke Adams is the last recorded lynching to take place in Orangeburg County.

1955
*Summer*
A petition by Orangeburg-area African American parents calls for the desegregation of schools.

1960
*March 15*
Water hoses and tear gas are used on civil rights demonstrators in downtown Orangeburg.

1960–1963
The Orangeburg Freedom Movement holds organized protests.

1967
Martin Luther King Jr. speaks in Orangeburg at Trinity Methodist Church.

1968
*February 5*
A group of students from South Carolina State College attempt to go bowling at All Star Bowling Lanes, a whites-only privately owned bowling alley.

*February 6*
South Carolina State students return to All Star Bowling and clash with law enforcement clash, sending eight students and one highway patrolman to the hospital. Students break windows of some local businesses as they go back to campus.

*February 7*
Campus and community leaders are at a stalemate over how to end student unrest.

*February 8*
Nine South Carolina highway patrolmen fire on a crowd of students gathered on the campus of South Carolina State College.

1969
*May*
The nine highway patrolmen are tried for the shootings and found not guilty.

1970
Former Student Non-Violent Coordinating Committee (SNCC) organizer Cleveland Sellers is convicted on charges of "rioting" in connection with the student protest at Orangeburg on February 6, 1968.

1993

*July 20*

Cleveland Sellers is pardoned by South Carolina Probation and Pardon Board.

2000

*July 1*

South Carolina removes the Confederate flag from the top of its statehouse.

2001

*February 8*

South Carolina governor Jim Hodges says, "We deeply regret what happened here. The Orangeburg Massacre was a great tragedy for our state."

2003

*February 8*

South Carolina governor Mark Sanford says, "We don't just *regret* what happened in Orangeburg thirty-five years ago, we apologize for it."

2007

*April 26*

Barack Obama and other Democratic Party candidates for president debate on the campus of South Carolina State University.

*December 1*

The FBI announces they will not reinvestigate the shootings of February 8, 1968.

2009

*February 8*

Orangeburg mayor Paul Miller issues an apology on behalf of the city.

# INTRODUCTION

It was a chance encounter with a book on a shelf. That's all it was. Out of the thousands of books in the Brooklyn Public Library at Grand Army Plaza, I bumped into the one that had the most relevance to my life, to my hometown, and to my childhood. It was a chance encounter while I was living in New York City and a strange antidote to the dislocation I was feeling as a southerner living in a bustling metropolis—this despite the fact that my reason for being there was to get as far away from the South as I possibly could.

Here I was on a bitter November morning in 2001, strolling up Union Street through Grand Army Plaza (built in honor of the army that defeated the Confederate rebels), passing the Soldiers' and Sailors' Memorial Arch in that windswept place, which on a autumn day reminds you that Brooklyn is on an island and that the Atlantic Ocean is near. A glance backward toward the harbor once revealed, above apartment-building and brownstone roofs, the boxy peaks of the World Trade Center and the blinking antenna on the North Tower. Now it was all gray sky, the creeping entrance of winter.

I was thinking about writing a poem rooted in another historical moment, about some past event or figure, an assignment to distract me from writing any more about 9/11 and the falling towers and men and women covered in soot hobbling home up Flatbush Avenue. After I entered the library, I walked up the broken escalator to the second floor and wandered through

Facing: A road to the Canaan community south of Orangeburg County the stacks. Biography. History. Pacing back and forth, I scanned the spines. And there I saw it—*The Orangeburg Massacre* by Jack Bass and Jack Nelson. I had heard about this book in whispered tones when I was growing up. I remembered a few conversations about the event that led me to believe it was not something discussed in polite (meaning white) company. In the early morning hush of the library, I felt like a teenager who had stumbled across a dirty magazine or a secret stash of bourbon. Opening the pages of that book felt somehow scandalous. Should I even look?

The book told how on the night of Thursday, February 8, 1968, Samuel Hammond, Delano Middleton, and Henry Smith were killed by South Carolina highway patrolmen as they fled the scene of a protest in front of South Carolina State College in Orangeburg, South Carolina, a rural community located between Columbia and Charleston and the place where I was born and raised. The violence was the culmination of weeks of disruption over continued segregation in medical facilities and in a local bowling alley. On the Tuesday before the shooting, an attempt to integrate the bowling alley had ended in a brawl between students and law-enforcement officers in the parking lot outside the alley. Communications between the college and the community reached a standstill. National Guardsmen rolled in. Patrolmen loaded their weapons. On Thursday night three young men were killed and at least twenty-eight black men and women were wounded, most of them shot from behind. South Carolina governor Robert McNair expressed his sorrow but claimed the students had been out of control and had fired first on the highway patrolmen. He blamed one man—former Student Nonviolent Coordinating Committee (SNCC) organizer Cleveland Sellers—for what had happened. Sellers became the only person connected to the events of that week to serve any jail time. The white highway patrolmen involved were eventually exonerated. The victims of the event received no restitution.

Turning to the index of Bass and Nelson's book, I saw some familiar names: Earl Middleton, E. O. Pendarvis, Pace. Right there among the *p*'s I had stumbled upon my great-uncle, Uncle J.C., or, as he was listed in the index, "Lt. Pace." Now I knew why my grandmother never wanted to discuss the Orangeburg Massacre. My great-uncle, her brother, was a highway patrolman and on duty in Orangeburg that night—though he wasn't among those who fired their weapons.

What happened in Orangeburg was one of the first violent protest confrontations to occur on an American college campus in the 1960s. The first was at Texas Southern University on May 16, 1967, when Houston police fired more than three thousand rounds into a campus dorm. There 488 students were arrested, and one police officer was killed, apparently from friendly fire. On May 14, 1970, unarmed student protestors from Jackson State College in Mississippi were fired on, leaving two dead and ten injured. Each of these three incidents occurred at historically black colleges. But the incident everyone remembers happened on May 4, 1970, two years after Orangeburg, when four students were killed by the Ohio National Guard at Kent State University. Everyone remembers Kent State as a central moment in American cultural history, but few remember the young men and women injured or killed in the other incidents. Indeed, the casualties in the event that has since been named the Orangeburg Massacre, have been little remembered outside South Carolina.

I stood in the Brooklyn Public Library amid histories and biographies visualizing the places the book described. The hill in front of South Carolina State where the shooting occurred. The railroad tracks opposite the hill, running between Highway 601 and Boulevard Street. A building that once housed East End Motor Company, immediately next to State's campus. Today, if you face the railroad tracks from that hill, off in the distance to your right you'll see a rotating McDonald's sign. (When that sign was first placed there, someone told me it was one of only two rotating McDonald's signs in the world. The other one was in Tokyo, Japan.) Across from the McDonald's sign is Taco Bell, which was, I believe, Orangeburg's first "Mexican" restaurant. Down Russell Street is the Piggly Wiggly, where you can get amazing fried chicken and fresh produce, good peanuts for boiling, and bottles of Duke's Barbecue sauce, a local mustard-based sauce that is, more or less, the elixir of the gods. On the other side of Russell Street, about a block away, is the old Glover house, where General William Tecumseh Sherman once spent the night before heading north to burn Columbia.

If you keep walking down Russell Street, you'll pass the spot where All Star Bowling Lanes used to be and where I bowled for the first time in my life while on a Cub Scout outing. I don't remember how well I played. If I bowled then as I bowl now, I was very inconsistent—alternating between gutter balls and spares. What I do remember is that I got into a shoving match with another scout and had to sit out a game. The bowling alley is closed now and sits amid start-up businesses and storefront churches in a withered postwar shopping plaza. The parking lot pavement is broken, and weeds stick up here and there.

On April 26, 2007, just half a mile from that parking lot, presidential candidate Barack Obama sat down with other Democratic candidates for the first debate of the Democratic primaries. The Democratic National Committee chose what now seems a rather auspicious location for each potential presidential candidate to tell the public why he or she would be the best person to lead the United States of America: the Martin Luther King Jr. Auditorium on the campus of South Carolina State University, one hundred yards away from the site of the shooting.

It was a huge deal for Orangeburg. The municipal airport saw more traffic than it had in years. Television trucks staked out spots in front of the campus while reporters searched for a good story. Some found their way to the row of barbershops and hair salons across from campus, a slice of small-town life. NBC did a spot on the Orangeburg Massacre. Tom Brokaw interviewed Cleveland Sellers, the man who, nearly forty years earlier, had taken the official blame for inciting the students and prompting the shooting.

Almost a year later, on March 18, 2008, Obama gave a speech titled "A More Perfect Union" addressing one of the United States' most mythic moments—the signing of the Constitution, a document that he claimed "was stained by this nation's original sin of slavery." This history must be addressed, he added; the divisiveness of racism in our nation must be acknowledged. He went on, "if we walk away now, if we simply retreat into our respective corners, we will never be able to come together and solve challenges like health care, or education, or the need to find good jobs for every American." Obama implied that, by not addressing what divides some Americans, genuine reconciliation—and thus genuine collaboration—will never emerge. We are a nation, he concluded, full of "different stories" but "common hopes."

How can we address those different stories, those common hopes, especially within our collective history of violence and in our current culture of reprisal? Weren't the wars in Iraq and Afghanistan rooted in the maxim "an eye for an eye, a tooth for a tooth"? But this is nothing new. American history is replete with stories of revenge—revolutionaries tarring and feathering tax collectors, Sherman burning a path through the rebellious South, Dresden destroyed for the sins of the Nazis; the list goes on. We have canonized revenge narratives, even when (as in Ahab's pursuit of the great white whale) they have led to bitter failure. Can we imagine other ways to move forward? Obama spoke of the *nation* needing to interrogate its past, the *nation* needing to heal, but what about small towns, human and local relationships? Is it easier or more complicated to resolve differences with the people you work with, go to school with, and stand in line with at the bank?

In 2007, when the FBI decided against reopening its investigation of the 1968 shootings, some folks in Orangeburg breathed a sigh of relief as they were concerned about the negative attention such an inquiry would bring. But victims and their families, and many other black residents of Orangeburg, remain outraged, believing that their suffering has yet to be truly acknowledged by the white community. More important, they claim, local, state, and federal authorities have yet to support any thorough investigation of the event. The nation was up in arms, they observe, when four white students were killed at Kent State, but when three black men were killed at South Carolina State, the truth was swept under the rug by a sloppy investigation and a trial that skirted the mechanisms of justice. Without another investigation (federal or state), they claim that reconciliation is a pipe dream.

Many white folks agree that something terrible happened, but they say it was in the past and to continue to discuss it simply pours fuel on the fire of racial animosity. They say those students weren't saints and point to evidence that someone was shooting in the direction of law-enforcement officers earlier on Thursday night. They claim that as proof that the highway patrolmen were under immediate threat when they shot at the students. And some say that the students didn't really know what they were getting into, that outside agitators had them riled up.

In Orangeburg, especially among white people, what to call this event has always been controversial. In popular conversation, in newspapers, and in the historical record, "massacre," "riot," "shootings," and "incident" have all been used at one time or another. Yet Bass and Nelson's book set the precedent. In an e-mail exchange Jack Bass told me that "Orangeburg Massacre" was the accepted name at the time for what happened—among victims as well as among a small group of civil rights advocates. The name was a reference to the Boston Massacre (five killed) and the Sharpeville Massacre in South Africa (sixty-nine killed). Initially Bass and Nelson included quotation marks around "Orangeburg Massacre." Later—without consulting them—their publisher dropped the quotation marks. Admittedly what happened in South Africa was more extreme; yet Bass noted that Thomas F. Pettigrew's foreword to *The Orangeburg Massacre* points to the similarities between the two events—the social justice efforts that precipitated the shootings, the tensions in the communities, and officers of the law firing into unarmed crowds. "Over time," Bass explained, "Jack Nelson and I concluded that based on the facts, as a summation of what happened in 1968 and placing those events in historic perspective, the quotes weren't needed." But some white folks in Orangeburg still aren't comfortable with that name. They're unsure what to call it. Some don't want to legitimize Bass and Nelson's book while others simply don't think what happened that night deserves being called a "massacre." Instead they bounce around from phrase to phrase. What you call it says a lot about who you are and where you come from. What you call it can start an argument. What you call it is absolutely everything. Call it an "incident," an "event," a "protest," or even a "riot." Or step out a bit further and call it a "shooting," a "murder," or a "massacre." To choose a noun from the first list is to situate what happened somewhere in time, to make it part of history. But to choose a noun from the second list is to claim multiple responsibilities, to assert that something horrific happened; it is to admit horror.

Back and forth the arguments go. The wave rolls in. The wave rolls out. Each time the wave gets closer and closer to the houses on the shore, the water licks their pilings, but the houses still stand. Discussions of the event, and the many and varied narratives they reveal, expose the fact that race relations in contemporary Orangeburg hinge on addressing this issue. One need only read letters to the local newspaper, the *Times and Democrat*, peruse online discussion boards, or ask someone from the town what they think to discover that the varied opinions expose differences—of race and class—that point to the problems Obama addressed in his speech. The event, and how people understand it, represents the stalemate. And yet it also represents the promise of reconciliation and change. Orangeburg is not what it was in 1968—thanks in part to time but also to the work of countless men and women who have attempted to address the racial divide and persistent inequities.

In response to the release of *Scarred Justice*, a 2009 documentary about the event, the *Times and Democrat* published an editorial acknowledging the horrors of the night and also what has come out of that disaster. The editors asserted: "While Orangeburg may be no panacea for race relations, it is a community in which progress in building unity is widely acknowledged." The Orangeburg Massacre brought notoriety to this community, they claimed, but it also brought change nearly half a century later. Is this true? And if so, what does that change look like? And is it possible to foster an even deeper transformation?

When political or social scientists speak of justice after gross violations of human rights, they often speak of two kinds—retributive justice and restorative justice. Retributive justice is revenge, Nuremberg, an eye for an eye. But what of that other response—restoration, recognizing that revenge will lead only to more revenge, that to move forward one must understand what happened and attempt to reconcile? The South African reconciliation project is one well-known example of such a response. The Truth and Reconciliation Commission (TRC) held hearings all over South Africa, and those who had committed politically motivated atrocities could petition for amnesty if they were willing to disclose their actions honestly in a public forum. At the same time, victims of these atrocities could tell their stories in the public sphere, often for the first time. According to South African author Antjie Krog, "It is ordinary people who appear before the Truth Commission. People you meet daily in the street, on the bus and train." The TRC put such people in an empowering position—that of expert witness—and gave them a public voice, a restoration of human dignity and human rights.

Desmond Tutu, who chaired the TRC, later stated that the fact that the process was guided by principles of restoration (of victims and perpetrator) rather than retribution, is admittedly problematic. Some wonder if this is justice; for example is it fair to the victims of heinous crimes? Tutu redefined the term "justice," claiming that "restorative justice is being served when efforts are being made to work for healing, for forgiving, and for reconciliation." Only then, he said, can humanity be restored for victim and perpetrator—for a nation.

Reconciliation isn't always about forgiveness. It can be, but forgiveness is not a requirement. Forgiveness is an ongoing process, but it can also carry an air of absolute resolution: "I forgive you," meaning, I think, it's over. I've moved beyond the wrong. We're reconnected. But it doesn't have to be this way—reconciliation can occur without forgiveness. Then what does it really mean to "reconcile"? In moments of linguistic confusion I often turn to my abused copy of the *Oxford American Dictionary.* I'm enamored of its simplistic responses to my supposedly complex queries. Its definition claims that "to reconcile" is "to restore friendship between people after an estrangement or quarrel; to induce one to accept an unwelcome fact or situation; to bring facts or statements into harmony or compatibility when they appear to be in conflict." If "reconciliation" does not always mean the same thing as "forgiveness," then the last two definitions work best. "Reconciliation" means accepting something you'd rather not. It means bringing seemingly conflicting ideas or parties into a functional harmony.

The TRC in South Africa was not about "forgive and forget"—indeed many perpetrators were brought up on criminal charges based on the evidence presented to the commission, and token reparations were collected for some victims. It was, however, a shared moment of national unity and disunity. It was a learning experience, and time will tell if it was a successful one. Yet, in the wake of apartheid's terror, something new was attempted; there were no mass hangings, beheadings, or firing squads. The TRC offered a mechanism for consciously building a new collective memory for the nation: *This is who we are, who you are, don't forget it.*

After the shooting stopped on February 8, 1968, many of the wounded were shuttled to Orangeburg's small community hospital. The hospital's "colored" waiting room was packed with injured college students. Something had happened. There was confusion. Stretchers came in and out. People were bleeding. Cleveland Sellers was escorted away by a few officers of the law.

He cried out to anyone who'd listen: "Y'all see I'm going with the sheriff. The sheriff's got me."

Meanwhile a young doctor named Henry Frierson was busy trying to repair the damage, trying to calm people down and to do his job. A highschool student named Ernest Shuler (no relation to me) was in another room having buckshot removed from his arm. Across town Clyde Jeffcoat was still on National Guard duty several hundred yards away from where the shooting took place. Johnalee Nelson, the wife of a local Presbyterian minister and civil rights activist, was answering a phone call from a friend who ran a funeral home. The news was bad. Three young men were dead or dying.

Eight years later, on December 31, 1976, I breathed my first breath in that same small municipal hospital, a place folks now call the Old Hospital. My mother was exhausted after delivering an eight pound, nine ounce boy, and rested in her hospital bed while my father sat in a chair next to her and grinned from ear to ear.

I checked out the book on Orangeburg from the Brooklyn Public Library and spent the rest of the year trying to write a poem that would do the event some justice and capture the complexities of the community that raised me. The poem was a disaster—there was no hope or possibility in it, only horror—and in the days, weeks, and months post-9/11, that wasn't what I wished to contribute to the universe.

This book is an attempt, using T. S. Eliot's phrase, to shore up the fragments of that poem and an opportunity for me to do some truth seeking. But this book does not pretend to be an authoritative history of what happened in Orangeburg on the night of February 8, 1968. Jack Bass and Jack Nelson (among others) have done that work. Nor is it an attempt to set the record straight or "crack the case" in an investigative sense (as one editor told me she hoped my project would do). It is, however, a book that I had to write. I was compelled to understand the most complicated dynamics of my own history and of the community that raised me. In order to be as honest with the reader as possible, I've made a conscious decision to document and account for that history from my own social location—a popular move by many scholars in the humanities these days. Ultimately my desire is that readers will recognize how researching and writing this book was a humbling experience for me, a project undertaken in a spirit of hopefulness.

Not only did I wish to learn about what happened that night in 1968, but I wanted to see what had changed in Orangeburg since then and since my own childhood. (I haven't lived full-time in the community since I graduated from high school in 1995.) Is Orangeburg a different place from the Orangeburg of my youth, and if so, how? Trying to answer that question, I intentionally interviewed only people who lived in Orangeburg, with two exceptions, Cleveland Sellers and Carl Stokes. Throughout this book, I have let those people speak for themselves, allowing them to tell their own stories and believing that such authenticity is the best route to open dialogue. I know full well, that this is the first part of a long process, but the best way that I (as a writer) can contribute to it.

What I have found on my journey is not necessarily one answer to my questions or one shining truth. Instead I have discovered a complex network of stories. This book shares some of those stories about the complexities of history, race, truth, reconciliation, and forgiveness. American stories. Stories about human beings trying to get along with each other—to wake up in the morning and go to work together, to pray together, eat together, and live together. This is a book about how we remember history, about the future and about the past, about the promises and problems of reconciliation. Walt Whitman wrote a poem with that word as his title. It begins: "Word over all, beautiful as the sky, / Beautiful that war and all its deeds or carnage must in time be utterly lost, / That the hands of the sisters Death and Night incessantly softly wash again, and ever again, this soil'd world."

Whitman wrote that the word "reconciliation" is "beautiful," but that it is hard won. Reconciliation emerges after intense struggle, after "war" and "carnage," after two sides slip away from one another in a clash of blood and bone. The whole is ruptured but then repaired in the calm that follows as the sisters "Death and Night" forever repair the breach. Whitman's prescription is no simple solution; it is idealistic perhaps, but it is also a realist's vision of the endless work of reconciliation. This book, I hope, will testify to that ongoing and timeless work—the work of small communities and the work of great nations, the different stories and common hopes.

# PART ONE

It is a remarkable fact that very many persons are prone to study the history of every other country while totally neglecting that of their own country and yet the study of local history is one of the most delightful studies.

A. S. Salley Jr., *The History of Orangeburg County South Carolina* (1898)

# 1   THE ARCHIVE AND THE ARCHIVIST

I wanted to start with paper, with documents, with what makes me (an English professor) comfortable. So, on a warm spring day in 2009, I began research for this book in the archives at South Carolina State University's Miller F. Whittaker Library, located at the back of the campus, a good distance from where the shootings on February 8, 1968, happened. The library's archives contain newspaper clippings, oral histories, and papers from the FBI investigation. As I drove into the parking lot in front of the library, I noticed to my right Sojourner Truth Hall peeking up over most of the buildings on State's campus. The building is a student dormitory and probably the tallest building in Orangeburg. It had been a long time since I'd thought about that building. I grinned.

The summer after my first year in college, I came back to Orangeburg and got a job installing cable lines in dorms on the Claflin and State College campuses. I was part of a crew of four that alternated between working hard and slacking off. The two men who had worked for the company the longest were an unlikely pair—a white guy from the country and a Parliament Funkadelic–loving black guy from Orangeburg proper. Their personalities showed in how and what they smoked. Country smoked Marlboro Reds, and Funk always had a Kool drooping leisurely from the corner of his mouth. They were yin and yang, black and white, but they were as tight as

Facing: Present-day view of the hill at S.C. State where students were standing on February 8, 1968 kith and kin. As part of their shared leadership, they determined how long and how hard our crew worked. Their preferred schedule was to work hard until early afternoon, take a long lunch, and then, ever so slowly, pick back up again. These lunches could last two to three hours depending on the presence or absence of our boss.

By the second week of August, we had installed cable in more than five dormitories. Summer was dragging on as it does in South Carolina, but I didn't care. I was a week away from taking off and going back to college. Our boss was away quite a bit that week, and we were finishing up work in Sojourner Truth Hall, within sight of Whittaker Library. We had worked all morning long, drilling holes and running cable. Tedious stuff. Lunchtime break was called, and Funk and Country made a run to the Quick Pantry at the corner of Chestnut and Magnolia. It sold two pieces of chicken and a biscuit for $1.99.

When they returned, loaded down with boxes of fried chicken, Country told us that he'd found a way to the roof. So we followed him up the stairs to the top. He pressed hard against a fire door, and all of a sudden, nothing but sky. The last time I'd had such a view of Orangeburg was in the seventh grade riding the double Ferris wheel at the county fair. From the rooftop we could see for miles. To the west a storm was coming, but it was far enough away that we didn't care. We all plopped down on the gravel roof and ate quietly, soaking in the view. Streaks of white lightning danced over fields in the distance. Clouds shook and shifted. Green trees bumped and swayed. The roof of the tallest building in town was probably not the safest place to be, but with the low rumble of thunder and the first drops of rain, it was an awesome spectacle. The storm rolled in, an ominous and lurching monster with a whip of thunder.

For the most part, the FBI's investigation of February 8 focuses on the shootings, but there's also evidence of interdepartmental bickering, letters from J. Edgar Hoover to Jack Bass and Jack Nelson criticizing their book, and pages and pages of information with most (if not all) of the names redacted. Some pages are completely blank with all the information missing, a thin black line indicating redaction—the only sign that there was once something typed on the page. Like the contents of the file itself, what is legible and what is not is haunting, the blocked-out names of people (some living, some dead) who are of another time and place.

FBI reports from the immediate aftermath of the shooting are contradictory and set the tone for what I found throughout the file. Some "facts" about the night of February 8 are consistent: there were 100 to 150 students on the front of campus; students built a bonfire; objects were thrown (some students mentioned throwing ineffective Molotov cocktails); firemen tried to put out the bonfire. Officer David Shealy was hit by some object (a piece of wood, a board, or part of a porch railing) around 10:30 P.M., and then there was the shooting proper, which lasted between eight and forty seconds. Victims of the shooting went to the Orangeburg Regional Hospital but also to hospitals in Charleston, Florence, and Summerville. Apart from these "facts," the stories told by black and white witnesses about what happened the night of February 8 diverge so much that it's as if they were reporting on two separate events. The students stated clearly that they were not shooting at the officers, and they noted a lag time of up to five minutes between the moment Shealy was hit and the moment when the patrolmen began shooting. From the other side, for example, one South Carolina Law Enforcement Division (SLED) agent described a scene of violent chaos claiming that as highway patrolmen escorted firemen in to douse the bonfire, the students rushed toward them as "rocks, sticks, and sniping continued from the crowd." In other words the patrolmen believed they were in immediate danger, so they fired on an attacking crowd.

Many white law-enforcement officers, National Guardsmen, and firemen report hearing gunfire (or what sounded like gunfire) throughout the night coming from the direction of State and Claflin. But in postshooting interviews of officers from the Orangeburg County Sheriff's Department, several men claimed they heard gunfire coming from the campus precisely at the time the patrolmen fired. (The sound is described as a "Pop! Pop!") In the same series of interviews, one man wondered if it could have been fireworks that he heard. Orangeburg policemen revealed a similar confusion and reported hearing "the sound of shots from in back of the crowd." Another said, "I heard some noise which I thought were fireworks." Security guards at State and Claflin also gave interpretations of what they heard. A security guard from State said he heard "small arms fire or fireworks" but didn't see students with guns. He witnessed the patrolmen's volley and noted that their gunfire "appeared to start all at one time and ceased at approximately the same time . . . the shots were fired as if there was a command." It must have been extremely loud out there with students yelling, several hundred people standing around talking, and a loud pumper on a fire truck working furiously. Indeed one fireman said it was so loud that he couldn't distinguish any of the noises he heard. Can we trust any of the witnesses' reports on what they heard?

In a report from August of 1968, several FBI agents who were on the scene gave their own sketch of what happened. According to them, just after the fire truck moved in, Officer Shealy fell, and that's when the patrolmen fired. One agent said he heard what sounded like "explosions made by relatively small firecrackers or the firing of small caliber arms" coming from the direction of State and Claflin. He claimed that first the fire truck went in, and later he heard a "burst of sounds" and then "a volley that followed" from the highway patrolmen. Another agent said he heard gunfire coming from the direction of Claflin and heard bullets hitting a nearby warehouse. He claimed, "I do not recall hearing any gunshots fired immediately preceding" the patrolmen's volley. This gunfire, then, was either disorganized or, perhaps, indiscriminate.

Throughout these reports, the students are described as being hostile, shouting obscenities, and throwing objects. As noted above, some students were forthcoming with agents and admitted to throwing objects in the direction of officers and to even trying to make Molotov cocktails. A State security guard reported that, around 9:30 P.M. on February 8, he found a box of soda and beer bottles filled with gasoline and rags, materials needed to make such incendiary devices. Clearly some students were angry and afraid and wanted to protect themselves. After the shooting, a group of students went to a security guard and demanded weapons—but to no avail. What's more, the head of ROTC at State said that he came back on campus at 11:15 P.M. and noticed a car in front of the ROTC building. He went into the arms room and noticed that a cabinet containing six .22 caliber match rifles (two Remingtons and four Winchesters) had been broken into. By 1:30 A.M. all the weapons had somehow been returned to the room. The ROTC head immediately locked the guns in the trunks of two cars for safekeeping. There were other well-documented outbreaks of violence on the part of the students, and these are included in the FBI report: some students broke shop and car windows on their way back to campus on Tuesday night after the first encounter with the police, and some threw objects at cars on Wednesday night.

A natural question is was all this violence part of an organized attack by students on the white community or simply a handful of young people letting off steam? The FBI reports indicate that they believed the students had malicious intentions, and the agents turned over every stone for evidence that at least some of the students advocated violence. Yet aside from noting that a black power organization, the Black Awareness Coordinate Committee (BACC) consisting of some twenty-odd students, existed at State, they reported little that indicates that the students had bigger plans. The FBI appears to have dug deep in search of such plans. One note in the file pertaining to the period before Cleveland Sellers's 1970 trial in Orangeburg claims that a "confidential source" reported having observed a woman selling the Black Panther newspaper at State. Included with this note is a brief sketch of the history of SNCC. More than one observer of the demonstrations on Tuesday and Thursday nights claimed to have heard students singing protest songs, a throwback to the early days of the civil rights movement, not a tactic of black power. If the students were foolhardy enough to be itching for a fight with so many armed white men, why did they turn and run when the patrolmen aimed their guns at them? Why were so many of them shot in the back?

If the officers of the law felt they were in immediate danger, why didn't they use tear gas? Why didn't they try other crowd-control methods? One fourth of the National Guardsmen present had tear gas (a fact that the highway patrolmen apparently knew at the time), but they claimed they couldn't use it because of wind conditions. They had observed the flames of the students' bonfire blowing around. Weather records from that day reveal that the wind was blowing in a northwesterly direction in Columbia (about forty-five miles away), but there are no official records from Orangeburg. Yet a reporter from the *Baltimore Afro-American* claimed, "The fire became so big it looked like it was going to burn some electric wires," indicating that the flames were rising upward and not blowing one direction or the other. Could tear gas have been used? If so, the patrolmen on the scene would have known how and when to use it; all had attended at least one of the training sessions concerning control of mobs and riots that were conducted by the FBI for South Carolina highway patrolmen in 1966 (August 9–11 and 16–18 and October 25–27). Around the same time each of South Carolina's highway patrol districts was given several copies of a short book called *Prevention and Control of Mobs and Riots,* published on behalf of the FBI and the Department of Justice.

The subsequent trial of the nine South Carolina highway patrolmen involved in the shooting was held in Florence, South Carolina, on May 19–27, 1969. The patrolmen were charged under a provision of the United States Constitution that prohibits authorities from imposing summary punishment. The defendants—Henry Morrell Addy, Norwood F. Bellamy, John Williams Brown, Joseph Howard Lanier, Collie Merle Metts, Edward H. Moore, Allen Jerome Russell, Jesse Alfred Spell, and Sidney C. Taylor—were, the charges claim, "acting under color of the laws of the state of South Carolina, [and] did willfully discharge and shoot firearms into a group of persons on the campus of South Carolina State College, which persons were inhabitants of the state of South Carolina, thereby killing, injuring, and intimidating persons in the said group, with the intent of imposing summary punishment upon those persons and did thereby willfully deprive those persons of the right secured and protected by the Constitution of the United States, not to be deprived of life or liberty without due process of the law. In violation of Section 242, Title 18, United States Code." Charles Quaintance and Robert Hocutt represented the Department of Justice while J. C. Coleman (South Carolina's assistant attorney general), Frank Taylor and Geddes P. Martin of Columbia, and Julian Wolfe of Orangeburg represented the defendants.

According to the prosecution, on Thursday night, February 8, 1968, there were about 150 students gathered near a bonfire on the front of the State campus and about an equal number of lawmen: sixty-six patrolmen and forty-five National Guard. The guard had fixed bayonets but no ammunition. The patrolmen were armed. At 10:30 P.M. they decided to bring in a fire truck to put out the bonfire. A patrolman (Shealy) was hit (by some sort of wooden object). Students moved back to the campus. "About five minutes passed." The prosecutor continued, "The students came back toward the front of campus. As they came, they got within about seventy-five or 100 feet of the front of the campus, some members of the Highway Patrol began to fire their weapons. Some fired into the air; some fired carbines; some fired shotguns; some fired revolvers. Eight men, defendants, fired shotguns in the direction of the group. One man, Edward H. Moore, fired his revolver six times into the group. The shooting lasted approximately ten, fifteen seconds." Three were killed and more than twenty-five were injured. Most victims were shot from behind. Finally—and the prosecution was clear on this—there was no shooting from the campus in the direction of the patrolmen immediately before they fired. In other words there was no immediate danger or provocation for the shooting.

Then J. C. Coleman spoke for the defense. The defense admitted the deaths and injuries were caused by gunfire coming from the patrolmen, but the defense focused on the things happening in Orangeburg throughout that week. They argued that a "state of extreme emergency" in Orangeburg had warranted the calling in of the National Guard as well as many police and sheriff's deputies—it was "a highly dangerous, explosive, a riotous situation." Coleman said that "this situation built up, and built up and built up until on Thursday night between 10:30 and 11:00 a line of squads of state highway patrolmen were faced with several hundred persons thundering at them, coming at them, charging, hurling brickbats, hurling pieces of concrete. Our evidence will show that there was shooting at the time from that group; and that there was nothing else that these state highway patrolmen, who did fire these arms, whoever they were, in defense of their own lives and the defense of other persons immediately in the vicinity; and more important than that even, in the defense of the entire population of Orangeburg." These two opening statements not only reveal the concerns of that historical and cultural moment—the fear of outsiders in small-town America, the South in the midst of a transformation—but they also represent two different worldviews bumping into each other in a southern courtroom.

Warren Koon, a reporter for the *Charleston Evening Post,* was the first on the witness stand. He noted that the patrolmen fired four or five minutes after Shealy got hit but also claimed that he heard small-arms fire coming from the campus earlier in the evening. Koon says he saw two "fire brands," objects that burned in the street. (Others have said the students were lighting toilet paper and throwing it.) But the most revealing part of Quaintance's questioning of this witness has to do with photographs that the prosecution had entered into evidence. The photographs depict patrolmen at the corner of Highway 601 and Russell Street, National Guardsmen standing around, firemen putting out the bonfire, and Koon standing near a patrol car that was preparing to take Officer Shealy to the hospital. Quaintance asked Koon if he felt he was in danger standing out there in the open with the protesting students close by. The witness replied that he did not.

This line of questioning gets to the heart of the issue: were the patrolmen faced with any clear and present danger? Were the highway patrolmen, government officials, firemen, National Guardsmen, and reporters—all hanging out opposite the students—in any danger? Koon, a man who served as a marine in World War II at Guadalcanal, Okinawa, and Guam—who had been shot at and, he said, hit on occasion—did not believe there was gunfire coming from the direction of the college prior to the patrolmen's shooting. But on cross-examination Koon noted that there was a lot of noise and that he couldn't be absolutely sure. In all about thirty-six witnesses said they didn't hear gunfire coming from campus right before the shooting, including several highway patrolmen, two soldiers, and FBI agent Charles DeFord.

Indeed much of the testimony focused on whether or not gunfire was coming from the campus and when it was or was not heard by witnesses. DeFord said he heard small-arms fire coming from the campuses, but he didn't recall, as other witnesses did, getting down when the shooting started. Two expert witnesses said that slugs found in the warehouse during the investigation came from the direction of students, but an "FBI crime lab expert from Washington contradicted the testimony." CBS cameraman Reginald

Smith said he heard shots throughout the night when he was standing by the Esso station near the railroad depot and by the warehouse. But Smith claimed he didn't hear any shots fired from the campus for about twenty minutes before the patrolmen fired their weapons. He did see the bonfire and the fire truck brought in to put it out. He did see Officer Shealy being carried away after being hit by some object. Then he saw an African American reporter from Baltimore escorted off campus by several patrolmen. After some time elapsed, the patrolmen moved up the hill and began shooting—it sounded like a "small war," he said. Yet we'll never know how many rounds were actually fired. A local photographer, Cecil Williams, picked up some shells and turned them over about three months later, but where the others went remains a mystery—they never showed up in court. The only real evidence that the nine patrolmen fired was their signed statements to that fact.

The prosecution concluded that there was no real danger for the lawmen while the defense insisted that there was. The defense's case focused not only on the night of February 8 but on surrounding events and on the role of Cleveland Sellers. The presiding judge, Robert Martin, told the jury to answer two questions: "did the defendants believe they were in imminent danger when they opened fire, and would a person of 'ordinary prudence, firmness, and courage' have believed himself to be in imminent danger under similar circumstances?" If yes, the patrolmen acted in self-defense, and they should be acquitted. This was not Martin's first high-profile case. In 1947 he had presided over the trial of the men accused of murdering South Carolina's last known lynching victim, Willie Earle. When they were not convicted, Martin famously walked out in disgust without observing the custom of thanking the jury for its service in upholding the democratic institution of the court. Martin's bold actions were duly noted and lauded far and wide. Twenty-two years later Judge Martin awaited another high-profile verdict, and after one hour and forty-two minutes, it was presented to the court. A jury of ten white people and two African Americans acquitted the nine accused officers. This time Judge Martin showed no sign of disgust with the jury's verdict.

There were other lawsuits, other trials, and other juries. One civil action, with William Bender from the Law Center for Constitutional Rights acting as plaintiff, attempted to put Orangeburg police under federal control, arguing that black people had been under "systematic violence" for years in Orangeburg. But U.S. District Judge Robert Hemphill ruled that the plaintiff didn't produce any evidence that city officials were responsible for what happened. The parents of Hammond, Middleton, and Smith filed a suit against Chief Highway Patrol Commissioner Silas N. Pearman in December 1968, claiming that the patrolmen worked on behalf of the commissioner. None of these cases went anywhere.

The only trial related to the shootings that resulted in a conviction was that of Cleveland Sellers. On September 28, 1970, Sellers was convicted on the charge of rioting and sentenced to serve one year in prison and pay a $250 fine, the maximum sentence for such charges. These charges were related to events in the parking lot next to the All Star Bowling Lanes on the night of Tuesday, February 6, 1968. Witnesses testified that Sellers was walking around talking to students, riling them up, and that at one point he stood on the back of a car and shouted, "Burn, baby, burn!" while pointing at the A&P grocery store adjacent to the bowling alley. The FBI and local authorities were concerned there would be "riots or demonstrations" connected to his trial. At one point about one hundred students showed up, but they were fairly quiet as they stood around outside the courthouse. There were no riots and no major demonstrations. In the end Sellers served seven months of his sentence.

Reading through the FBI's investigation materials, which contain no summary of findings, and the Florence trial transcript left me with more questions than when I started. If someone was shooting from either the campus of South Carolina State or Claflin, did anyone try to find the person responsible? Nothing from the FBI investigation gives any indication that any law-enforcement officers went in pursuit of the shooter. Even if someone were firing a small-caliber gun, was it necessary for the police to load their weapons with buckshot? Couldn't they have used tear gas? The students needed to blow off steam, so why didn't the city allow a march? Why didn't the college organize a rally or bring in a heavy-hitter speaker or attorneys to talk to students, to investigate what happened Tuesday night at the bowling alley, or to help plan a way forward? Why didn't anyone formally acknowledge the students' complaints?

Those complaints and the obvious tensions in the community were seemingly relegated to the dustbins of history, to the archives of South Carolina State University. The case was apparently settled. An editorial published in *Times and Democrat* on May 29, 1969, said as much: "We hope that the great majority of the white and black people of Orangeburg and the state, particularly the students, will accept the verdict by the jury as a manifestation of democratic justice. We hope that future racial understanding and relations will continue to improve and that the bitter memories of the night of February 8, 1968, will fade away. We consider the case now closed." But the case was far from closed. That night lived on in the stories of those who were there, those who lived and worked in Orangeburg then, and those who still try to understand what happened and why it happened. What you don't get from the FBI investigation or from the court transcript, are these people, their stories, and their history. You don't get the people of Orangeburg at all. Their sorrow, their biases, and their anger—all that is buried beneath inter-departmental memos, elevation drawings, petty squabbles between Hoover and his minions, Hoover's rants to Jack Bass, wind-direction charts, sketches of the train tracks in front of the campus, photocopied pictures, redacted names of people, many of whom have long since passed away. After sifting through the debris of that investigation, I understood that I had to talk to Orangeburg.

South Carolina State archivist Ashley Till is proud of the university's collections, which include—among other things—the papers of Congressman James Clyburn (a 1961 graduate of S.C. State) and college records dating back to its inception in 1896. When I was finishing up work in the archives one day, Till started talking about them. "We have the minutes from the first board meeting all the way up the present. And we can tell you who the students were from then on," she said, with an excitement that told me she's a true librarian. "But I'm most proud of our collection on the Orangeburg Massacre, and I wish more folks from Orangeburg would come look at it. I think it would help—people need to see this stuff to know what really happened. I think it would help Orangeburg. Lord knows, it needs some help."

Ashley Till knows what she's talking about. She grew up in Orangeburg. Her family is from Orangeburg. And her schoolteacher mother was always committed to the community and to public education—to helping Orangeburg. This, Till told me, made a deep impression on her as a child. When it came time for young Ashley to start school in Orangeburg, there was no question that she'd be going to a public school, despite the fact that many white families pursued other avenues to education—private school, home school, or school in other predominantly white districts. Till's mother would have none of that. Ashley Till began her education in a public elementary school and graduated from a public high school.

After high school, she attended Emory in Atlanta and lived out west for a while, but came back to Orangeburg to be closer to her family and to work at South Carolina State in a job that intrigues and delights her. But being a white librarian at this historically black college has been complicated. She feels a lot of pressure from white people in the community. They ask her constantly, "Why are you at State? Why would you want to work *there?*" What concerns her is that anyone would ask her that at all. Why not work at State? She's an archivist. This is what she's trained to do. Where some see a problem, she sees an opportunity.

She's been responding to such bias-infused questions most of her life. And meeting her, one wonders who would have the courage to ask them in her presence: Till is small in size but comes with a mountain-sized will. She never gives an inch, and she'll be glad to take a mile. She's confident almost to a fault, but she needs to be. She has a tough row to hoe as an anomaly in a divided community. She all but fell over when I said that I think the town has changed quite a bit from when I was growing up. "Where?" she asked with defiance. "'Cause I don't see it." Till pointed out that Orangeburg is a black community with all the trappings of a white community clinging to the plantation myth. Look around, she said—the stretch of Highway 301 that runs through Orangeburg is named after proslavery advocate John C. Calhoun. There's a monument to the Confederacy smack dab in the middle of the town square. "Obama won in Orangeburg, but we have a Confederate soldier in the town square?"

"But it's heritage, right?"

"But what about the rest of the town's heritage?" When Till was growing up, she doesn't remember slavery ever being brought up. She does remember being confused—not understanding why, since this happened so long ago, there was still so much hatred, so much anger. "I also thought it must be very hard for black people to like white people. I mean, how would you ever, really?"

She told me she's glad when she sees that history recovered and her students engaging with that history, some of them for the first time. A while back there was a lecture here on the Gullah people, a culture and language developed by slaves and their descendants on the Sea Islands off the coast of South Carolina and Georgia. One woman who had graduated from State discussed how she had traced her family's history back to Sierra Leone and explained the relationship between that part of West Africa to the Gullah culture and to South Carolina. Many students at State are from parts of the state where the Gullah language and culture doggedly persist; they were mesmerized. "They couldn't stop asking questions! They'd say they were ashamed of their accent and how they tried to lose it, but it had never occurred to them before that connection. It's putting pieces together . . . making that connection of who I am and where I'm from. That my family is from West Africa."

Despite (or because of) this history, Till insists on progress, but she's not sure there's much hope for Orangeburg. "I think Orangeburg's an anomaly. And I don't understand why anyone would want to live here if they're not from here because I think the history here is so complex." This history has shaped how folks relate to one another, how they see each other and do not. She remembers going to dinner at Shoney's in high school with a couple of black friends, and the hostess seated her and the other white person in her group, leaving her black friends behind. The assumption was that they couldn't possibly be together. Some folks' racism is just below the surface, but such subtle actions and gestures are dead giveaways. "Friends that come here who are black, from California and other places, comment on this attitude . . . you could call it."

"Like white people talk differently to them?"

"Yeah, well, or for instance, the use of the 'N' word. That's a word I don't allow to be used around me but I've had to tell people that. I've had to *tell* people, 'You're not welcome in my home if you use that word.' [Some white] people my age still see themselves as separate from the black community and think that it's still okay to use language like that."

This is learned behavior, she told me, acquired by young people who don't go to school together, play together, or hang out together, and by institutions that foster that separation. "I think the private schools in Orangeburg are ridiculous," she said. Because they exist, she believes, there's no community commitment to public education. She's proud to have gone to public schools but recognizes that it made her social life tricky. "I felt alienated from the white community. I never had friends at my church because I was the 'public school' girl. All of my friends from first grade on were black, and when I had birthday parties all my friends that came over were black."

Till doesn't feel that much has changed since those birthday parties. Orangeburg frustrates her, and she wouldn't be here if not for her family and her career. But she's a cynical idealist—always working to effect change but pragmatic about how much change she can effect. In order to maintain her sanity while living in the community, she stays involved. She's active with an organization that combats domestic abuse and with a multigenerational women's group called Discourse Divas, made up mostly of retired schoolteachers from a variety of backgrounds. "It's a mixed crowd. There are black, white, and Filipino women." They talk about everything. They go out to dinner together in order to make a statement. "How often do you see that? An integrated table at a restaurant? We go to places to be seen and go as a group. I think that's one of the things that changes people." She stays involved, she said, because she doesn't believe in complaining. Till's mantra, it seems, is that if you want something to change, then you have to get off your ass and make that change.

Something that she hopes to have a hand in changing is the public understanding of what happened at South Carolina State on February 8, 1968. "You can read about something, but unless you've experienced and you were there then it's really hard to know. That's why with the Orangeburg Massacre we need to get out in the community and talk about it. What white people thought—it's okay. Just say it. Or what black people were thinking. We need to get a dialogue going." She's well acquainted with public discussions about difficult topics. She saw the whole nation of South Africa stop in its tracks for the Truth and Reconciliation Commission hearings when she was studying there in college. "I've always thought a truth commission would be a good idea here. But that means that there would have to be a true dialogue." A state investigation is still warranted, and she's not giving up on the idea because it's an important one, especially for the families. But in South Africa, the public hearings exposed victims and their families to what really happened and were an important step toward closure. She wonders whether the victims of what happened in Orangeburg have had that kind of closure. If this had happened at any school in South Carolina other than State, she told me, you can bet your left eyeball that there would have been investigation and heads would have rolled. There would have been closure.

"From talking to black people," she said, "and this is the side I'm coming from, there's anger. If it had been your child you would want an answer. I'm not even talking about compensation. What is a conversation going to do? It's going to get some of the hurt, the anger, the pain, out. People were treated in a way that's not right. Until we get some sort of recognition and validation of that, then there's going to be anger and things aren't going to change. It's not to blame anyone; it's to talk about it."

"But it was forty years ago," I pointed out. "Won't an investigation or truth and reconciliation commission make things worse?"

"They can't get any worse."

Walking out of the library and back to my car, I felt a deep dread about this project that I hadn't felt up until that point. I couldn't figure out if Till was being negative or simply observant and critical. And I couldn't figure out why that bothered me. This *is* what I wanted to do, right? Talk to people about what happened in Orangeburg in 1968 and how far (or not) the community had come since then? But I was feeling doubly depressed—the files left me with more questions, and my conversation with Till was demoralizing.

I felt as though she was attacking my childhood, my upbringing, and my people. And yet, what did that mean—"my people"? White people? Was she forcing me to confront something vastly more complicated—was this no simple narrative of crisis and change in a southern community? Was I and am I, a part of that community and, as such, a part of that community's problems?

I unlocked my car and sat down. I pulled my digital recorder out of my messenger bag in order to take some notes about what I was thinking. I turned the recorder on but quickly turned it off. I turned it on and off again. I couldn't think of what to say. I knew then that this was going to be a difficult story, more difficult than I had imagined. Not only would I be confronting my hometown, but I would be confronting myself and my own privileged status. I turned on the recorder once more and started talking.

# 2  THE BYSTANDER

When you're young, there are some things you don't or can't notice. You don't notice the social norms, cues, and realities of the adult world. At times you think that something must be amiss, but the thought slips quickly away, and you continue living in your world, whatever world that is at the moment. The past does not haunt you. You live in the present; you are where you are. As a child in Orangeburg, I gave little thought to the fact that few black folks lived in my neighborhood. They *worked* there—mowing lawns, cleaning houses, delivering mail, and picking up garbage. But they didn't *live* there.

In some ways things have changed since then, but Orangeburg still has its "train tracks," so to speak. Driving over to Ernest Shuler's house in March of 2009, to interview him for this book, all the way across town, it dawned on me what I was really doing—driving to the black part of town. I crossed Highway 21, Columbia Road, which more or less divides the community along racial lines—white people to the west and black people to the east. Shuler lives to the east of that dividing line and northeast of State College, off a muddy, pot-holed cul-de-sac that juts off Belleville Road. This is no middle American suburban cul-de-sac; it is just four or five old trailer homes surrounded by pine trees. One home proudly flies a green, red, and black African National flag. Cars and other mechanical debris litter the yards, the detritus of working-class America.

Facing: The old Orangeburg jailhouse, known as the Pink Palace, still in use during the 1960s

Ernest Shuler and I share the same last name, but my skin is white and his is not. Ernest Shuler and I share the same last name, but our material experiences of Orangeburg have been completely different. This is painfully apparent in the geography I have to cover to reach his house. That last name and the reason it is shared is a delicate subject that I'm not sure I have the courage to speak to him about.

I maneuvered my rental car around a few enormous holes and parked in front of Shuler's home, a modest single-wide trailer, white with brown trim, a gray Chevy truck parked in front. Shuler was standing in front of his house wearing a black baseball cap and a red hoodie with "Orangeburg Preparatory Schools" (the largest private school in town) written across the center. Limping, he walked over to greet me with a smile and a strong handshake.

His house was damp and cold and smelled of stale cigarettes. I sat on a leather couch and he in an armchair. Carolina wrens sang in the pine trees outside, and a patch of spring sunlight drifted across the floor as we talked. Looking at Ernest Shuler, I saw that his frame has been sculpted by work. His whole life has, in some way, shape, or form, been constructed by manual labor, bending down, picking up, building, making, cleaning, and doing. In fact he was coming home from work on the night of February 8, 1968, when he stopped by State College, despite his mother's warning, to join the gathering protest. That night he was shot in one foot and an arm.

Shuler was born in Orangeburg and remembers a segregated community. On Saturdays some blacks would go downtown to shop at the Winn-Dixie or go to the Dairy-O to eat curly burgers (hamburgers topped with pimento cheese) or soft-serve ice cream. They parked their cars, if they had them, in a lot next to the old jailhouse, the Pink Palace, so called because its stucco walls were painted pink and it looked like an old castle. Built in 1860, this neo-Gothic landmark was often the site of executions, public or otherwise. Today rumors abound that the building is haunted.

When Shuler was about six years old, he wandered away from his parents on one of these Saturday excursions downtown. Scanning the stores on Russell Street, he and his brother headed for the Kress Store, typically off-limits to black children. "We were excited to be there!" he told me. "And we saw some sling shots with the toys and of course we wanted to look at them." Then they made the mistake of picking up one of the slingshots. A white manager ran over and accused them of stealing. They protested, but the manager carried them to their father and told him what had happened. "My dad said, 'My kids don't steal.' The manager said he didn't care, that he didn't want us in his store anymore. But I had a good life, my dad took good care of us, but I always wondered about places we couldn't go." Shuler was politic as he brushed off Jim Crow racism as though it were a minor hindrance.

When he was eight or nine, Shuler began working in white people's yards, taking his lunch on the back steps. As he got older, he graduated from yard work to more stable employment delivering food in the hospital and working at the local Elks Club. He would walk from one job to the next, carrying a change of clothes with him. It was grueling, but it was necessary. There were five boys and two girls in his family, so everyone worked if they could. Each child was responsible for one of the bills as his parents were trying to save enough money to buy a house. Shuler worked, and he worked a lot. But he didn't mind; it was a way to meet people and to learn about the world around him. He even had white friends where he worked. But they never talked about race, never talked about segregation, the different schools they went to, and the different rules they lived by. While they were working, they were friends, but after work, about town, they lived on different planets. Shuler's voice rose for the first time in our conversation: "It made me feel pretty bad, but there wasn't nothin' I could do about it. You know? And as I got older. . . ." He trailed off, effectively ending that discussion.

Shuler graduated from Wilkinson High School, the black high school, in 1969. After graduation he moved around the country in search of employment opportunities and lived in California for three years, then Florida, and eventually New York City, where he stayed for more than thirteen years. After all the time away, he missed Orangeburg—the quiet calm, his family and connections. When he moved back, he went from job to job until he found something he really liked. "The last place I worked before I became disabled was Orangeburg Preparatory Schools. You know where that is?"

"Yes," I replied, "I went to Orangeburg Prep."

In addition to living separately, whites and blacks in Orangeburg, more often than not, learn separately. (Ashley Till is an exception to this rule.) When the push for integration began in the late 1950s and early 1960s, private schools catering to whites were created. Two of these schools, Wade Hampton Academy (founded in 1964) and Willington Academy (founded in 1970), survived until 1986 when they merged and became Orangeburg Preparatory Schools, Inc. While the schools pitched themselves as elite institutions of learning, they also created "safe spaces" for parents not interested in sending their children to schools with black children. In South Carolina this was a statewide phenomenon. According to historian Walter Edgar, "In 1956 there were only sixteen private or denominational schools in South Carolina.

Between 1964 . . . and the mid 1970s, nearly 200 schools appeared." Seventy of these schools (or academies) established the South Carolina Independent School Association or SCISA in Orangeburg, where its headquarters remain to this day. The organization was led by Dr. T. E. Wannamaker of Orangeburg, who also founded a chemical plant that later was sold to Ethyl Corporation and then Albemarle Corporation—a plant that employed many folks in the community, black and white. But Wannamaker was also a supporter of the White Citizens' Council.

Reading through the FBI investigation files, I discovered how important these schools were to some in the white community—at least two deputies were stationed at Wade Hampton on the night of the shootings. Wade Hampton and Willington were poorly funded, with teachers receiving low wages and parents paying significantly lower fees when compared to more established elite private schools on the East Coast—Wade Hampton was no Dalton or Woodberry Forest. (I count myself among the lucky to have been taught by some amazing teachers at both Wade Hampton and Orangeburg Prep, teachers who encouraged my desire to write and learn.)

But these schools served their purpose. For many years, they had all the trappings of entrenched segregation—especially Wade Hampton, the school I first attended. Wade Hampton's mascot was the Rebel—a bearded figure dressed like an antebellum planter, nonchalantly leaning on a cane and often depicted with a Confederate flag fluttering in the breeze behind him as it actually did in front of the school. When Wade Hampton and Willington merged in 1986 to form Orangeburg Preparatory, a debate ensued: what would the new mascot and team name be? Neither the Rebels nor the Patriots (Willington) would suffice as team names any longer. I remember the classroom discussion and some of the proposed names—Eagles, Cougars, and Rams from the boys and—from one girl—the Rainbows. I was a fan of the Rams. An upperclassman had stopped by our classroom and told some of us to vote for the Rams. Then he curled his biceps and said, "See, Rams, the horns on the ram are like my arms—tough!" We were impressed. We wanted to be tough. But the unified school board chose from all the students' excellent recommendations . . . the Indians. To my third-grade mind, this new mascot seemed innocuous, even boring. Ten little Indians dancing around. Thanksgiving. Pocahontas. But that Indian was anything but innocuous: the Indian resonated through the years and brought back specific memories for older members of the community. The mascot for the old whites-only public Orangeburg High School had been the Indian.

The merger of Wade Hampton and Willington created a school with about seventeen hundred students, making it the state's largest private comprehensive school. Today enrollment is about half that number. Many children attend private schools outside Orangeburg County, including Calhoun Academy in St. Matthews or Heathwood Hall and the Hammond School in Columbia. Education in Orangeburg remains basically segregated. In 2009 Orangeburg-Wilkinson High School (Orangeburg's public high school) was approximately 96 percent African American and 3 percent white. A year earlier Orangeburg Prep was 90 percent white and 4 percent African American.

In the 1980s and 1990s Orangeburg Prep was a quiet manifestation of Jim Crow. Though it expressly advertised that it would admit anyone regardless of race or creed, few people of color attended Orangeburg Prep. There were a few notable exceptions, including 1989 graduate, now South Carolina governor, Nikki Haley, the daughter of immigrants from India. But for the most part, this avenue of integration—the classroom—was effectively closed for my generation in Orangeburg and perhaps for future generations. When I attended, black people did on occasion appear on campus. For example once a year the Jarvis Brothers, a local African American gospel group, performed; it was the only school assembly I enjoyed attending. The Jarvis Brothers were doing the kind of singing I wished we would do in my church. The deep base of "Swing Low, Sweet Chariot" resonated in our gym. There I was, a privileged white kid clapping along to gospel music with slave roots, for the most part clueless about the system I was a part of.

The other black men who were regularly visible on campus were the custodians—the Ernest Shulers of the school. In dirty T-shirts and jeans, they mowed grass, mopped floors, and worked their way through my memories. But I don't remember ever talking to any of these men, don't remembering knowing their names. By the time I was a senior in high school, however, there were several African American students. In the high-school grades there were at least two—I'll call them Johnny and Cyrus. I imagine they were uncomfortable in their lily-white surroundings, but white students, as far as I knew, never openly questioned their presence.

Yet beneath the surface, as I discovered one day, resentment bubbled. Apparently Cyrus got into an argument with some white students at a football game, saying things they didn't want to hear—that the school was racist, that he felt out of place and was treated differently than white students. A few days later this conversation was brought up in my economics class by several students who'd been there and heard his accusations. Cyrus wasn't there to defend himself, and it seemed that the whole class was against him.

"I can't believe he'd say that."

"I don't care what color you are, I'll judge you by how you act."

"I'm not a racist. I treat everybody the same."

I couldn't believe what I was hearing and spoke up: "Y'all have no idea how he feels! How can y'all possibly know how he feels? Look around!"

The classroom turned on a dime from engaged discussion to heated argument. And this argument was beyond our just-out-of-college teacher's control: the entire classroom siding with the girl who couldn't understand how Cyrus would feel uncomfortable at Orangeburg Prep, and me, alone, playing devil's advocate. In my memory they are yelling at me—voices upon voices. I'm in the middle of it all, trying to speak. I'm sure it wasn't that intense, but it seemed so in the moment.

"Fuck y'all!" I shouted. Silence. The other students were aghast. About that time the bell rang, and school was out for the day.

A few days later, I apologized to one of the students in that class, and he admitted that maybe I was on to something. I never heard anything else about my little outburst. I'm not surprised, though. Now that I teach, I can empathize with that teacher: a charged conversation, growing frustration, and an angry student dropping the F-bomb. She never said anything to me, perhaps understanding that I was in a difficult position—in a room full of history in a town where clear lines had been drawn. But by no means was my outburst heroic. Johnny and Cyrus walked into that school building every day.

With delight, Ernest Shuler asked, "What year you come out of OP?"

"1995."

"You graduated in '95? Yeah, I came there after you."

"Did you like working there?" I asked.

"Yeah, I loved it. The kids were good. Predominately white, but I enjoyed working there." The school was like one big family to him. When he became disabled and couldn't do the work anymore, he was upset because he hated the thought of leaving that job. But he'd always known that that bullet in his foot might be a problem at some point in his life. He'd known since the moment in 1968 when he was in the hospital, and the doctor said that as he got older, the bullet they left in his foot could touch a nerve. And when it did so, the pain could be intense. That's what's happened. "I'd be working out on a tractor mowing grass and that old nerve would come in, and I'd have to stop. Or I'd be doing maintenance, moving tables or something." The pain became too much, and he couldn't work. He had to quit.

Shuler was coming home from work on the night he was shot in his foot and in his arm. He had a brother who went to State, and it was on his route to and from work, so he was always stopping off to hang out at the student center—playing pool and eating french fries, sometimes with his cousin Delano Middleton. (Like Shuler, Middleton was interested in sports and was an excellent basketball player with plans to play at State the next year.) But this day Shuler's mother told him not to stop, that trouble was brewing and he best not get involved.

Sure it was common for black people to come together to protest segregation in this community. But that night there were National Guardsmen stationed here and there, and tanks over by East End Motor Company. Things felt different that evening, she pleaded. Shuler didn't listen, and when he got off work at the Elks Club, he stopped by the campus to see what was happening. There was so much excitement and everybody was out protesting. He didn't care that he was disobeying his mother's orders. He just wanted to be involved.

Shuler went to the student center just as tensions were boiling over. The talk was mostly about what had happened at the bowling alley earlier that week, the meeting with the mayor, the fact they felt nothing would ever change in Orangeburg. And rumors were flying that a policeman had slapped a female student. Not a local student, but a girl from out of town, from "up north." This, he says, really got the crowd going. Some folks went down to the hill on the front of the campus. "And they built a bonfire right in the street. Right in the street, right down the hill. In front of us were troopers, and guardsmen behind. We were just yelling, yelling, yelling."

He remembers exactly what he was wearing—a beige suede jacket, blue jeans, and white sneakers. Everybody was yelling, some were even taunting the officers. And then he heard a bottle break, one, maybe two. "And then I remember hearing a 'click' noise. Click. And that's all it took. Next thing I heard—pow, pow, pow. I told Delano, 'Man, come on let's go, let's go!' I used to run track at the time, and he was a football player. So we started running. And he was behind me, and I heard him hollerin'. I went to turn around but bullets were flying. I couldn't do nothing. I had to run."

He was running in the direction of some bushes when a bullet hit his foot and knocked him down. So he crawled. That's when two football players who knew his brother recognized him and came over to help. They picked him up and threw him over the bushes and out of harm's way. Those two good Samaritans were shot from behind in the process. Lying on the ground, writhing in pain, Shuler could see through the bushes as patrolmen dragged his cousin Delano down the hill and onto a sidewalk in front of the campus.

The next thing he remembers is being in the infirmary, or maybe the student center. (He's not sure.) Wherever he was, the floor was covered with students and their blood. Blood everywhere. Somehow he made it to the hospital, where he was immediately recognized as the kid who delivered food to patients and whose mamma worked in the cafeteria. Because he was recognized by hospital staffers, he thinks, he was quickly pulled from the crowded "Colored Emergency Room" and put in a private room.

"They took the bullet from my arm, just above my elbow, but they couldn't take the one from my foot. Recently the doctor told me that maybe after all this, he'd be able to take it out. With the technology they have now, they can remove it." Most students were hit with buckshot, but Shuler told me a bullet from a .38 is still in his foot.

Someone from the hospital contacted his parents to tell them where he was. But all routes to the hospital were closed, and there was no way they could get to him. And then, in one of those strange and generous turns that will forever complicate the narrative of the southern racial divide, Shuler's father reached out to Senator Marshall Williams, one of the most powerful white men in Orangeburg. Williams served as a state senator for forty-three years and was always decked out in a suit and bow tie, a chewed up (but never lit) cigar hanging from his lips. He was almost a caricature of the southern lawyer-legislator. Calm and cool, Williams was known for making waves behind the scenes, not on stage. "My daddy used to work for Senator Williams," Shuler told me. "And so Williams had one of the sheriffs or whoever it was get my dad and my uncle and my mother and bring them to the hospital." Yet at a meeting of the White Citizens' Council in August 1955, this same Senator Williams had stood up and "encouraged 'every white man in the area' to join the organization." Thirteen years later, however, Williams was helping some black people reach their injured son in the hospital. A gesture of simple human kindness? An example of old school white paternalism, a sort of noblesse oblige? Or just another one of Williams's behind the scenes maneuvers?

When Shuler's parents finally arrived, he remembers that their mood quickly turned from relief to anger. "Man, they were serious! They were mad at me! 'Cause I didn't do what they told me to do—I was kind of a hard head back then. But I thought what we were doing was right. We didn't have equal rights."

# 3 GARDEN CITY AND PALMETTO STATE

You must know this: Orangeburg is beautiful. In the summer it is a lush paradise. Deep green ivy climbs oak trees draped in Spanish moss, while yellow pines sit sentinel over fields of soybean and cotton. And the din of cicadas provides citizens soft comfort as they sip sweet tea or cold beer and try for a moment to forget the humidity and heat.

Those terrible twins are inescapable. During the day you race from car to house and back to car and from car to store or to work. You're always getting away from them. But in the evenings the temperature mellows, and you can sit on a porch and listen to the fabulous insects and the occasional owl. Bullbats dip and rise over your backyard. You're glad they're around to keep the mosquitoes at bay. A Carolina wren sings its last song of the day. Light shifts west, a scrap of pink cloud. You might hear the rumble of thunder or the slow march of the Southern Railway crossing John C. Calhoun Drive and shuffling by Mirmow Field, where the lights shine on a summer game and fans sit on concrete bleachers, eat boiled peanuts, and blame umpires for their miseries.

In the fall cotton brightens the roadsides on the town's edges, off toward Calhoun County or toward Santee on Highway 301. Cold snow might come once every ten years to Orangeburg, but every fall the fields sparkle white with cotton. Sometimes traces of the South's fabled fruit will fall off trucks and come to rest at intersections or loll about Russell Street.

Facing: Railroad crossing where Lawrence Brown's lynched body was likely found in 1897

In the fall the leaves turn a deep brown and slowly make their way down. Cool comes in the evenings; yet days of Indian summer sometimes stretch into November. In the fall the fair comes to town as it has since 1910, and folks with accents you've never heard before cook amazing treats—elephant ears, Polish sausages, and french fries served with salt and vinegar. You wander through the old wooden fair building and get free pens and buttons from political candidates. (Your parents will tell you later which ones to keep and which ones to toss.) You race by the needlepoint and crochet exhibits to the display of motorcycles and four-wheelers. Then the double Ferris wheel beckons and gives you the glimpse of your hometown you've been waiting for. As you climb high above the pecan and oak to see the downtown lights, you see the grain elevators blinking in the distance. Above, so many stars.

Winter brings deep cold, brown grass, and bare trees. The landscape settles and rests like a bird in a nest—readying for the glory to come. Only the flowering camellia bushes give you hope through it all. The camellia bushes and the brave moon, steady still despite the wind. The cold digs deeper because you live in South Carolina and have never owned a proper winter coat. You wear your dad's old army jacket. You do the best you can. It doesn't matter because winter doesn't last long.

Then spring and so many azaleas your eyes hurt. Pink and purple flowers dotted here and there by the magisterial dogwood and its cruciform flowers that every churchgoing boy knows is the sign of the cross, the sign of God's love. But who can't think of God amid a southern spring? The yellow jasmine snakes across fences and bushes, wrapping around trees. And in the Edisto Memorial Gardens, thousands of rose bushes burst forth and give the Edisto River something to look at as it wanders by. Giant oaks, cypress, crab apple, and wisteria. Intense colors—green and pink and yellow and red and white—speak up to the blue sky and the deep, dark, and ancient river.

But you think about that river and what it has seen while passing through this land. That river irrigates the crops that feed you and quenches your thirst. It cuts deep through this place. The Edisto (originally called the Pon Pon) slips through eleven counties in its three-hundred-mile jaunt to the Atlantic Ocean. It is, you've heard, the longest black-water river in North America, the dark color coming from the tannin-rich soil and decaying cypress trees. The river connected the first colonists to the coastal ports and beyond to the Atlantic world. A bridge crosses the river in the gardens, and at that spot Confederate rebels last defended the town from the onslaught of Union troops. The defense failed, and thus slavery ended in Orangeburg on

February 12, 1865. But the vestiges of that pernicious practice persisted in the community, and the river knows all about that. When your parents learned to swim in that river, white people swam upstream and black people downstream. It would have been indecent for the two to swim together, or for white folk to catch the germs of black folk by swimming downstream from them.

Sometimes history reveals absurdities such as this. Sometimes history reveals horror, and then that river can look like a deep wound across this beautiful land. Fix your senses on time's accumulated stories and walk down to that river. Sit down on those muddy banks and tell your story to the wind and the moonlight; maybe the world will listen. But tell it—that's all you can do. And if you explain this history, maybe the sun will rise again over freshly planted fields.

The first white person to settle in the Orangeburg area was an Indian trader named George Sterling. In 1704 he set up camp in what is now Calhoun County and traded with the Santee, Congaree, and Wateree peoples. About three decades later, a group of more than two hundred colonists arrived in what was then called Orangeburgh District and settled on the North Fork of the Edisto River. They were led by a man named Ulrich Giessendanner of Lichtensteig, Switzerland. Most of these colonists were from Germany and from the Swiss cantons of Zurich and Bern. My own story begins here, as Shulers show up in Giessendanner's records. The head of the first Shuler household in Orangeburg was a man named Hans Joerg Schuler of Bibern, parish of Ferenbalm, in Bern, Switzerland.

Hans and the other intrepid pioneers landed in the city then known as Charles Town, South Carolina, on July 13, 1735, having traveled by way of Rotterdam. The folks in the port city must have been delighted by their arrival, as they had been for some time encouraging settlement in the back-country and had created eleven townships for any takers. The colonial government had set aside two hundred thousand acres of land for the township of Orangeburgh, named in honor of William IV, the Prince of Orange, son-in-law of England's King George II. (More recently a shopping mall was named after this prince—The Prince of Orange Mall, a hop, skip, and a jump from Orangeburg's Wal-Mart Supercenter.)

The colonists trekked into the "howling wilderness" to begin the Orangeburgh experiment, each family having been given fifty acres of rich Carolina soil. Most went to work raising indigo, wheat, and cattle, shipping their wares down the somewhat navigable Edisto River. Few Native Americans remained in the area on account of diseases brought by the earliest settlers to South Carolina, and many more were killed in the Yamassee War of 1715–18. Bears and wolves still roamed the swamps, and snakes fell from the trees during the torpid summers. Yet these minor inconveniences were far better than what Europe offered.

Some early residents may have first learned of the colony of South Carolina from promotional literature that was being passed around Western Europe at the time. In 1731 Jean-Pierre Purry (also known as Peter Purry) published a proposal targeting Swiss farmers. He wrote that the land in South Carolina "will not be difficult to clear, because there are neither stones nor brambles, but only great trees, which do not grow very thick; so that more land may be clear'd there in one week, than could be done in Switzerland in a month." It is "in general an excellent country," Purry proclaimed.

Because word had spread abroad that South Carolina was not that excellent or healthy, Purry took great care to address the naysayers: "Some perhaps will object, that this country is feverish and unhealthy, and all the advantages which might be found in other respects, would not make amends for the loss of health: besides, that you are plagued there with several sorts of insects, and especially with great rattle-snakes; so that you are in danger of your life every moment. To this we answer, that if people are sick there, 'tis generally an effect of their bad conduct, and not knowing how to regulate themselves suitably to the country where they live."

According to Purry, bad behavior produces illness. Good behavior and a sound approach to one's environment will produce happiness and healthiness. Purry offered this advice for dealing with the pesky mosquito: "if a house is troubled with them, it is easily remedied, by opening the windows about sun-setting, and shutting them again a little before the close of twilight, the muscatoes never failing to quit the house about that time." One historian noted that all one has to do is read Purry to see why "the Switzers must have fancied that province to be . . . the El Dorado of America—the second Palestine of the world." Purry's prospectus—and many others like it—may seem ludicrous today, but to struggling European farmers, Purry's Carolina must have seemed like Canaan. Indeed these were hopeful people who believed they could strike out into the unknown and find paradise.

Today, about fifteen miles south of Orangeburg, between Highways 301 and 21 is in fact a tiny community called Canaan. In Canaan the trees creep toward the road, and moss hangs down here and there while the alternating cool and warm air from the swamp disconcerts the visitor. This is the

Orangeburg to which all those ambitious colonists came—ready to farm and sculpt a new world out of the rich lowcountry soil.

Bill Hine was just beginning to understand this history when three students were killed at South Carolina State College. A native Ohioan, Hine arrived in Orangeburg in August 1967 to teach at the college. His teaching experience was limited, to say the least—he had spent the previous half year teaching high-school English in the suburbs of Cleveland. But he needed the income and, more important, he had recently passed his military preinduction physical and his status was about to be changed to 1-A. Moving to Orangeburg to teach at State was a quick way to get a deferment from military service in Vietnam.

"I was twenty-three years old at the time and kind of impetuous," he admitted when I first interviewed him. Besides, with his age and experience, he was lucky to have found a job, any job. Hine didn't know anything about South Carolina State College. "I was naive in my own way. I had never been in the South. And on top of that, I'm white and back then didn't know anything about historically black colleges, and certainly didn't know anything about Orangeburg."

Hine accepted the job on a Friday afternoon. The next morning, at nine o'clock, he got a phone call from the college to go over the details of his new position. Hine was confused as to why anyone would be working on Saturday morning; they must be putting in extra hours or something. And that's when he found out that State held classes on Saturday mornings, some starting at 7:30 A.M.

Saturday morning classes or not, Hine needed the job. So he drove down to Orangeburg in August, and that's when he learned about South Carolina heat. "I can't tell you how hot it was," he exclaimed, "and I stayed in a dorm and there was no air conditioning. God, it was hot!" But the real baptism by fire came when he began to explore the town itself. It became obvious that there were few places for students or professors to hang out. The town was, it seemed, a throwback. "It was stuck in time. I think the best word for it was 'gothic,' it was a gothic community."

When Hine met white people in Orangeburg they did their best to hide their shock at his place of employment. As a Yankee below the Mason-Dixon line, he was outsider enough, but in a community so sharply divided along racial lines, he didn't know where or how to fit in. He didn't feel as though he were a part of Orangeburg, black or white. Whites didn't like where he worked, and blacks weren't exactly rolling out the red carpet either. He walked the line between two worlds and did so carefully. On occasion he did go out in public, venturing off the campus in mixed company. But those adventures were rare and inevitably uncomfortable. During his first or second year in Orangeburg (he's not sure which) he joined a small dinner party at the old Holiday Inn restaurant on John C. Calhoun Drive. The group was mixed by race and gender, and their entrance did not go over well. It was clear that some diners didn't want them there. Some gave them dirty looks or complained to the wait staff; one man stood up and yelled at them from across the restaurant.

Hine remembers that at the time Afro hairdos were catching on, and some State students were becoming "very nationalistic." The spring semester of 1967 had been marked by a series of protests at State, which resulted in the early retirement of President Benner C. Turner. It was obvious to Hine that students were awake, aware, and thinking seriously about their civil rights. As on any college campus, there were also many students who were serenely apathetic, but they were overshadowed by a core group of students who were anything but apathetic. Among this group, said Hine, were veterans who had traveled beyond the South and were shocked by Orangeburg's persistent segregation and inequities.

In the fall of 1967 these politicized students showed up for their first history class of the semester, and their history professor was white. Many of State's students were products of the old segregated school system and had never had white teachers, so Hine was kind of a curiosity. But others, Hine told me, "were just distant or aloof and a few were hostile."

Given the sociocultural milieu into which he'd been thrown, Hine was assigned the rather auspicious task of teaching American history. "I still remember the book, a book by Avery Craven, an old Quaker historian in the nineteenth century, called *Experiment in Democracy*. And I thought the title was perfect because in Orangeburg everything was controlled by white people even though there was a black majority. Orangeburg *was* an experiment in democracy!" The book was devoid of African American history, a fact that Hine says didn't seem to faze most of his students, who were accustomed to American history books that ignored black people. He decided to supplement Craven's version of history with Benjamin Quarles's *The Negro in the Making of America*. Ignorant of this history himself, he eagerly read it along with his students. The history teacher was busy teaching and learning history during the first week of February 1968 as history was unfolding all around him.

There was, he said, a strange feeling in the air that week. It began with confrontations at the bowling alley on Monday and Tuesday nights. Students were arrested, and some were beaten by law-enforcement officers. The fact that young women had also been beaten amplified student anger. But no one sensed that things would end up the way they did. "There was cause for alarm but there was also a kind of strange lightheartedness that brought people together," Hine said. "It was like when you have a natural disaster, a flood or a big blizzard; it brings people together who haven't talked to each other for a while—it was sort of like that." Except for the fact that the National Guard was on standby and Orangeburg was in lockdown. No one was supposed to go off the campus. Bill Hine was a long way from Ohio and stuck on an island.

And then late Thursday evening, while reading in his room in Nix Hall, he heard some yelling and looked out his window to see people running across the campus. Someone shouted that students had been shot by officers of the law. He heard cars racing. More shouting. His first thought was that the campus had been invaded and was about to be occupied. Curious to know what was happening, Hine left his room and walked over to Hodge Hall. Outside he learned about the shooting for the first time and overheard some students suggest breaking into the ROTC barracks. He doesn't know if that happened, but given the vulnerability they all felt in that moment, it seemed like an appropriate step, he said. Soon the campus grew quiet as many students went to the infirmary or to the hospital. Bill Hine, like many others on the campus and in Orangeburg, went to sleep that night knowing that something had happened but not knowing exactly what.

In the morning he got into his car and drove to the front of the campus, close to where students had been shot the night before. "It was eerie. There was nobody around and I didn't know whether there were classes or not. I just didn't know what had happened at all. I had no newspaper; there were some things on the radio, but that was it."

Hine stuck around the front of campus, combing the scene of the previous night's violence. He came across several double-ought buckshot casings and an unexploded firecracker. An FBI agent showed up, and Hine showed him what he'd found. He never heard from the FBI again. Later the FBI and the state circulated stories that students were firing at the patrolmen. He wonders if what law enforcement thought was gunfire was only firecrackers.

Professor Hine spent another year in Orangeburg, but decided that if he wanted to continue teaching in a university, he'd need to get his doctorate. So he went back to Ohio and enrolled in the history program at Kent State University. Given this timeline, I didn't even have to ask. "And I was out there," he said, "when they shot four more students on May 4th of 1970. I didn't hear the gunshots in Orangeburg, but I heard Kent State. I heard that. I heard that."

There was an uncomfortable silence. And then, haltingly, he admitted that he still had a hard time dealing with what happened at both schools—personally and as a historian. The people involved with what happened in Orangeburg and at Kent State were friends and colleagues, but they were also part of the larger American historical narrative—a narrative in which race and violence chase each other endlessly in awful circles.

"As a historian, it seems to me, that you've got your personal life, but you've also got your responsibilities as an historian to try to depict the past as accurately as you can. So I know that it's one of those peculiar twists in history that slave patrols went out after slaves who ran away, escaped, incited rebellion. And the patrols were fairly active, especially in times of tension. And it was the highway *patrol* here in Orangeburg in 1968 that shot the students. So you go from the eighteenth century to the twentieth century, and it's still the patrol and the patrol was all white and the victims were all black. There's a tenuous connection there but maybe in terms of this state's history it's a little more than tenuous or coincidental."

If you delve into the annals of Orangeburg's history, you'll encounter more than a few moments of violence, more often than not, moments that expose the community's problematic historical roots. That violence began when African slaves were forced on ships and brought to the English colony of South Carolina. Unlike the journeys of most white settlers, theirs were not by choice. By 1735, when Europeans first settled in Orangeburg, slavery was well established in the South Carolina lowcountry, and it wasn't long before it became a fact of life in Orangeburg. Slavery first came to South Carolina in 1526, when a group of Spaniards led by a man named Lucas Vásquez de Ayllón came ashore near present-day Myrtle Beach. Among Ayllón's company of about six hundred men were about one hundred black slaves. The colony was short-lived because of illness, power struggles, and a slave rebellion.

English speakers brought African slaves in 1670, when the colony of Carolina was first settled, at the behest of the Lords Proprietors, a group of investors based out of London. The Lords Proprietors were headed by a man named Anthony Ashley Cooper, Baron Ashley (later Earl of Shaftesbury), who had recently hired an upstart man of letters named John Locke to act as the group's secretary. Locke, under the watchful eye of Lord Ashley, wrote the

Fundamental Constitutions of Carolina, the colony's first guiding document. Among its provisions for establishing the colony were several permitting slavery and a clear social stratification along racial lines.

By 1720 there were some 18,000 people in South Carolina, and 11,828 (almost 65 percent of the population) were slaves. By 1735 in South Carolina, there were roughly 15,000 free white residents and 30,000 black slaves, who spent the bulk of their time cultivating rice and indigo for export. Agriculture was big business, and slavery was an integral part of its development in South Carolina; indeed slavery was central to the colony's success. Thousands upon thousands of men, women, and children were kidnapped from Africa and brought to the bustling port city of Charles Town. In fact, "More than 40 percent of all blacks who came to North America from 1700 to the end of the colonial period, probably came through Charles Town."

For these "immigrants" the journey began through a series of terrible acts and personal indignities—kidnappings, wars, cross-continent treks, shackles, and prisons. In his *Interesting Narrative,* Olaudah Equiano described slavery in the eighteenth century as essentially an act of terrorism—an economic system that begins and ends in terror: "The first object which saluted my eyes when I arrived on the coast was the sea, and a slave-ship, which was riding at anchor, and waiting for its cargo. These filled me with astonishment, which was soon converted into terror." Over the course of his narrative, he acknowledged his genuine shock and awe, writing of "fears," "dejection," "sorrow," "horror," "anguish," "consternation," "despair," and "terrified Africans." The conditions on slave ships, he noted, were "a scene of horror almost inconceivable," so horrible that many preferred suicide to the ship.

The trauma of the Middle Passage experienced by South Carolina's first African Americans left deep psychic and physical wounds. It also fostered a sense of community and resistance. Slave rebellions were a common occurrence, especially during the 1730s. In 1739 for example, a group of slaves led by a man named Jemmy or Cato broke into a store about fifteen miles south of Charles Town, killing the storekeepers and taking valuable guns and ammunitions. They killed more than twenty whites and burned houses as they marched southward toward Spanish Florida. This rebellion, known now as the Stono Rebellion, was eventually suppressed, and many slaves were executed, their heads placed on pikes along the public road leading to Charles Town. In the wake of the Stono Rebellion, the South Carolina government established a set of laws meant to better control slaves. These laws, called the Negro Act, reinforced extant laws that were modeled on the slave codes of

Barbados, where many of South Carolina's first colonists came from. The Negro Act prohibited slaves from learning to read or write, playing drums, gathering in public, or moving freely.

The prohibition on free movement was reinforced by groups of white men patrolling the countryside. The slave patrols (and any white person) had the right to stop any black person (free or enslaved) and request his or her papers. Historian Robert Weir has suggested, "Perhaps here—in the perversion of the laws making every white man a guardian of law and order—lay one of the tangled roots of vigilantism and nineteenth century lynching." Colonists "terrified at what the large number of slaves might be able to do, attempted to terrorize the slaves into not doing it." This system, Jim Crow's great-grandfather, was rooted in terror.

As an additional precaution to prevent future rebellions, the South Carolina government wished to attract more white colonists to the townships (such as Orangeburg) that had been created years earlier. They were somewhat successful. Orangeburg chugged along, attracting more residents and with them more slaves. Orangeburg County, however, was not home to the enormous rice plantations that developed along the coast, and it was therefore home to fewer slaves. But slavery was still a fact of life in the community as it was elsewhere in the colony. As early as 1753, John Tobler wrote, "There lives there [in Orangeburg] a man from the area of Bern, name Christian Myny, who owns about 2,000 head of livestock and, in addition, many horses, Negroes, and other things." Myny was not the only slaveholder, of course; slavery was widespread, not just for wealthy planters with two thousand head of cattle. In fact, many families owned several "hands," as slaves were often called (signaling their value only as workers). And with the cotton boom, beginning with Eli Whitney's gin, came a growing number of slaves in Orangeburg and the rest of the state. By 1860 45.8 percent of white families in South Carolina owned slaves giving, the Palmetto State "the highest percentage of slaveholders in the nation." Those white families controlled the lives of South Carolina's black majority.

In this manner racism and inequality were firmly established in the social, political, and legal structures of South Carolina from the beginning. Indeed in early America the narrative of arrival and settlement is dramatically different for whites and blacks. This is crucial for understanding what happens next—the development of separate cultures, separate worlds. In the wake of all these oppressive laws and despite slavery, blacks in South Carolina developed a distinctive culture known for its foodways, Gullah language, and moving spirituals—indeed most of these songs were developed in the lowcountry.

Historian Daniel Littlefield has noted that in many places throughout South Carolina (as in parts of Orangeburg County) where blacks outnumbered whites, black people "created communities shaped as much by their own interactions as by their relationships with whites." The development of these two separate public spheres is integral to understanding contemporary South Carolina. Racial division and inequality were a fact of life: two worlds side by side, and one of those worlds had considerably more resources and power.

The first strike against the wall of legal racial separation seemed to come with the Civil War. White South Carolinians played a major role in initiating this bloody war by firing shots at Fort Sumter on April 12, 1861. The coast was blockaded during much of the fighting that followed. Few battles occurred within the state until Sherman and company made their entrance, at which time Orangeburg found itself in their torch-lit path. Much of the center of the town was burned to the ground, including the courthouse, the jail, a cotton storehouse, and the old First Presbyterian Church on Russell Street, a few blocks away from the future location of All Star Bowling Lanes.

Today at the center of Orangeburg's town square is a statue of a Confederate soldier, a monument erected in 1893 by the "Women of Orangeburg County" in honor of those who died fighting for the Confederacy. The statue faces forever southward, glaring in the direction from which Sherman and his men entered Orangeburg. The model for the soldier was Captain John S. Palmer, who—according to local historian Gene Atkinson—"at that time in the 1890s, had the 'shape and bearing of a man from the 1860s.'" The irony was that in 1893 many white men had grown out of the physical body type of the antebellum man but still retained his ideals. The inscription on the statue's pedestal for the statue reads: "A grateful tribute to the brave defenders of our rights, our honor, and our homes. . . . let posterity emulate their virtues and treasure the memory of their valor and patriotism."

You can still find traces, remnants of these so-called virtues, in the most unlikely locales. Today, if you hop off I-26 at exit 145 as you're heading south to Charleston or north to Columbia and drive down Highway 601 into Orangeburg, you will pass a community health center. Just after the health center, take a right onto a dirt road appropriately called Ruff Road. Drive down that road, and you'll pass a few burned out homes and falling down fences—remnants of old farms. Keep going, and the road will soon intersect with some train tracks where, in the early hours of January 6, 1897, a black man was found hanging from a railroad crossing, most likely at this intersection of Ruff Road and the Georgia–South Carolina railroad. The bullet-riddled body of Lawrence Brown had been left there the night before with a note attached to his blood-stained shirt: "Notice to all whom it may concern: Judge Lynch's court is in session tonight for the protection of our property, and by the help of God, he will convict and execute any man, woman, or child that burns or destroys property. We will protect our homes and property, and our neighbors shall not suffer loss from the firebugs. Let this be a warning to others." "Judge Lynch's" findings led to three bullet holes in this twenty-year-old man's back and abdomen. Conjecture-laden reports are found here and there in newspapers from the period, but the truth of what happened seems as elusive as a cool breeze in an Orangeburg August.

Some believed Brown was responsible for burning a barn belonging to R. E. Wannamaker and that area residents took the law into their own hands. But an opinion piece in the January 8, 1897, edition of the *State* newspaper asserts that Wannamaker's evidence for this claim was shaky at best. A short article in the *New York Times* posits that Brown's murder was the work of those who actually burned Wannamaker's barn, an attempt to displace the blame. While Wannamaker himself claimed that he heard a few shots the night of Brown's death "but thought nothing of it." Brown's family eventually sued Orangeburg County based on a provision in the South Carolina state constitution that held each county liable for any lynching that occurred within its borders. The family held the county responsible for the death of Lawrence Brown, but the local judge disagreed.

Like many lynchings in South Carolina, the details behind Brown's are murky. But lynchings in the state and in the South increased dramatically in the wake of the South's defeat in the Civil War and the freeing of slaves. A radical shift in social structure happened overnight—literally in some cases. During Reconstruction white people lost political power, and black people went about constructing new free communities from the ashes of the worlds they had constructed as slaves. But there was never any great moment of reconciliation, no moment of racial harmony or uplift, when white people recognized the humanity of freed slaves and set out to work with them to build a new South Carolina. There was only lingering animosity and ever-widening division along lines of race and class. Dreams of a reimagined social and political landscape were shipped away when Union soldiers exited the state at the end of Reconstruction.

Well before the end of Reconstruction, the Ku Klux Klan began to flex its muscles, particularly in counties in the upstate and west, where there were few black people. White people were on a quest to regain control of the state, and the Klan and their lackeys attacked anyone who attempted to protest their terror tactics. When the federal government finally cracked down, few accused Klan members were found guilty for the murders, whippings, and arsons they had committed. White Democrats wrested back political control was from black Republicans when Wade Hampton, a representative of the old-school antebellum planter class, came to power with his Red Shirts in 1876. "Politically and socially," Walter Edgar has written, "they intended to re-create as much as possible the world of antebellum South Carolina." Like the Klan, Hampton and company used violence and intimidation to prevent black people from voting.

At times ballot-box hijinks were employed. In 1882 Edward McCrady Jr. of Charleston proposed the Eight Box Law, whereby each voter had to know in which box to deposit his vote. If it went in the wrong box, it was invalid, a ruse to keep the vote out of the hands of black people. South Carolina's black electorate continued to shrink. In the last decade of the nineteenth century, literacy rules for voters played a crucial role in the political juggernaut of "Pitchfork" Ben Tillman, as did his racist populism. As Edgar has noted, "At the turn of the century there might have been about ten thousand registered black voters, but only two thousand to three thousand bothered—or dared—to vote in what was now the meaningless general election."

In addition to the all-white government in Columbia and monuments in town squares dedicated to the Confederate dead, the continued prevalence of lynching was the most obvious sign that blacks held little power in "reconstructed" South Carolina. According to literary critic Elaine Scarry, "Physical pain does not simply resist language but actively destroys it." In South Carolina the threat of being lynched, real or otherwise, was a powerful tool for social control—intended to destroy language, to destroy the voice of a community, and to disrupt any dissent from the social or political status quo. Between 1880 and 1947 there were at least 180 lynchings in South Carolina. In Orangeburg County there were 11 known lynchings (including Lawrence Brown's). Of these 11, 10 of the victims were black men: Lewis Kinder (March 10, 1880), Jack Williams (October 12, 1881), John Barnwell (June 22, 1895), Lawrence Brown (January 6, 1897), Charles Evans (July 1, 1903), Keitt Bookhard (July 11, 1904), Wade Tyler (October 28, 1911), Joe Felder (December 21, 1912), Manson Shuler (July 28, 1915), and Luke Adams (April 20, 1924). Orangeburg County was one of the most violent counties in the state of South Carolina; only Aiken, Barnwell, and Greenwood had more victims.

One of the earliest post-Reconstruction lynchings in Orangeburg was that of Jack Williams, accused and convicted of raping a young girl named Jennie or Linny Hughes. In response to his trial, an October 3, 1881, article in the *Times and Democrat* claimed that lynching is wrong, but in the Jack

Williams case, it might serve a purpose. Weeks later another article in that paper detailed his lynching on an oak tree near the Edisto Bridge: "On last Wednesday night a posse of men, variously estimated at from one to three hundred, went in a body to the jail, and in the silent hours of the night, while the whole town was asleep, took out the prisoner Jack Williams, and, carrying him to the riverside, hung him to the limb of an oak tree until he was dead. . . . It is said . . . that he was allowed time for prayer, and that he said the Lord's prayer before he died. The dismal spot by the dark and quiet river at which this terrible deed was performed, and the gloom and the silence of the night, lends a horror to the scene which is calculated to impress upon all a feeling of awe." His body was hauled in a cart to the courthouse with a note attached claiming, "Our mothers, wives, sisters, and our daughters, shall be protected."

The accusation of rape was all too frequent. Often a glance—or as in the case of Emmett Till in Mississippi in 1955—a whistle, could constitute rape or "attempted rape." Most such accusations were dubious at best. In South Carolina many lynchings appear to be the result of accusations of murder. Popular sentiment held that the courts weren't effective, so white folks took the law into their own hands, especially if the accused murderer happened to be black.

Lynch mobs did not always kill the accused; in some instances the accused was whipped (publicly or otherwise). The pages of the *Times and Democrat* reveal many incidents of vigilante justice: a black man named Israel Gordon, accused of making "indecent proposals" to a young white girl, was given eighty-nine lashes and told to leave town (November 2, 1887); a "colored boy grossly insulted a lady on the street" and was given forty lashes by her friends (August 29, 1888); Alice Thomas, "a negress, . . . was taken from her home near Norway and flogged" (April 22, 1924). In 1883 the *Times and Democrat* went so far as to propose a whipping post in the town square for punishment of minor crimes (February 15, 1883). Thus "Judge Lynch's" midnight work was sanctioned by a community both immune to, and supportive of, violence.

Over time, however, community sentiment began to shift, and by the turn of the century South Carolina newspapers were often quick to condemn lynchings publicly. On May 3, 1893, the *Times and Democrat*'s editors hedged their bets, condemning the practice while still managing to condemn the accused, the victims. The editors claimed: "*The Times and Democrat* regards lynch law as one of the most hideous things that can become prevalent in any land or among any people, but at the same time it believes that any monster, be he white or black, who ravishes any pure woman, it makes no difference what her color may be, forfeits his right to breathe the pure air of heaven and should be out the way as soon as his guilt can be positively determined."

Thirty-eight years later, the paper's editors offered another excuse for lynching, claiming that it's an expression of distrust in the government: "The laws in South Carolina are made by white men. The courts are managed by white men. The jurors are white men. There is no reason for white men to distrust their own courts as agencies of justice." In other words, there's no need to lynch African Americans, our segregated courts will do the job. But no amount of editorializing could change the reality in South Carolina: if you were black, you were always in danger of horrible violence perpetrated by whites without due process of law. This fact of life was made all too clear on February 17, 1947, when a black man named Willie Earle was accused of murdering a cab driver near Greenville. Earle was shot in the face after a severe beating by an angry white mob. Governor Strom Thurmond called for swift justice for those involved, but that justice never came. The thirty-one men accused of the crime were not convicted. An all-white jury—a jury, as it were, of their peers—found them not guilty.

For his part Bill Hine wonders if a better understanding of this long history of racist violence might have changed things in Orangeburg on the night of February 8, 1968. "Sometimes you hear about these brave students who demonstrated on the front of the campus knowing full well they might be shot. But, I mean, no one went out there with any anticipation that that would happen. Maybe if I'd had a better grasp of South Carolina's history back to the slave patrols or earlier, and I certainly didn't at the time, I'd have said, 'This is very volatile. It's night, white law enforcement, black students. We've got a recipe for disaster.'"

# 4 SPITTING AT JIM CROW

I was in the fourth grade when I first heard about the Ku Klux Klan from a classmate at Orangeburg Prep. One day he told me (and anyone else within earshot) that his uncle belonged to a club who wore white robes and masks and looked like ghosts. And when anybody, especially "niggers," did something bad, like hit a woman or steal money from an old man, they'd go to his house and beat him up. And then, turning to the group of boys listening to him with rapt attention, he told us in no uncertain terms that if we bothered him, his uncle would beat *us* up. How much of what he said was true, I'm not sure; all I knew then was that I'd pushed that boy waiting in line at dismissal a few days before. For weeks after his dire warning, I dreamed of mean men in white sheets coming to my house to beat me up.

For African Americans growing up in the Jim Crow South, the Klan was a reality, not a dream. In his autobiography Orangeburg businessman and respected civic leader Earl Middleton acknowledged the horror that many Americans felt watching the events of September 11, 2001, unfold on their televisions and then observed, "As I reflected on these horrendous tragedies, I came to realize that blacks in America have lived with terrorism inside our borders for centuries." Middleton remembered the first time he encountered it: he was twelve years old, and a Klan march passed by his house. "We watched from our darkened windows as they passed between our home and the railroad tracks." Ghostly figures walked slowly, rubbing the intimidation

Facing: Jailhouse door in the Pink Palace

in deep. That night they carried torches, just as Sherman's men had done decades before.

Earlier that day Middleton had read about the impending march in the paper and asked his father about it. His father responded with silence. In that moment Earl Middleton began to understand the significance of racism in the United States: his father "was terrified. He expressed his concern by his silence, and that made an impression on me." This moment stood out as a turning point in his memory because, Middleton explained, his parents typically avoided any and all discussions about race with their children, perhaps out of a desire to protect them from "psychological damage" or from the idea that somehow white was better than black.

Middleton's parents were also protecting their children from the very real threat of physical harm that Jim Crow posed for African Americans. In that sense Middleton's acknowledgment of racism as a grand act of terrorism is apt. For black people during Jim Crow, whiteness itself was terrifying and terrorizing and represented terrible possibilities. Through his father's silence, Middleton was experiencing the consequences of Jim Crow—generations of men and women who felt as though they weren't in control of their life choices. That they could be arrested on a false charge at any moment. That they could be accused of acting "all uppity." That they could look at someone the wrong way. That at any minute the Ku Klux Klan could march down their street.

Sociologist Ron Eyerman has referred to the experience of Jim Crow as part of a kind of "cultural trauma" that has had lasting effects on African American culture. This trauma began with the Middle Passage and chattel slavery, experiences that Eyerman claims are lived again and again as the narrative of those traumas are passed on from generation to generation. Compared to Jim Crow Mississippi or Alabama, there was less public violence in South Carolina (or at least fewer recorded lynchings), and thus the trauma may not be as obvious in this state as it is elsewhere in the South. Indeed the popular narrative of the Palmetto State is that it made a relatively peaceful transition out of Jim Crow, what happened in Orangeburg in 1968 being one obvious exception. But racial violence in South Carolina was not simply the overt manifestation of hate—lynching and Klan rallies—but the less obvious ways in the late nineteenth and early twentieth centuries that blacks were pushed down onto a lower rung of the ladder through the oddly elaborate social framework of Jim Crow.

South Carolina's Jim Crow laws began to take shape during Reconstruction, but it was the 1895 state constitution that firmly established a legal structure for them. A year later, the *Plessy v. Ferguson* "separate but equal"

Supreme Court decision, which opened the door for legalized segregation, was for many whites a ruling allowing them to take any and all political and social power from black people. Laws were established requiring separate medical and educational facilities, banning intermarriage, creating separate sections in theaters and restaurants (if not barring entrance altogether), prohibiting blacks from trying on clothing in stores, requiring separate recreation facilities, and establishing that most unholy symbol of Jim Crow—separate drinking fountains. One fountain for white people. One fountain for "coloreds."

An indication of the deep structural and economic inequalities fostered by Jim Crow may be seen in a 1923 study of economic and social conditions in Orangeburg County by two University of South Carolina sociologists. The study reveals that in 1920, 81 percent of white children and 71 percent of African American children attended school. White children attended an average of fifty-four days and black children twenty-eight. White schools were open about sixty-six days and black schools thirty-one; $26.67 was spent on each white child and $1.96 on each black child. The value of white school property in 1920 was $341,835, and black school property was worth $30,775. The average annual salary for white men working in the public schools was $1,030 and $510 for white women. For black men it was $197.50 and for black women $145.

Jim Crow fostered attitudes and customs that persisted, as far as I can tell, into the 1980s, well after the legal code that once supported them had perished. Many white people still believed that black people were below them, and this attitude showed in their interactions. More important, the paternalistic attitude—that blacks were to be pitied because they were not of the same social class or mental aptitude as most whites—was omnipresent. My father once told me that, when he was growing up, most whites were kind to blacks. They treated them well. They took care of them. They let black people live on their land. They visited them when they were sick. Baked them cakes. And with more than a dose of sarcasm he added, "Sort of like how someone would treat an animal. They were like the S.P.C.A."

This "good treatment" was especially extended to black men. Black men were the most dangerous of all and had to be reminded of their "place." My own "education" about black masculinity didn't take place only in school, it also happened at my grandmother's house, in the library, and at public gatherings. As far as I knew when I was growing up, there were two kinds of black men: great leaders such as Martin Luther King Jr., whom I read about voraciously as a child, and poor, deferential workers.

I knew a little bit about the great leaders, having met Earl Middleton and legendary South Carolina State football coach Willie Jeffries on outings with my father. They were the kind of men who owned any room they walked into. With his well-deserved pride and propriety, Middleton stood tall in his business suits and, I remember, gave me a firm handshake. Jeffries won me over with his smiles and generosity, making sure that a wide-eyed kid was introduced to the biggest, toughest-looking players on the football team. These men were in my mind the gold standard. But I encountered the humble and deferential workers more often.

For me the stereotypical deferential worker was a man named Leon who worked in my grandmother's yard. Some days he'd be out there in the hot sun, sweating buckets, a beat-up trucker's hat over a mess of hair, a torn T-shirt covering his slim frame.

"Hey, Leon," I'd say.

"Hey, Mister Jack. How you doin'?" he'd reply, the "mister" sounding almost like master—the two words colliding, touching slightly, but never making that much noise. It wasn't polite to talk about the differences between those two words in small southern towns. I suppose the "a" was replaced with an "i" sometime after Reconstruction by black men and women seeking social dignity and physical survival. This slight alphabetic shift was always greeted with a polite nod by appreciative white people. Those two words—"mister" and "master"—carried similar weight. And obviously a young white boy being called "mister" by a middle-aged black man in the 1980s was an action that reverberated with the plantation culture's racial hierarchy. To be honest, though, I was never completely sure what he was saying to me after that deferential greeting. Leon spoke with a thick low-country accent, a close-cousin to Gullah. It was so foreign, so unusual, that it almost frightened me. But Leon didn't really say that much—he just worked. And when he ate his lunch, he sat on the back steps of my grandmother's house. She would bring him a sandwich on a plate, a piece of fruit, a glass of milk. He'd tell her "thank you." The two would then exchange pleasantries.

Leon would wipe his brow. "Sure's hot, Missus Shuler."

"Yes it is," she'd answer politely.

They might talk for a second about the bushes that needed more trimming, the grass that would surely need mowing next week. Then she'd go back in the house leaving Leon on the back steps with his meal.

This is how I learned about Jim Crow and his father, plantation paternalism. The principal rules of these ideologies were bound to the long history of the South—blacks have their place in this world, and whites have theirs. Good white people take care of "their blacks." Good whites feed "their blacks." Good whites dole out work to "their blacks." But good whites never eat with "their blacks," never set foot in "their blacks'" houses, never get too close—socially, romantically, or geographically. When they do, terror may erupt spontaneously, as if the act of straying from these rules could set off an almost natural landmine. History, time and again, demonstrates this.

Earl Middleton always found this history and the system of Jim Crow quite puzzling. He wrote, "The 'system' was the problem. Individuals were our friends; the system was the obstacle preventing black people from being viewed as equal human beings. It can be argued that whites controlled this system, which is true, and that has long been the dilemma for the black minority." This system was in full effect when Middleton settled down in Orangeburg after returning from fighting in the Second World War. He wrote that there were two very different worlds in the town: "We had our church, our families, our friends, our work, 'our' stores, and 'our' side of town." And then there was the white side of town with its own institutions and decidedly more power and privilege. When blacks entered this world, no matter what position of authority they held in the black community, they did so on the white people's terms. But Middleton found a way over and through the system: he made money. Middleton started his own real estate business and became quite successful. Because he was his own boss and therefore didn't rely on the white community, he was able to combat Jim Crow on his own terms and in public ways. His reputation as a leader eventually earned him a spot in the South Carolina House of Representatives.

Despite this infernal caste system, there were white people who challenged it or cut around its unseemly edges. Middleton wrote that rather than focus on the indignities of Jim Crow, he wished to remember those white people in Orangeburg who risked a lot to do the right thing, the human thing. This, he claimed, helped him avoid feeling "bitter" about the past. Middleton recalled a local pharmacist who provided medications needed to keep a young black man, a hemophiliac, alive. The widow of that pharmacist, Mary Williams, was also active in breaking down racial barriers in the community: "She carries forward the spirit of love for all people, regardless of their skin color, that her husband and his father demonstrated during their lifetimes."

Mary Williams moved to Orangeburg in 1937, soon after graduating from Winthrop College, at one time South Carolina's state-supported school for white women, now a thriving coed university with an excellent basketball program. Two years later she married a local pharmacist, Sumter Williams Jr. At that time Orangeburg was Jim Crow. It was a vastly different place from the small upstate village of Shelton, where she grew up. Shelton was cotton and red-clay hills. It was farm country through and through. Twenty-five miles from the town of Union, twenty-five from Chester, twenty-five from Winnsboro, and twenty-five from Newberry. Today there's nothing left of this rural outpost, not even a post office. Back in the day though, Shelton was a close-knit community where everybody knew everybody. Black and white people alike were all a part of the hardscrabble social fabric of struggling farmers always praying for a better year than the last. In small-town Shelton, Williams learned some valuable lessons about what she calls "human relations." Because times were hard for everyone there, no one person was better than any other. They took the Golden Rule to heart. This egalitarian vision of the world was owing in part to necessity: for miles around there weren't many people.

There were so few families around that white children had to play with black children or play with no one at all. In the cool of the late afternoon, as soon as they'd rushed through supper, a group of children—black and white—would gather on the front steps of her cousin's house and play a game they called "shoo turkey." When I interviewed Williams, she remembered the game with a grin. "One of us would be the leader standing out in the yard while the rest of us sat on the steps. The leader would say, 'You been down by the river?' 'Yes, ma'am,' the ones on the step would answer. 'Did you see a black turkey?' 'Yes, ma'am.' 'What did he have around his neck?' 'A golden chain.' 'What did he have in his mouth?' 'A silver spoon.' 'Will you help me catch him?' 'Yes, ma'am.'" And then the gaggle of gigglers would rise and follow the leader around the yard calling out, "Shoo turkey, shoo, shoo, shoo turkey!" Running and skipping until it was someone else's turn to be the leader.

"Then we had a game called 'Andy over.' You'd have two teams—one on one side of a house and one on the other," she explained. One team would throw a ball up and over the house, and it was caught by somebody on the other team. And then they'd run, and you'd have to run to try to catch them, and anyone you caught was on your team. It was a hoot!" As she told me these stories, her face lit up, eyes wide behind her glasses. Her dress was never ostentatious but her hair, each time I met with her, was always well set. She was a grand dame, an old-school southern type. I knew she was in her early nineties, but I was too much of a gentleman to ask for specifics. I was also intimidated by her reputation. Mary Williams was an unusual woman because she commanded respect not through wealth or political power but through her genuine kindness. Doors were opened before her, and glory trailed in her wake. She was a treasure. But don't let that fool you; she wasn't afraid to get her hands dirty or speak her mind. And she had plenty of opportunities to do both.

The first thing Williams saw in Orangeburg was segregation, and it appalled her sensibilities. Schools were segregated in Shelton too, but there was something more palpable about the kind of segregation she encountered in Orangeburg. Perhaps it was because she was older and more aware of her world, but she could see the injustice in Orangeburg's starkly separate school systems, the all-white government, and the signs in store windows. She became involved in positive community changes wherever and whenever she could. She never took part in any activity that wasn't integrated. When a Head Start program began at Nix Elementary School, she joined the effort and worked alongside Lula Wilkinson, whose father was the second president of South Carolina State College. Williams helped to form the only integrated hospital auxiliary in the state at the time and later became involved with the Girl Scouts. Her troops were all mixed. "My intent," she said, "was to just peacefully do what I was doing. A lot of people didn't like it, and at church I was put up for elder way back, and some businessman in the church remarked, 'We don't want her elected because she'll have the church filled with blacks.' But I never let that kind of stuff affect me."

"So, you had a reputation about town?" I asked.

"Sure, but if you do what's right you can live with a reputation," she responded.

But that church member's fear of integration was widespread among whites, and she knew it. She also knew that that fear was rooted in ignorance and a lack of understanding, so she got involved in the search for a solution. Williams organized an interracial discussion group to help smooth the process of integration. The group included her husband, Sumter; school superintendent Bill Clark; Reverend Dr. McLeod Frampton of the all-white First Presbyterian Church; a Mrs. Worthy; a Mrs. Austin; a high-school student; and Reverend James Herbert Nelson, pastor at St. Luke Presbyterian Church, the historically black Presbyterian church in Orangeburg. The group met regularly and secretly at churches around town. They met, she said, because they "wanted to act instead of having to react."

"People's hearts have got to be changed. *Now* there are black people that have responsible positions in Orangeburg, and whites have gotten used to it, whether they like it or not. And today we've got some of the finest young black people and young white people that are choosing to stay and live in Orangeburg. So from my own standpoint I see so much change, but a lot of people don't even know it because they're not even involved." She talked about events in the recently renovated and slowly reviving downtown, about a gala at the local hospital—times when blacks and whites interact socially. Such moments, she said, reveal just how far the town has come.

"I once went to a meeting about improving race relations up in Spartan-burg. But they were so far behind us because they were not getting together socially. Until you do that, you can't make any changes. I don't think people can be friends unless they can get together some way and get to know each other." It never made any sense to her that folks could assume so much about a person or a group of people without even getting to know them as individuals. Case in point, in the late 1950s or early 1960s (she can't remember when exactly), Duke Ellington was performing at State College. There was no way she was going to miss a performance by the "duke" in her own backyard, so she went. Her husband, Sumter, and Earl and Bernice Middleton—a white couple and a black couple—got all dressed up and went to the show together. "And the interesting thing was," she said, "we were received beautifully."

She was no Pollyanna. She was aware there's still a lot of work that needs to be done. Racism still exists, and it has a long and violent history in Orangeburg. She saw it with her own eyes. She could remember a time in the late 1950s and early 1960s when the White Citizen's Council and the Klan were active. When black people were standing up, protesting, picketing, and organizing. When they pushed, white people pushed back, violently at times. Mary Williams remembered this violence. "I was downtown, almost at the corner of where the Eutaw Hotel was on Russell Street, a block away from where the bowling alley was. Some students were marching uptown, and the fire trucks were coming down the street the other way and just spraying the crowd with water. I was absolutely horrified. It was like I was looking at a movie." What bothered Williams the most was that this was her community. She was invested in it, and she didn't like the way some folks in her community were treating black people. The hardest thing was when her own friends suggested that force was the best way to respond to the protests. This strained her relationships in ways she hadn't imagined: "People that were my friends just thought that was what needed to be done. They didn't have any bad feelings about what was happening at all." Mary Williams walked away from that scene out of a movie determined to be a force for good.

Geraldyne Zimmerman was also on Russell Street that day. She also saw those protestors get sprayed by fire hoses. She too was horrified by the violence. But the world and her hometown have come a long way since then. And she would know. Zimmerman was born in the house she lived in her whole life, except for when she went off to college at Fisk University. You wouldn't expect someone who chose to stick so close to home base to have an independent streak. And yet, Zimmerman was all herself and no one else. She said she went to Fisk in order to escape her stern parents and stretch her legs, if only for a short while. She loved her parents and didn't mind coming back to them when her husband took over her father's position at South Carolina State College. From them on she was in Orangeburg, living on Treadwell Street.

Orangeburg and her neighborhood had always been safe for her, and because of that, she said, she never experienced some of the harsh realities of segregation. She understood that there were places she couldn't go, things she couldn't do. But in her world, a bubble crafted by her parents, she was treated fairly. Her father was a respected member of the community with an important position at State College, and he somehow managed to stay in the good graces of the white community. She explained that her parents never talked about slavery because they weren't direct descendants of slaves. Her father's mother was Cherokee, and father was "mixed black and white." Zimmerman's mother was also racially mixed, and her grandfather on her mother's side was a stevedore in Georgia who owned his own business. Nothing but proud, independent people as far back as she can tell. She wasn't fazed by Jim Crow in any deep way until her students at State College began to protest, and Jim Crow's fingers reached deep into her own life.

She remembered a time when her students were on strike, and the college president made it clear that any teacher who walked out in solidarity could pack up and hit the road. So class went on, often with few or no students in attendance. Instructors were told to mark absent those students who weren't there. But Zimmerman and many others refused to do so. One day, after all her other students had walked out to join a march, one young man stayed put. She asked him, "What are you still doing here?" He replied, "Well, I'm coming to class 'cause I have to." Her instincts told her that someone was pressuring him to go to class so she nipped that in the bud. "Son," she said, "if you don't get out of here, if you are not going to join those students in that march, I'm going give you an F." He lit out of that classroom, she said, as though his desk was on fire.

Negotiating the political world of the campus was complicated at State College. Zimmerman often felt as though she were being watched by the administration. Her fears were confirmed when she found out one day that her immediate supervisor had been rifling through her office trash can. At the time, Zimmerman belonged to the National Association of College Women (the NACW), and he had found a piece of paper with the letters "NAC" on it. She laughed when she told me, "I don't know whether my boss man saw the 'W' and took it off or what. But he took that to the chairman of the trustee board and told him that I was doing something for the National Association for the Advancement of Colored People [NAACP]!" In those days, she explained, you could lose your job at State if the administration found out you were working with that organization. Then-president Benner C. Turner viewed any involvement with the NAACP as a threat to the establishment. Zimmerman was prepared for this and defended herself when her job was threatened. Indeed there wasn't much she couldn't take. She'd been inducted into the movement for racial justice by her mother a long time ago, and there was no way her "boss man" was going to slow her down.

Her mother, Hazel Pierce, a well-known local activist and long-time supporter of the NAACP, had looked Jim Crow directly in the eye and spit on a regular basis. In 1932 she had decided she wanted to register herself and her daughter to vote, even though she knew they might not be allowed to cast their ballots on Election Day. She wanted to try. When they went down to the board of elections, the people at the board gave the two women a little bit of a run around—go to this office, that office, take this form, that form. Zimmerman, however, had no problem registering; she was a schoolteacher, and many black schoolteachers and doctors and ministers were registered back then; of course actually voting was something else. But they wouldn't register Hazel Pierce because she was "only" a housewife. The white man at the voter-registration office decided to test her literacy and handed her a copy of the Constitution. "Read this," he sneered. And she did—loudly and as fast as she could. After a speed-read through the Preamble and most of Article I, she shoved that auspicious document back into the hands of the registrar and demanded, "You read it that fast!" His white faced turned red, and he offered her a few choice words. But mother and daughter went home, heads held high, as registered voters in the state of South Carolina.

According to Zimmerman, "My mother and I never missed an opportunity to vote when they finally let us. We used to laugh and say if you were voting on a cat or a dog, we were there." Hazel Pierce was fighting Jim Crow's social rules long before any organized movement. One day a young white man came knocking on her door and called her "auntie." She replied, "I'm sorry, are your mother or father kin to me?" Another time she was in the Belk's department store with her grandson. He was young and not reading yet, and he made the faux pas of going to take a drink from the water fountain marked "whites." Pierce ran over and grabbed her grandson shouting, "Oh, no, no, no, no! Don't drink from there. That's filthy!" The store clerk who witnessed that encounter just about died.

But Zimmerman's mother's showdowns with Jim Crow weren't always peaceful. One day Zimmerman was driving her mother (who didn't and wouldn't drive) home from the grocery store. In the distance they could see a large group of students marching down Russell Street past the Eutaw Hotel. Suddenly the police turned water hoses on the students. Hazel Pierce demanded her daughter pull the car over. "And my mother got reaaaaal upset. And she got out of the car and went over to where they were hosing the students down. And I can remember the police bringing my mother back to the car and saying, 'Please take her home. We don't want anything to happen to her.' You know, she might have gotten hurt at her age."

Zimmerman didn't know until I told her that Mary Williams was also out there that day. The coincidence isn't lost on her. In 2000 both Mary Williams and Geraldyne Zimmerman were both recipients of one of South Carolina's highest honors—the Order of the Palmetto. That award came because Williams and Zimmerman were two friends who chose to thumb their noses at Orangeburg's color line at a time when it wasn't an easy or safe thing to do. They had a radical idea: start an interracial Girl Scout Council.

Back in the 1970s there were white troops and black troops in Orangeburg, but there was no mixing or shared governance. Both Mary Williams and Geraldyne Zimmerman had been working with Girl Scouts for years, but they didn't know each other. When a controversy arose over support from a donor, Williams and Zimmerman came to an agreement over the issue and in the process became friends. "Mary was a peculiar person. As far as she was concerned, there was no race. You know, there was no black-white. They were just people to her. Really, we didn't talk about black-white. I don't think Mary ever thought about race—even though she was mixed up in it. As far as she was concerned, we were just friends. We worked together. And that was it." Williams and Zimmerman worked together for many years to integrate some of the Girl Scout troops. At times they succeeded; at times they didn't. "We started what we call the Daisies, which is for the four- and five-year-olds. And in the beginning, our troop, we would have whites as members." But often, as those girls got older, they would leave the integrated troop and go to a white troop that was in their school or elsewhere.

But Zimmerman saw a lot of changes. Being able to vote—not to just register to vote—changed a lot of things. Blacks are employed throughout the community, and anytime anyone wants to put together a committee for anything, there will be black members on that committee. She admitted that she didn't suffer the worst of segregation because of her family, but she did not look at history or the present through rose-colored glasses either. "A lot of people are still saying that there's an element of prejudice, that they still feel that there's an air of prejudice in Orangeburg. Sometimes I think it's your attitude. You've got that attitude of racial hatred that you haven't got rid of. But you don't get anywhere with hatred."

It's surprising that Geraldyne Zimmerman had any time to think about the past at all. When I interviewed her, she sat in her home like a queen, having audiences with friends and neighbors throughout our conversation. The phone rang constantly. "This is Grand Central Station," she exclaimed after about the third phone call during our conversation. A coffee table next to her was loaded down with blank greeting and sympathy cards waiting for her kind words, with medicine bottles and magazines, while behind her an elaborate cabinet displayed the family silver. She was the ninety-eight-year-old conductor, in charge with a sincere directness and sense of humor that infected the room. Like her mother, she was not afraid to look you in the eye, and like her mother, she was never afraid of Jim Crow.

One summer she was teaching at Benedict College in Columbia. On weekends she came back to Orangeburg on the bus. One time when she got on the bus, all the seats were taken except for a spot up front next to a young white soldier from Fort Jackson. "So I just went on and sat on down beside him. And the bus driver came to me and told me, 'You can't sit there.' And I said, 'Uh, why?' He said, 'Well, colored people supposed to sit in the back.' I said, 'Well, this is the only seat available.' And he said, 'Well you just can't sit there.'" She paused, letting a big smile light up her face. "I remember just what that soldier from Fort Jackson said. He said, 'Why can't she sit there? It's all right with me.'"

In the mid-1950s a robust and well-organized civil rights movement emerged in Orangeburg and throughout South Carolina. The impetus for this movement was in part a collective outcry over the inadequate education black children were receiving in comparison to their white counterparts. Orangeburg County's neighbor to the northeast, Clarendon County, was home to the Summerton School District, which was involved in the *Briggs v. Elliott* suit, initiated in 1950, one of the cases that made up *Brown v. Board of Education,* which the Supreme Court decided in 1954. Change was afoot across the South and the nation, but some white segregationists didn't want to go down without a fight. The South Carolina legislature established a committee in 1951 to explore ways for the state to avoid integration. Called the Gressette Committee, it was named after Senator Marion Gressette of Calhoun County, another neighboring county to Orangeburg. Indeed Orangeburg County's "neighborhood" was rife with segregationist sentiment.

In the town of Orangeburg, however, black parents and college students became organized in ways that not only challenged laws but defied local social norms. The first act of defiance came in late summer 1955 when fifty-seven parents petitioned for the desegregation of a local school district. After the *Times and Democrat* published the petition, including the names of those who signed it, many were quickly fired by their white employers. A local economic war ensued. Black leaders were not about to back down. They organized a boycott of white-owned businesses and raised money for a fund to help the black community ride out the boycott. This economic tit for tat became a battle for hearts and minds.

Orangeburg white people then formed a chapter of the John Birch Society and the first White Citizen's Council (WCC) in South Carolina. Chapters of the WCC soon appeared in six other towns in Orangeburg County—Cope, Eutawville, Holly Hill, North, Norway, and Cordova. For a while the WCC was everywhere, including the front page of the *Times and Democrat,* where it once ran a recruitment ad. The WCC attacked local black leaders and the NAACP, whose ultimate goal—the WCC claimed—was miscegenation. South Carolina State and Claflin College, they claimed, were at the beck and call of the NAACP. Tensions were high across the community. When some black ministers invited a group of white ministers to meet and discuss these tensions, the white ministers refused.

White-run businesses addressed the boycott by refusing to supply black-run businesses connected to it, including Jim Sulton's Esso Station on Russell Street. For the black boycott to work, it was crucial that black business owners sign the petition. They didn't have to worry about being fired; yet they were still putting their businesses at risk. Sulton was willing to take that risk. Despite the white counterboycott, Sulton's business survived. Like other black business owners, he milked his connections outside Orangeburg. Standard Oil continued to supply him with gas, and he bought merchandise from distributors in Charleston. Sulton was even able to hire a worker who had been fired by his previous employer for supporting the black community's boycott.

This boycott revealed that black citizens in Orangeburg knew how to organize, and it had the additional effect of inspiring others outside the community to do the same thing. A young preacher in Montgomery, Alabama, Martin Luther King Jr., was particularly interested in the Orangeburg boycott. In late 1955 several Orangeburg area civil rights leaders—including Earl Middleton, Leroy Sulton, and Julius Washington—drove all night to hear a twenty-something King speaking at Dexter Avenue Baptist Church. Afterward they sat down with King and told him about their boycott and the tactics they had used.

The late 1950s and early 1960s were a pivotal period for the South Carolina State students who participated in marches and toed the boycott line. Their activism did not end with the boycott. They continued to organize and discuss ways that they might foster change in the town. In the winter of 1960 State students began a series of sit-ins at the Kress Store in downtown Orangeburg, just across from the monument to the Confederate dead. The sit-ins were often thwarted by customers and employees who removed lunch-counter seats. But students and community members persisted in their efforts to desegregate local businesses. On March 15, 1960, tear gas and water hoses were turned on a crowd of more than a thousand demonstrators near the old Eutaw Hotel downtown. About 350 were arrested (among them future U.S. House of Representatives Majority Whip James Clyburn and future State College football coach Willie Jeffries). A front-page photograph in the *New York Times* showed the students "corralled" in a stockade of sorts outside the local jail singing "God Bless America." Many were eventually taken to the state penitentiary in Columbia on a cattle truck.

Three years later, a group formed the Orangeburg Freedom Movement. The movement submitted a list of demands to city council, calling for widespread, if not complete, desegregation. The refusal to take the demands seriously prompted mass demonstrations. More than 1,350 arrests were made of Claflin College, State College, and Wilkinson High School students, as well as local activists. In 1967 Martin Luther King Jr. paid a visit to Orangeburg, giving a talk at Trinity Methodist Church (now United Methodist), the center for many of the town's civil rights activities. Despite all the petitions, boycotts, marches, and arrests, many of Orangeburg's institutions remained segregated. During the summer of 1967, Orangeburg hosted the American Legion Little World Series. A few kids from a California team tried to go bowling at All Star Bowling Lanes, but manager Harry Floyd told them that black people were not allowed inside. At the time Orangeburg County was roughly 40 percent white and 60 percent black. And yet because city limit lines were drawn by white people for their own benefit, the percentages in town were the exact opposite. Median income for whites was $2,603 in the county and $4,617 in the city. For blacks it was $1,461 in the county and $2,075 in the city. According to one study, before 1968 only 48.8 percent of eligible blacks in the county were registered to vote, compared to 99 percent of eligible whites.

The social tensions and economic inequities in Orangeburg mirrored those in the United States and beyond during the first few months of 1968—a year of auspicious beginnings and dramatic conclusions, a year of violence and protest, and a year in which the media began to play a major role in telling about and showing that violence and protest. On January 23 the USS *Pueblo* was seized by North Korea. On January 30 the Viet Cong launched its Tet offensive. Two days later Nguyen Van Lem was executed by Nguyen Ngoc Lon, an event photographed by Eddie Adams, who later won a Pulitzer Prize for this infamous image. The My Lai Massacre happened in mid-March, while on April 4 that young minister from Montgomery, Alabama, who met with civil rights leaders from Orangeburg in 1955, was gunned down in Memphis. On July 17, Saddam Hussein became vice chair of the Revolutionary Council of Iraq after a coup d'état, laying the groundwork for future wars and genocides. Nineteen sixty-eight was also the year of student protests in Belgrade, Warsaw, Paris, Mexico City, and Rome. At the summer Olympic Games, American athletes Tommie Smith and John Carlos raised their black-gloved fists. In the same there were struggles in Northern Ireland, the Prague Spring protests, demonstrations at the Democratic National Convention in Chicago, and the Farmington Mine disaster. Operation Commando Hunt was launched, during which some 520,000 U.S. bombing missions dropped more than 2 million tons of ordnance onto Laos. Many of those bombs didn't explode and remain on the ground today, history's menacing detritus yet to detonate.

# 5 EIGHT SECONDS OF HOLY HELL

Oscar Butler ended up in Orangeburg and at South Carolina State College in 1952 because of an athletic scholarship. A graduate of Pearl High School in Nashville, Tennessee, he was a standout on the basketball court and on the baseball diamond, but because of the color of his skin, his college options were limited. For black athletes in the 1950s, historically black colleges were the only game in town. So it was that this strapping young athlete from a fancy, big-city high school ended up at, as he saw it, an under-funded college in a southern jerkwater.

Indeed Butler and his friends thought both the school and the town were backward, from another time and place. They had better facilities back at Pearl, and the town offered little entertainment for students. Because of Jim Crow, there were basically two options—the soda shop across the street from the college or the "Negro" balcony at the movie theater. Neither seemed that appealing to a big-city kid. Butler wasn't particularly angry about the restrictions of Jim Crow; he thought the whole charade was sad to the point of being funny. In general being a student at South Carolina State in the 1950s was making the choice to live on an island amid a strange sea of white faces, odd laws, and conspicuous surveillance.

After he graduated, Butler worked in New York City for a while, but he came back to Orangeburg a few years later when he was offered the job of dean of men at State. The college and the community—like the nation

Facing: Sign for the bowling alley where students protested on February 6, 1968 itself—had begun to transform in his absence, attracting students from further afield, many of them military vets, who balked at the racist ideology underpinning Jim Crow. But rather than laugh it off, they began to resist. These students came from the Northeast or from bigger cities in the South. The shifting demographics at State led to shifting ideas. Shifting ideas led to tension. And tension eventually led to violent confrontation.

Butler says it all started with a bowling alley in April 1967. This bowling alley, however, was in Sumter, South Carolina, not Orangeburg. The statewide youth chapter of the NAACP held a conference in Sumter, and students from State attended. At some point during the conference, some attendees wanted to go bowling but discovered that the bowling alley was for white people only. They threatened to demonstrate and said they would close down the city in the process. Sumter city officials and the bowling alley manager reacted quickly to their demands. An agreement was struck, and the students were allowed to bowl.

When the State contingent returned to Orangeburg, they couldn't wait to tell Dean Butler about their success in Sumter. They were eager to desegregate All Star Bowling Lanes in Orangeburg—one of the last segregated businesses in the area. After what had happened in Sumter, Butler was convinced they wouldn't meet too much resistance in Orangeburg. He believed there were enough folks in town, black and white, who would support the effort to integrate the bowling alley. Butler had a vested interest in the matter: he was an avid bowler and part of a successful team that regularly burned up the lanes in Columbia. If only they could bowl in Orangeburg. When I talked to him on March 19, 2009, he laughed: "Now you talk about a dreamer, I was a dreamer!"

In the summer of 1967, Butler and three others—Earl Middleton, Lamar Dawkins, and Reverend James Herbert Nelson—opened up a conversation with Harry Floyd, co-owner of the bowling alley and the man in charge of the lanes. They met with Floyd on his turf and reasoned with him. They talked about the civil rights laws, about all the business the students would bring, and about what happened at the bowling alley in Sumter. At one point Floyd said he had "just about made up his mind" to open up the bowling alley. But, Butler believes, Floyd was feeling pressure from a small group of white people in the community who told him that desegregating his business would be "giving in to the niggers." They weren't going to let that happen. Though he can't prove it, Butler thinks, "They gave Floyd a large sum of money not to open it up," effectively ending Butler's behind-the-scenes negotiations.

That fall there were more official conversations about Floyd's business among the city, the chamber of commerce, and local black leaders, but to no avail. Floyd asserted that his business was not covered by federal civil rights laws and that he could serve whomever he wished. By the spring semester of 1968, the students were tired of these negotiations. They wanted change now. To them the bowling alley was just one more example of white Orangeburg's continued resistance to change. Some students remembered the protests in the 1950s and early 1960s; some had even participated in them. So they understood that sometimes it takes organized dissent—sit-ins, marches, and bodies in the streets—to raise awareness about an issue and change the direction the wind is blowing. Negotiating with Floyd would get them nowhere. They had to act.

By Monday, February 5, 1968, a group of students—including a well-known State College activist named John Stroman and a white student from Orlando, Florida, named John Bloecher—had organized to take care of the problem themselves. Butler was out of town attending a funeral for most of the day. When he returned to his campus office, a student office worker told him that Stroman had stopped by to tell him they were going to the bowling alley.

"Gone *where?*" he asked the student.

"The bowling alley. He left about twenty minutes ago."

Butler jumped in his car and raced down there. Floyd had recently placed a "Club Members Only" sign on the front door, but Butler went in anyway. Inside the "private club" Butler found Stroman and Bloecher and several other students. "I asked them what they were doing. And Stroman says, 'Well, it's for club members only, but you know all these folks aren't club members.'"

This was not the first time that John Stroman found himself at the center of controversy. Stroman was on everybody's radar. The year before he had been central in a movement by students to protest the actions of then-president Benner C. Turner. Conservative and Harvard-educated, President Turner was never popular with students; many thought of him as an "Uncle Tom." Some students and professors openly questioned the academic and social situation at State—Turner's old-school ways, the facts that few faculty members had doctorates, that freshmen and sophomores had to attend chapel on Friday, and that the college received so little money from the state in comparison to the other state-funded colleges. Apparently Turner took such criticisms to heart and failed to renew the contracts of three popular white professors in February of 1967. He also suspended several student activists, including John Stroman, who at the time had helped organize the Black Awareness Coordinating Committee (BACC)—an activist group with more radical leanings than the mainstream NAACP. Turner was eventually forced out, and Stroman was reinstated. So it was that in early December 1967, Stroman met a fellow student named James Davis, an air force veteran, who told him that he'd gone over to the bowling alley and been run out by Harry Floyd. Could Stroman help? When I interviewed him on July 15, 2009, Stroman explained that he was reluctant. He'd been catching hell for his involvement in protests the year before. He wanted to keep a low profile. He wasn't interested in getting into any more trouble.

But the thought of integrating All Star wouldn't leave him. Traveling on the Greyhound bus back home to Savannah for Christmas break, he pondered the situation. In Savannah he talked to some activist friends, and they told him to visit the local bowling alley and talk to the manager. "So I went down to a bowling alley in Savannah, and I talked to the manager and he said, 'Well, I didn't want to let any blacks in my bowling alley either.'" But the manager explained that if the bowling alley in Orangeburg had a lunch counter, which it did, they would have to integrate. The manager was referring to the clause in the 1964 Civil Rights Act that stated businesses conducting interstate commerce, such as most eating establishments, must be integrated. So Stroman wrote AMF (the bowling-gear company) and the American Bowling Congress and told them about the situation. "I got a letter back from AMF, but never heard from American Bowling Congress. AMF told me they only rent the machines, they couldn't tell him how to run his business so I had to go to a higher authority than them. I got that letter on Monday, February the fifth, and after that we went to the bowling alley." Stroman insists that what happened in Orangeburg was not about some college students who just wanted to go bowling; it was a planned civil rights demonstration. It wasn't as though Stroman himself was going to bowl any frames; his arm was in a sling at the time because he'd recently had an operation on his shoulder. He reminded me that he was a pretty good bowler. He played his first games at a black bowling alley in Savannah. "I started bowling when I was a teenager. I used to be a pin boy before that. I set up pins in the white bowling alley before they had automatic pin spotters. And, you know, the man used to let us bowl after a certain time of the night."

That Monday evening Stroman sent John Bloecher, the white student, ahead to the alley to start bowling. The plan was for Stroman to come in next and pose the question, "Is this really a *members* only bowling alley or a *whites* only bowling alley?" Before he left he consulted with some other students.

Not everyone was on board. It might be dangerous, some said. You might get kicked out of State again. But Stroman wasn't going to hang Bloecher out to dry. "So I said, 'I'm going to the bowling alley.'" Along the way he ran into fellow BACC member Wayne Curtis, who joined him and about a dozen others. When they got there, Bloecher was bowling. Some of students who came in with Stroman and Curtis went over to the lunch counter and started touching things. And everything they touched, one of the workers would throw away. So they began touching salt shakers, forks, knives, spoons, whatever they could get their hands on. Stroman walked over to the jukebox and hugged it asking if they'd throw that away too. About that time Dean Butler rolled in. A furious Floyd begged Butler to make the students leave, insisting his establishment was for members only. That's when Stroman pointed to his white classmate who was bowling away, no questions asked. "Well, he's not a member," he said. "He goes to State." Floyd immediately turned the lights off and closed the bowling alley for the night.

The students had to leave then, and Butler warned them to be careful and keep a low profile on their way back to campus. As they were leaving, Orangeburg Police Chief Roger Poston pulled Stroman aside and asked him to stop by his office before he went home. That semester Stroman was living off campus with his aunt. As he walked back to her house, he did stop by to chat with Chief Poston. "We talked for about thirty to forty-five minutes, and he said he didn't need any of that stuff in Orangeburg. He wished they would just open the door or close the door on that. And so I said, 'Chief, we're going back.' And he said, 'You'll be arrested.' I said, 'Well, that's the plan.' They always make it sound like we just went to the bowling alley one day." Stroman says it was better planned than that.

Chief Poston, Harry Floyd, and the rest of Orangeburg, had no idea what kind of trouble was coming their way. Dean Livingston of the *Times and Democrat* wrote in a story that "Floyd and black power were on a collision course." He was referring in part to Stroman's group, BACC, decidedly the most radical civil rights organization at State but with a membership of maybe twenty on a good day. To many folks in the community, white and black, BACC was akin to the increasingly radical Student Non-Violent Coordinating Committee (SNCC), despite the fact that the two groups were unaffiliated. Livingston may also have been referring to the presence in the community of Cleveland Sellers, whose ties to SNCC were known far and wide. Originally from Denmark, South Carolina (about thirty miles from Orangeburg), Sellers came to Orangeburg in October 1967. He was a well-connected veteran organizer, having spent time in Mississippi and Alabama, and most folks believed he came to Orangeburg to organize on behalf of SNCC. In fact Sellers had made some contact with students in BACC, but he hadn't made a significant impact on the campus. Local officials didn't know the extent of Sellers' work in Orangeburg. All they knew his friendship with radical activist Stokely Carmichael linked Sellers to SNCC and to the black power movement and maybe to the Black Panthers. In small-town Orangeburg, Sellers' presence did not go unnoticed.

When I spoke to him on February 5, 2010, Sellers told me they got it all wrong. He came to Orangeburg because of a promise he'd made to his mother. When he dropped out of Howard University in the early 1960s to get involved in the work that SNCC was doing in Mississippi, he promised his mother then that he would eventually go back to college. After stepping down from his position as program director for SNCC, he decided to fulfill that promise. South Carolina was home, and it would be a fine place to restart his education. South Carolina felt familiar, comfortable. He sensed too that there was a change in consciousness taking place, a shift from a focus on civil rights to a focus on black power. The African American community in South Carolina was coming together, recognizing the importance of collaboration and collective effort.

According to Sellers, some of the students at State were recognizing this as well. But most were still interested in the tactics of the early civil rights movement—marches, sit-ins, and demonstrations. "I did not agree with the effort to protest the bowling alley. I just thought we had passed that; that was the 1964 Civil Rights Act." The urban rebellions of Newark and Detroit had happened, and many people were killed. "It became very clear that nonviolence and confrontational politics weren't going to cut it anymore. At that point SNCC supported efforts to organize in African American communities and began to organize around a kind of political empowerment." Sellers agreed with this focus on community-based empowerment and believed that once organized and empowered, African Americans could effect real changes in their lives. But the majority of students at State were not there yet; they were still focused on integration. Sellers said he had to learn to keep his mouth shut at times. But, he added, the last thing he would have advocated would have been a nighttime protest at the bowling alley.

Yet on Tuesday night a group of students led by John Stroman went back to the bowling alley. This time they walked over with more students and a plan to get arrested so they could launch a court case. Stroman claimed that this time not only did Chief Poston know it was going to happen but so did

Chief J. P. Strom of the State Law Enforcement Department (SLED), who worked directly under Governor Robert McNair.

Rather than approach the bowling alley from the front by walking in full view of the community down Russell Street, the students went to the bowling alley the back way, down Amelia Street. They tried to enter at about 7 P.M., but the door was locked. Chief Poston arrived, and when the door was opened for him, a group of students barged in. Inside the students immediately sensed something amiss. The place was full of plainclothes officers as well as a few in uniforms. "Chief Strom walked up to me. and he said, 'Mr. Stroman there isn't any use to all this trouble.' He said, 'We need to just get it on record, and that's all we need. All of you don't need to go to jail.'" Stroman agreed that that was the sensible thing to do—just a few would get arrested, it would go on record, and they could take this thing to court. A handful agreed to be arrested. But because so many students were still milling about the bowling alley parking lot, Strom and Poston didn't want to leave just yet. So Stroman and the others who agreed to be arrested walked from the bowling alley to the jailhouse uncuffed and on their own. "We weren't trying to raise any hell," he reiterated. They wanted, he said, to do this thing the right way.

But by the time they got to the jailhouse and were signing in, Robert Scott, president of the State College student government association, ran inside to tell Stroman that hundreds of students were pouring into the bowling alley parking lot. And they were upset. They wanted to see the students who'd been arrested to make sure they hadn't been mistreated, and they weren't going to leave the parking lot until they did. With police permission Stroman and the student leaders turned around and walked back to the bowling alley, hoping to calm the crowd.

When Stroman reached the parking lot, he went over to a group of football players he recognized figuring if he could persuade them to leave, they would encourage others to do so as well. At that moment, a fire truck pulled into the parking lot. The last time a fire truck came to a civil rights protest in Orangeburg, the hoses were turned on the crowd, soaking protestors on a cold day—a scene straight out of Bull Connor's Birmingham. This fire truck brought back those memories, and many students became incensed. They knew what the fire truck could be used for. According to Stroman, "Somebody started lighting matches, a book of matches, and said, 'Put *this* fire out.'" Cleveland Sellers remembers that some of the students who had left and were walking back to campus turned around when they heard the fire truck. Then a window in front of the bowling alley was broken, either by the pressure of the crowd or by someone's foot. Stroman said, "When the window broke the cops grabbed the smallest fellow they could grab. I heard a girl say, 'Hey! What are you going to do with him?' Man, after that, it all broke loose. And they started hitting girls, fellows, everybody." It was chaos.

The police had billy clubs and used them on the protesting students; many were beaten or thrown to the ground. Others ran as fast as they could away from the melee. Some students smashed windows in businesses and damaged cars as they fled back to campus. That night, eight State students ended up in the hospital as did one highway patrolman, who had gotten tear gas in his eyes. Some things happened that night that couldn't be cured in the hospital, couldn't be healed or washed away: the students were now angry not only about the bowling alley but about the way law enforcement handled the protest, in particular the fact that women were beaten. "I don't care if you're white," Stroman said. "A man don't have any business beating on women. He's supposed to be king of the jungle so why should he beat on a woman? But they didn't care."

Later that night students and faculty members met at State psychology professor Roland Haynes's house. They were trying to figure out what to do next, how to respond. Stroman, Sellers, and Butler were there, as well as Robert Scott and the student government president from Claflin. Sellers apparently suggested a student blockade of intersections around town the next day, but most students wanted to have a march through town. The meeting ended with the consensus that they would seek a permit to march.

As Oscar Butler was telling me about the events of Tuesday night, all of a sudden he stood up. He's still a burly man, tall and imposing. "Let me show you something." We walk from his kitchen into his living room, the walls of which are covered with awards and citations and photographs, the kind that lead you to believe that he's a man who has been there and done that.

He points to a photograph of a much younger and leather-jacketed Oscar Butler surrounded by white men in uniforms and business suits. His hand is up in the air, and his eyes are downcast. The photographer has captured him in midmovement so it's difficult to read Butler's expression. At a glance, it appears he's grinning, but closer scrutiny reveals a kind of sadness or fatigue. Bags appear under his eyes, lines on his cheeks, all of this under the gaze of many of the white men in the photograph. You can also see the backs of several students' heads. Their eyes are also on Butler, still a young man but under an immense amount of pressure. "This was outside the bowling alley Tuesday night, and a captain from the highway patrol was getting ready to pull his gun, and I asked him, 'Please don't pull your gun.' That was two nights before they got killed."

Early Wednesday morning Butler met with Mayor E. O. Pendarvis and city manager Bob Stevenson and requested a permit to march. They wouldn't issue the permit but asked if they could go to the college and talk with the students. Butler was surprised. "For what?" he asked. "What are you going to say? If you're not going to say you're going to open the bowling alley, then don't even come." That wasn't Stevenson's intention, but he wanted to meet with the students anyway. Flabbergasted, Butler told Stevenson he must be the most "courageous" person he'd ever met.

The on-campus meeting of Bob Stevenson and Mayor Pendarvis with the students is legendary. The two white men had no idea what they were getting themselves into. They and a few other white businessmen sat on a stage in front of a packed auditorium filled with irate college students. "That meeting caused holy hell," Butler told me. Stevenson and Pendarvis responded to the situation as best they could, but they were in way over their heads. Stroman laughed when he told me, "They're lucky that they got off of that campus alive, because first of all when they got there they could not say 'Negro.'" What they said sounded like "nigra," which sounds a lot like "nigger." The students saw them as just two more white men trying to explain to them the way things should be. They responded to Stevenson and Pendarvis's platitudes with hoots and hollers while student Wayne Curtis asked them probing questions. Curtis, it turns out, was mistaken for Cleveland Sellers. From up on the stage, Pendarvis and Stevenson saw a black man with an Afro asking questions. They saw a crowd of shouting black students. One can only imagine that those two men were thinking: "So this is what black power looks like!" According to Butler, Stevenson, more than Pendarvis, seemed to understand what was happening. "And truthfully, in all honesty, if the city leaders would have listened to Bob Stevenson and police Chief Poston, what happened next would never have happened."

Instead officials working for Governor McNair—for the state—rolled in. And that disrupted any kind of communication among local white leaders, the college campuses, and the African American community. "McNair actually interceded in 1967 at S.C. State and was able to see the student's point of view, and that's when they retired Turner," Sellers pointed out. "But this time he decided to send surrogates, which was a tragic mistake." Now that the state was in charge, along with the FBI, local law enforcement wasn't able to draw on personal relationships and connections throughout the community. "It would have been better to leave it in their hands." When the locals were in charge, Cleveland Sellers lamented, change was slow, but at least the locals knew who to talk to and who to make deals with. Take for example what happened on Monday and Tuesday when John Stroman and Chief Poston were in close and constant conversation. When SLED and the FBI entered the picture, so did the idea that Orangeburg was under threat of black power advocates. And that, Sellers said, convoluted everything.

But after the Wednesday morning showdown on campus, the students and many white city leaders were beyond the point of listening to each other, and there was little communication between the state and the students. Attorney General Daniel R. McLeod met with city officials and was alarmed; he said they were "parleying back and forth like a couple of warring nations." For their part the students had seen it all before and were frustrated by the slow pace of change. So was Butler. "Everything that you're told that you should do in a situation like this, we had done. We had written the bowling congress. We had written the government. We had written the FBI. But none of it worked." Later that day, students submitted a list of demands to city officials. This list made it clear that the students (while still interested in bowling a few frames at All Star) had moved well beyond the issue that precipitated the standoff:

1. Close down the All Star Bowling Lanes immediately and request the management to change his policy of racial discrimination before opening.
2. Police brutality—The action taken by the . . . officers was uncalled for, especially the beating of young ladies.
3. Immediate suspension, pending investigation, of the officer who fired a shot unnecessarily into the State College Campus.
4. The establishment by the Mayor of an Orangeburg Human Relations Committee of a biracial nature, with the recommendation that each community select their own representation.
5. A request should be made for a public statement of intent from the Orangeburg Medical Association as to its determination to serve all persons on an equal basis regardless of race, religion, or creed.
6. Formulate or integrate a fair employment commission in the city of Orangeburg.
7. Change the dogmatic attitude of personnel at the Health Department and the segregated practices used there.

8. Extend the city limits of Orangeburg so as to benefit more than one segment of the community.

9. Give constructive leadership toward encouraging the Orangeburg Regional Hospital to accept the Medicare Program.

10. Eliminate discrimination in public services, especially in doctors' offices.

11. The integration of drive-in theaters.

12. Fulfill all stipulations of the 1964 Civil Rights Act by leading the community so that it will serve all people.

The city made no immediate response to these demands, further frustrating students and faculty. Off campus, some white business owners were holed up in their stores, heavily armed. Meanwhile Governor McNair made public comments about the black power advocates infiltrating the community. He had called in the National Guard, which—along with the South Carolina Highway Patrol—had set up roadblocks around the colleges. The town was fit to pop. But not everyone was interested in the direction things were headed. Butler recalls walking down the street in front of the campus and having to walk between a few guardsmen he recognized. "Some of them were local business figures, people we knew. And a few actually walked up to us and said, 'We're here because we have to be here, but we're not in support of what's going on.'"

As darkness fell on this beautiful southern town, some students headed to the edges of their campuses and threw rocks at passing cars. Three students from Claflin College were shot at by a man who said they were trespassing on his property. Later that evening a blue Mercury Comet with a white man behind the wheel and another riding shotgun, drove onto State's campus. Someone from the car whipped out a gun and began shooting at students. Stroman remembers hearing gunfire and then being pulled to the ground. When the driver drove into a dead end, the car was pelted with rocks and bottles. Eventually campus security guards chased the car off campus, but not before its presence increased students' distrust of the law enforcement. They wondered how the car got onto campus in the first place. A few students reacted to this incident by going to the front of the campus and throwing more objects at passing cars. In some instances they connected with their targets. A State security guard got wind of what was happening and walked over to investigate. He told the students he saw to get back to their dorms, and said that most of them complied. The two white men in the blue Mercury

Comet were never brought to court because a weapon was never found. The driver was charged with reckless driving and fined twenty-five dollars.

Cleveland Sellers could see where all this was headed—no communication between the various factions, a public whipped up by a fear of black power, and a bunch of angry college students. On Thursday morning he held a press conference in his apartment (which was just across from State's campus) and told the journalists present, including Jack Bass and Dean Livingston, what he believed was about to take place: somehow he would be arrested or his apartment raided. He said that, if he were arrested, SNCC leader Stokely Carmichael would come to town. Sellers's fear was that things might end with him either injured or dead. "And I explained to them what was gonna happen, how it was gonna happen, and why it was gonna happen." Sellers knew at that point that his apartment was no longer a safe place. A friend on campus told him he could stay in his room for the time being; Sellers took him up on that offer. With the National Guard milling about in the streets around his building, he figured that was his best option. He'd be safer on the campus surrounded by students.

Despite escalating tensions, there seemed to be an understanding that the students would hold off from further protests. "We were trying to get some sense of what was going on to prevent anything serious from happening" said Butler. "We thought, Sellers included, that there weren't going to be any more demonstrations. And lo and behold somewhere the lines of communication got crossed. There was one group saying there weren't going to be any more group meetings and one group saying, 'Oh, yes there are.'" In other words no one was really in charge, and there was no agreed-upon course of action. Students milled about campus while McNair called up more National Guardsmen and sent them to guard public utilities.

By Thursday evening the campus was locked down, and students were prevented from leaving. Earl Middleton recalled driving up to the campus early in the evening with his wife, Bernice, who taught at State. As he got closer to the campus, "Someone in the crowd threw a brick and broke a headlight on my car." Undeterred, they continued driving onto the campus. All of a sudden, Bernice told Earl to stop the car. She rolled down her window and called over a student she recognized. The student walked up to the car with a few empty Coke bottles in his hands. She pleaded with him to not get involved, to go back to his dorm room, but he didn't seem to be listening. When Earl asked her who that student was, she said "Henry Smith."

Butler was in Bethea Hall when a student came to him and said, "You need to go down to the front of the campus. Somebody is going to get hurt."

Butler wasn't sure what that meant, but the student told him things were tense between the students and the state highway patrolmen. He went first to the campus police command post and listened in to the chatter on the police radio. What he heard sounded ominous, so he headed for the front of campus. Students had built a bonfire on Watson Street, close to the campus entrance. Some were standing near the fire, while others were hanging out in a field just beyond an embankment that ran down into the street. A few students were apparently throwing more bricks and rocks at passing cars and in the direction of the law enforcement. More than sixty highway patrolmen stood there, backed up by forty-five National Guardsmen, twenty-five SLED agents, and a handful of deputies and city police. Some law-enforcement officials claim that they heard sporadic gunfire coming from the campus in their direction. But students mostly just shouted at them—"Hey honkies! Come and get us!" Others sang "We Shall Overcome." They were stuck somewhere between Malcolm X and Martin Luther King Jr.

Sellers was settling in for the night in his borrowed dorm room, when he heard a frantic knock at the door. Something was happening on the front of campus, and he might want to get down there. When Sellers arrived at the bonfire, his first thought was, "Hey, this is not good." Students were just standing around, directionless and agitated, with the highway patrol lined up opposite of them, white helmets disguising their faces. He saw a State College security car over by the campus gate and figured that was a positive sign. they seemed to be level-headed and would get students out of the way if things got dicey. He walked toward a group of students. He was not sure what they were doing—strategizing, preparing a chant, a song. In the group he saw Henry Smith. "I can't remember now whether or not I actually called his name out or whether or not I got close enough to stick my hand out to shake his hand, but I saw Henry, and I recognized him. And I wanted to go to him and say, 'Let's move this group out of here. It's dark, and we're in an open field. Ain't no barriers, no obstacles, no nothing. And these policemen are right at the bottom of the hill, and they have their weapons drawn. This is the wrong place." But Sellers never got to talk to Smith.

The flames from the bonfire leapt upward into the cold February sky. Someone ordered firemen to put out the bonfire, and the patrolmen moved in to protect the truck. What happened after that is less certain. Sometime around 10:30 P.M. patrolman David Shealy was hit in the head by a banister ripped off an empty house nearby. Mass confusion ensued. The students ran back toward one of the dorms on campus. About five minutes passed between the time Shealy was hit and when a group of patrolmen moved up the embankment, from the street and onto the campus proper. Some say one patrolman fired into the air—as an intentional warning? Mistakenly? Some say they heard a whistle. Some say they heard nothing. There's no question as to what happened next. Nine members of the South Carolina Highway Patrol began shooting. No order was ever given. For about eight seconds they fired their weapons. Most students were hit by double-ought buckshot fired from 870 Remington 12-gauge pump shotguns, a standard-issue police riot gun. One patrolman fired his service revolver, a .38 caliber Colt. Later the highway patrol and the governor claimed that the officers were returning fire, though no guns were ever found on the students. State president Maceo Nance later speculated that, with all the armed law enforcement on hand, "they could have arrested the entire college community if they had wanted to."

The students fled in terror from the spraying buckshot. Thirty-one or more were hit, most of them from behind. Sellers described seeing Henry Smith, "spin and crumple to the ground. . . . I was certain that they had shot Henry thinking he was me. He looked just like me." Sellers himself was hit in the left shoulder. He knows that the shooting lasted only about eight seconds, "But it sounded like it was much longer than that. It sounded like an eternity." He remembers being alert yet confused in those anxious moments. A dizzying mix of cacophonous shots, gun flashes, and the acrid smell of powder and bonfire ashes shocked his senses. Part of him wanted to look behind to see who was shooting, but another part of him wanted to get the hell out of there. He scrambled to get off the ground. He remembers grabbing someone by the arm and pulling them along as far as he could. Some yards away he saw a trash can and ran for it. He knew that if he was laid out and the police found him, he was a goner. "I was convinced of that. I had no misunderstanding about that."

Oscar Butler was running to the front of campus when a bullet hit a trash can he passed. He knew it was all over. "I was right in the middle of the campus, where they have a monument to the victims of the shooting now. I was on the sidewalk. It seemed like it lasted two minutes, three minutes maybe." After the shooting stopped a student from Lowman Hall came running to him and said, "They shot in my room!" Butler asked him what he meant. So the student showed him what he meant—a bullet had landed right in the book he was reading. The next morning Butler found more bullets. He was combing the bushes on the front of campus with local photographer Cecil Williams, when they discovered some shell casings. "I gave all of mine to the FBI, and I think Cecil gave some of his, not all of his, to the FBI. We thought we were, well, doing the right thing."

That night Geraldyne Zimmerman awoke from her sleep to find her husband quickly putting on his clothes. "What's wrong?" she asked. "I gotta go up to the campus," he answered. He was in charge of State's physical plant and had been told to come to the campus immediately. Something was happening. Then she heard gunshots—their house was only a few blocks from campus. Now she was nervous and didn't want her husband to leave. She told him as much. She feared for his life. She knew the gunshots had something to do with what had been happening that week. She knew. She just knew. Her husband left despite her pleas. She walked over to her window and watched him race up Treadwell Street. Moments passed, and she was still in front of the window when cars began screeching around the corner from Boulevard onto Treadwell, screaming, horns blaring. Students were taking the injured to the hospital on Carolina Avenue. Car after car barreled down her street, bright white lights blurring into red lights trailing off into the distance.

When the shooting had stopped, Oscar Butler made his way to the hospital to keep an eye on the students. "All the mayhem you hear about in the hospital is true and some of the doctors coming in saying that the 'niggers died' and 'they asked for it' and all that kind of stuff. It did happen." He can't remember who said what, but he does remember who was working that night. "Dr. Campbell was the one that worked on Delano Middleton. Campbell said they just shot him up so bad he could not stop the bleeding. I was there when he came out and operated on him. He said the more they tried to patch him up, the more they couldn't."

Dr. Henry Frierson didn't witness the shootings, but he did see their impact. Frierson was attending a meeting at the Holiday Inn on John C. Calhoun Drive, a few miles away from campus. As he drove home, he heard sirens throughout the city, but wasn't sure what to make of them. He had been asleep for a short while when the phone rang; it was an emergency-room nurse. She told him he was needed at the hospital even though he was not on call. The surgeon on call that night was Dr. Roy Campbell, but the emergency room was overflowing with students who had been shot, and it was all hands on deck. Indeed, of the approximately thirty physicians on the hospital staff, at least half of them showed up to help.

When Frierson arrived on the scene, victims were still arriving in the emergency room. He told me he saw a man acting rather frantically in a hallway and he thought it was Cleveland Sellers. But Frierson wasn't sure. He didn't know Sellers. Didn't treat him. He was not even sure Sellers was injured. Besides he wasn't contemplating Cleveland Sellers or the civil rights of African American college students—he was too busy. There were more than three dozen injured people who needed to be helped. He has no earthly idea how many of them he treated. He and his colleagues worked nonstop for several hours. With each patient it was the same: get an X-ray, locate the bullet, and figure out the next step. Two of the young men who died were operated on by Dr. Campbell and Dr. Wolfe, but Frierson is not sure about the other student.

According to Frierson, there was a lot of justified hostility among the people who had been shot, and that complicated the work. He mostly treated gunshot wounds, which, he reminded me, are not typically life threatening: "A bullet does its harm when it's moving. Very seldom after it comes to rest does it migrate." He remembers one gunshot wound that he treated many years ago where the bullet found its way into a vein and then into the victim's heart. But that's an anomaly. Trying to explain this reality to college students who'd just been involved in one of the most intense experiences of their short lives was a challenge. Most folks learn about the treatment of gunshot wounds from watching television, he said. "On TV they grimace, and the doc removes the bullet, and they walk out, and they're well. That's not the case. Now if it goes through the heart, it may be fatal. But a lot of the students had been shot in the shoulder, and you can imagine trying to tell them, 'This does not have to have surgery. You're going to be all right without it. You can leave the bullet alone.' Everybody assumes a bullet has to be removed, which is not always the case."

Apparently there wasn't much that could be done to save Delano Middleton. The seventeen-year-old Wilkinson High School student had been shot in the chest, heart, thigh, hip, wrist, and forearm. He had joined the students at the bonfire while waiting for his mother, who worked on the janitorial staff at State, to finish work. He was an athletic teenager who hoped to win a college scholarship. Lying in a hospital bed waiting to die, he asked his mother to recite the Twenty-third Psalm. When Middleton's mother finished reciting the psalm and in the creeping calm of the hospital, at 1:10 A.M. Delano Middleton passed away to thoughts of green pastures and a merciful God whose shepherd son would guide him to calm waters, carry him through the geographies of death and evil to a place far from the blood and bones of that evening. At his funeral a few days later, with law-enforcement officers on call and FBI agents on the scene, about two hundred mourners filed into Warren Chapel Baptist Church. The church bulletin read, "A busy life came to a close Thursday night February 8 when Delano Middleton was called to his heavenly home." His high-school classmates carried his casket while his sister repeated over and over, "They didn't have to kill him. They didn't have to kill him." Again and again and again—they didn't have to kill him.

Middleton's sixteen-year-old cousin, Ernest Shuler, had been hit in the back of his right arm and in the bottom of his right foot. Shuler and many of the others who had been shot that night recovered to some extent. But others did not. Eighteen-year-old State student Samuel Hammond died at 11:20 P.M. He had been shot in the back. Hammond's classmate, Henry Smith, died a few hours later, at 1:45 A.M. Smith had been shot in the right torso and neck. A pregnant woman named Louise Kelly Crawley was beaten and arrested while shuttling students to the hospital. She later suffered a miscarriage.

Cleveland Sellers has always wondered about the possibilities the lives of those young students represented. His initial involvement with the struggle for civil rights came when he learned about the 1955 lynching of Emmett Till, another young black man killed well before his prime. Sellers told me that's what he carries with him still, those young men, those young women. They were killed, or they were injured and carry those injuries; they carry that moment with them. Sellers's own life was also disrupted that night. He was arrested while waiting in the hospital's "colored" waiting room and driven to the Orangeburg County courthouse, where he was charged with inciting riot, attempted murder, and arson. His bond was set at fifty thousand dollars.

According to John Stroman, what happened on February 8 surprised the entire community. "Orangeburg is a tough town, but I never thought they'd stoop that low." He wasn't there that night, so he's not sure what exactly went down. The night of the shooting, Stroman was at his aunt's house, and he didn't hear about what had happened until the next morning. Yet Stroman thinks a lot about what happened: Why didn't they just let them have the bonfire to get whatever out of their system? And why were students shot in the back? If they were attacking the law-enforcement officers, they would have been shot in the front. Right? Some highway patrolmen, he noted, shot in the air. What if they hadn't? How many more would have been killed? And the patrolmen's claim that they were returning fire? Lies, Stroman said. The students by the bonfire didn't have guns. After the shooting, some of them did break into the ROTC building and steal guns. But those guns didn't have firing pins. "That's like having a gun with no bullets."

Stroman thinks the highway patrolmen opened fire in a planned fashion—that what happened was part of a conspiracy. Someone blew a whistle, he told me, and then opened fire on the students. "I think the highway patrolmen were angry because of what had happened to the guy that got hit with the banister. But anyway, they blew a whistle. The highway patrolmen blew a whistle. Shot. Blew a whistle. And stopped."

"This is what you heard? This is what people told you?"

"Well, yeah. The whistle, too many people talked about the whistle." He added that Henry Smith was targeted because they thought he was Cleveland Sellers. And what's more, Stroman thinks Smith wasn't dead when he got to the hospital but was beaten to death there. "They beat him to death in the hospital. That's what I say to you."

"And they thought Smith was Cleveland?" I asked.

"That was our feeling. I can't say what they thought."

The morning after the shooting Stroman's aunt woke him up early and told him to come listen to the radio. Exhausted from the week's events, he got up slowly. Then he heard the report coming over the radio. He picked up his pace after that, threw on his clothes, and raced over to campus. By that time parents were arriving to see if their sons and daughters were okay. Reports in the media were all over the place about how many students were shot, who was shot, who shot first, and who was responsible. Fingers were already being pointed at black power advocates, Cleveland Sellers in particular.

Stroman doesn't like most of the books about February 8, 1968, because too many things have been left out of them. And by books he seems to mean one book, Bass and Nelson's. The books don't mention the white student who went with Stroman and company to the bowling alley on Monday. They don't mention a lot of things. But they *do* talk about Cleveland Sellers. Everybody talks about Cleveland Sellers. Stroman's speech intensified as he got to the crux of what bothers him about the aftermath of the shooting.

John Stroman's white hair indicates his age though it could also come from intense deliberation, worry, anger, or sorrow. He's clearly very intelligent, and he's been around the block a few times. More than once he said he'd tell me some of the story but not all of it—he doesn't want to let go of certain memories. So he'd circle back and repeat himself, reworking the past and his theories. But there's a stark sadness wrapped up in his efforts to understand this complicated past. For all his deliberations about what happened that night, Stroman can't escape one painful fact—he was not there when those three young men were killed.

# 6  THE STATE'S MEN

Carl Stokes said it happened often. His phone would ring at one, two in the morning. On the other end of the line would be his boss, Chief J. P. Strom, who would tell him to get dressed and come pick him up pronto. Strom would direct him to drive to some small town a few hours from Columbia—Bamberg, Allendale, Barnwell. The two would travel through the dark Carolina night on back roads, deer darting across occasionally, passing hamlets and farms and speaking few words, an anxious air of caution hovering between them.

Stokes remembers the first such trip—remembers it as though it were yesterday. When I interviewed him in February 2010, he explained that he was more scared than cautious because he understood the seriousness of their venture. They drove into Allendale, in the western part of the state. Strom directed him to turn into a cemetery in the middle of town. In the car's headlights they spotted what looked like a group of men standing beneath an oak tree. Strom told Stokes to cut the lights and pull up closer to the tree. Stokes parked the car, and Strom got out. Stokes watched nervously from the car as his boss walked up to and greeted about a dozen black men. They seemed to know each other. The men told him what they were planning—a march to a local lunch counter, where they expected to be arrested. Strom was in on the protest from the beginning. Local black leaders wanted things to go

Facing: Historical marker commemorating the events of February 8, 1968 smoothly and didn't want any violence; they didn't want Alabama or Missis-sippi in South Carolina. And neither did some white leaders in the state. To this day, said Stokes, it bothers him that few people know about this behind-the-scenes work.

Some white leaders in South Carolina, he believes, realized by the early 1960s that segregation was wrong and wouldn't last. "We in the South knew that, know that, and had tried to make it right by separate but equal, but Governor Byrnes and then McNair realized that that was not going to be, that the federal government was going to push farther and rightly so. Congress doesn't go in and just change laws; they adapt laws to whatever they want done to carry on a peaceful society. The only way to change laws is to put them in the courts." For that to happen, Stokes explained, some white leaders understood that whites and blacks in the state had to communicate and work together to effect changes in laws. It was clear to them that, in states such as Alabama and Mississippi, blacks distrusted whites. So South Carolina took an approach that involved behind-the-scenes meetings be-tween whites in law enforcement and black leaders to establish open lines of communication in order to build something that resembled trust. It had to happen under the radar, Stokes believes, because if it happened in the open whites or blacks might think one group was taking the side of the other. Appearances were everything.

The South Carolina Law Enforcement Division (SLED) was always involved. It was the premier law-enforcement agency in South Carolina and was charged with providing technical and logistical assistance to local law-enforcement agencies and conducting special investigations. They worked directly under the governor. In the days before the advent of a police acad-emy in South Carolina, SLED provided crucial technical services, such as dusting crime scenes, for undertrained and understaffed police forces across the state. It wasn't particularly glamorous work. Stokes was in forensics and was often called out to some podunk crossroads to dust a house or a coun-try store for fingerprints. He said they were called for just about anything. It never happened, but if Strom had called him at home in the middle of the night and told him that some police chief in Walhalla or Beaufort or wher-ever was writing a report and needed a pencil, he'd hop out of bed and hit the road. He'd take that chief a pencil. He'd take him two.

It was an exciting job for a twenty-something son of a former minor-league ball player turned sheriff from Darlington County. Stokes was always on the go. Traveling about the state. In the know. Behind the scenes work—important work. Indeed Stokes and another agent, J. Leon Gasque, were

Strom's go-to guys. He depended on them, especially when it came to civil rights matters. In conjunction with local law enforcement and community leaders, they helped organize security for demonstrations. Strom confided in Gasque and Stokes and trusted them enough to call them early in the morning to drive with him to some clandestine meeting. Stokes said that, through these meetings, Strom was able to build relationships with local black leaders. "And that's what people don't realize about South Carolina," he insisted; "that's why we did not have any troubles in the state until Orangeburg." Unfortunately Orangeburg was different. According to Stokes, things got out of hand quickly there; the standard operating procedure didn't work with a group of college students riled up by outside agitators, such as Cleveland Sellers, he claimed; and because of Sellers, local leaders weren't able to take charge of the situation.

On Monday, February 5, Stokes and Strom went to Orangeburg. They conferred with Orangeburg Police Chief Roger Poston about what was going to happen the next time students tried to go bowling—who was going to be arrested and how they were going to get arrested. Stokes and Strom went back to Columbia thinking they'd be back the next day to have a demonstration and arrest some students and take this bowling alley controversy to the courts.

"Now were you talking to any of the students?" I asked him. "Were you talking to people like John Stroman?"

"I don't know John Stroman, but there were some blacks we were talking with together with the owner." Stokes said, but he doesn't remember exactly who they were in communication with in the community (preachers, college administrators), other than Chief Poston.

When they returned to the bowling alley on Tuesday, they found students gathering in the parking lot. "They were not belligerent, were not agitated. I remember standing there talking to a small group, and they told me they did not understand how they could go over to Vietnam and come back and not be allowed in this establishment. And I agreed with them, and I said this is the way to get it changed: change the law, without any violence. But somehow or another as the night went, each little group we talked to was friendly with us, and we'd leave them, and next thing you know they're belligerent, start hollering and cursing us. We'd try to calm them down and go to another group, but each time we'd do that, one individual in that area would go talk to them." It was Cleveland Sellers, he said. Sellers was out there talking to students, riling them up. The violence that night had nothing to do with the arrival of the fire truck, as others have said, and memories of water hoses turned on civil rights demonstrators in Orangeburg in the early 1960s. The fire truck was in the parking lot for only a brief period of time—long enough for law enforcement to realize it was a bad idea. The agitation, Stokes believes, was caused by Cleveland Sellers. It was all Sellers.

According to Stokes, the fighting started when a student came forward and kicked in the glass door of the bowling alley. When the glass broke, "It sounded like a shotgun. Pow. He kicked it. Pow."

"You said you saw him kick it?" I asked.

"I didn't see the act. I was blocked out. But I was close enough to hear and see the commotion. That was the one thing that set everything off; that's when the melee took place. Everybody started running and swinging."

"A lot of students, men and women, were hit. There was a lot of violence, wasn't there?"

"If you can imagine a crowd that is standing there, and all of a sudden something happens, and they started swinging, and when one starts swinging, everyone starts swinging, and there was commotion every which way." Eventually the students ran off, he said.

"Was it excessive, would you say?"

"Nah. Well it was just, it lasted four or five minutes and the whole parking lot was empty. Excessive? I don't know if 'excessive' would be the proper word. The force that was used was enough to break up what was happening." Stokes said he was disappointed that things had not gone as planned, that students hadn't been arrested the way they usually were. And he was frustrated that "one guy had set all this off." That "one guy," he claimed, was Cleveland Sellers.

I told him about BACC and John Stroman, that it wasn't a large organization, that there were clear disagreements between Sellers and students about what to do next after the confrontation at the bowling alley, indicating that the students were not all on the Cleveland Sellers bandwagon.

"They did not let that be known to us," Stokes answered. "Because it was common knowledge throughout law enforcement that Cleveland Sellers was there on purpose to cause violence and that's what was occurring." From Stokes's perspective, and that of others in South Carolina law enforcement, Sellers was dangerous. This is what the FBI was telling them. This is what they believed. And then there is this confrontation at the bowling alley. Sellers, they must've thought, was in town to create havoc. "Another thing always concerned me—from the very first civil rights demonstration—the outside media would come in from up north. They would try to get the police to do something so that they would have something to report back.

They were always pushing for violence, pushing for violence, pushing for violence. The media tried to stage things that would cause papers to sell in other parts of the country."

"How did they do that? By talking with the police, the students?"

"Well they tried to get us to arrest some students for nothing to start with, and then they tried to get students to do things that police would react to." He didn't have any examples, though (none that he could remember).

By Wednesday, Stokes and Strom and the others from SLED were hunkered down in Orangeburg. They had stayed overnight. "The next day we started planning what needed to be done, talking to the chief, talking to the governor. That's when they set up a curfew. We set up roadblocks 'cause at first dark when cars were coming down Highway 601 in front of the college, they were being bombarded by bricks and things." Again there was little communication between SLED and the campus. "We didn't know anything. Nothing was coming from the campus, and nothing was coming to us other than that they were upset. I think they were upset that the kid that kicked in the window was arrested. It seemed like they were disgusted with that."

Wednesday evening he was standing near a roadblock on 601, closer to Claflin College. All of a sudden, a red-striped number-fifteen pool ball landed about ten steps away from him. Rather nonchalantly, Stokes reached into a bag and pulled out what he said is the same ball. He said he also heard "rifle shots" while standing out there. "We had a SLED agent and an FBI agent down at the depot telling us the bullets were zinging over their heads, hitting that building. If I had to put a number on it, I couldn't, but it was a lot of shots on Wednesday."

"So you knew that there were rifle shots, coming from a .22 probably, on Wednesday?"

"My background was as a forensic examiner. And my thought was that it was a .22 rifle."

"But no one found any bullets the next day?"

"We didn't look for any." They didn't go up on either campus to investigate that night or the next day because, he said, the campuses were closed.

"So did anyone try to find the person shooting?"

"We confided in the security on campus to let us know what was happening. From an investigative standpoint, we did not go on campus to try to pinpoint, but we got word that that stopped, and we needed to find out who was doing it if possible, but we never got to first base with it."

Because students had been throwing things at passing cars, the roads around the campus were still closed the next day. And still, he said, he heard the occasional round of gunfire. "It wasn't any continuous wailing. It was a shot here and maybe fifteen to twenty minutes later another shot. I don't know what they were shooting at. It seemed to be coming from the dormitories at State but also right where Claflin joined State."

As darkness fell on Orangeburg, students began gathering in an open space close to the edge of the South Carolina State campus. "And they were sitting out there because the campus was closed down. After having been there a little while, they built a bonfire in Watson Street." Stokes and Strom were not there at that time; they were out checking on various utilities around town that were being guarded—water, electric, and gas. At about ten o'clock Chief Strom got a call that the fire in Watson Street had grown. "I was driving, and Gasque was next to me, and Chief Strom was in the back with the FBI agent in charge of South Carolina, Charles DeFord. And we pulled up to the railroad track." They could see the flames from the bonfire almost touching the lights on the telephone poles. Strom made the decision to put the fire out. Because they were concerned that students might prevent the fire from being extinguished, he ordered ten or twelve highway patrolmen to escort the fire truck with a squad of National Guardsmen following. "That group of highway patrolmen stood at the foot of that little knoll, and the firemen began to put the fire out," Stokes told me. "There was some cement steps just to the right of where the patrolmen lined up. I was standing at the top of those steps. The students had moved back—all the way back out of the light. For whatever reason, I don't know, they started whooping and a hollerin' and throwing and charging back. What set off the shooting, I don't know. Whoever you talk with heard something different. But I believe that whoever or however that shooting had come from the campus the night before, shot the first shot. And I think the volley of shooting that followed was an answer to that shot."

"You don't think it was because Officer Shealy was hit while y'all were standing near the fire truck? That that incident raised tensions that led to the shooting?"

"I was standing there, and Officer Shealy was hit, and I didn't have any ideas whatsoever of anyone having been shot. From looking at Officer Shealy, I would have never thought he was shot because he was bleeding in the face. A gunshot wound is not going to cause that kind of damage. . . . It happened while they were back, before they charged forward."

I ask Stokes why, if the students were charging, did law enforcement use lethal buckshot? Why didn't they use gas or some other method to hold them off? He said gas wasn't used because the wind was blowing down 601, and gas wouldn't have helped their situation—it would have either blown back into their faces or impeded their ability to get to the students. "There was no expectation of having to use those guns," he claimed. "Those were mostly for show. The carbine, nobody ever thought the carbine would be used. Those were a show of force hoping that nothing would happen. But that split second of whatever triggered, and you hear the one patrolman saying he heard this and another one heard that. . . . I was standing right there, and when the students started back, 'cause they had backed up all the way to the end of that open space, that grassy lot. As they started back, they were shot. When they were shot, they were in the middle of that open space; they had charged that far. That's probably close to fifty yards."

Stokes continued, "But I'm telling you now that something caused it, and with the gunfire that we had the night before, that could easily have happened."

"Did you feel in danger out there at all?"

"I did not feel danger then until they started charging back. The thought went through my mind, 'How we gonna stop them?'"

"And you were up on those steps?"

"I was up on the top step."

"You were on the top step, and the troopers were?"

"The troopers were to my left, in fact, a split second, all I heard was yee-tuuuuttt-tuuut-ttuuuut. The guy, the patrolman beside me, I don't know who it was, but the patrolman beside me had a carbine on full automatic. Dddddeeetttttteeeeee."

"How many shots can you get out of a carbine?"

"I don't know how many a clip would hold, I'd say nine or ten. I would think that would be about right. And the shotguns, double-ought buckshot is all we had because in a riot situation we aren't concerned about what size shot we're shooting. In a riot situation this is our normal training. And that is what we train for, not a civil rights demonstration but a riot demonstration."

"Are you talking about the training manual from the FBI about riot control? Had you been through that training?"

"I don't know when that book was published. I'm a graduate of the FBI National Academy, and I went through that in 1961. They did not offer any riot or civil rights training at that time. All we had was training dealing with criminals, and riots meant to overthrow the government, and so at that particular time having anything less than buckshot would've been for naught. Normal issue for a riot situation at that time was double-ought buck."

"And that's because it can spray and do more damage?"

"Well a double-ought buck has nine in it. One shell has nine buckshot, and they're about the size of a .32 caliber. So you got nine pellets going out at one time—depending on the choke of a shotgun, as to whether they stay together or whether they scatter. That's the principle behind bird shot. Bird shot's got I don't know how many pellets in it, but the design is if you got an open barrel then it starts spreading the time it leaves and you got bird flying. You just cover a whole area. You don't really aim at them; you just point and shoot."

"But most of the wounds on the students were from behind?"

"The FBI report indicated that there were gunshot pellets, bullets, found in the third floor of that dormitory. The highway patrolmen were shooting up. It depends. Some were shot on the legs, in the back, but let me tell you, they had come halfway back down whenever they were shot. In fact, the three that were moved from the middle, they were probably in the front of the line. And so that the shots weren't level, were shooting up. Now some might have gotten hit in the foot because of buckshot scattering."

"After the shooting, what did you feel emotionally?"

"I did not know anybody was shot, anybody was hurt. It reminded me of going to a western movie when I was kid, and the cowboys are shooting right into a herd of buffalos, and they fall. Well the students started coming and next thing I know, they all went down. The thought went through my mind, 'They killed every one of them.' And then when they started getting back up and running. So I was relieved that maybe they just fell, not been shot but fell."

"What were you thinking about at this time, besides 'I'm doing my job, et cetera'?"

"The thing that went through my mind, I did not think anybody was killed. I did not. And I thought how much we had tried to keep something of this sort going because we had been going to civil rights demonstrations since '61, '62 and how hard we had worked in trying to keep this from happening, and here this all of a sudden blew up in our faces."

What caused it? Why did things get so far out of hand? For one, Stokes said, there wasn't much communication with college administrators or faculty. "When that fire got as big as it did," he said, "they should have put it out. They should have come and made sure that was extinguished not us to go forward and do it. But they did not." As far as SLED knew, no one was in charge, or if anyone was in charge, it was Cleveland Sellers. "That is what we thought and that is what was coming from the black leaders that we were dealing with, that Sellers had control of the students. And that he would not let them agree to do anything and they lost control of the students because of Cleveland Sellers. And that's the reason we got to looking for him and arrested him that night. And me and a deputy sheriff named Livingston drove him to the penitentiary at two o'clock in the morning. I was driving the car, and Sellers was in the backseat, handcuffed."

"Mr. Stokes, you said that the truth needs to be known and to be honest with you, every single person I interview has a different truth. So what do we do?"

"Well, I think until the black community over there realizes the State of South Carolina was doing its darnedest to try to keep this from happening. And there were supposed to be arrests made on Tuesday, but for some reason it didn't happen. And we blame Cleveland Sellers for that not happening. And that's the part that others don't know. They know he was convicted but they think he was convicted for Thursday night but that's not true. He was convicted for Tuesday night."

Stokes wants to be clear on one thing—SLED worked hard to prevent things like what happened in Orangeburg from ever taking place. Orangeburg got away from them. There was no midnight meeting in a cemetery. There was no cabal of white and black leaders. There was no open communication. SLED had better success elsewhere. Because of their work and that of local law-enforcement officers, the Klan became a nonfactor in South Carolina. Bass and Nelson noted that Strom himself was "a central figure in South Carolina's record of racial peace," that he was responsible for disrupting the Klan and had "won respect for his handling of civil rights demonstrations." Indeed Stokes remembers sneaking around parking lots at Klan rallies and copying the license-plate numbers of parked cars at Strom's request. That, he told me, was scary, but necessary, work.

"Jack Bass's book has got some facts in there that are accurate, but he tries to persuade so many others that there was no gunshots being fired from campus, and he tries to make out that we were villains, when in all honesty we were trying our best to settle everything. We had no idea that anything like this would happen in Orangeburg. And we did everything we thought we could to try to alleviate and we thought we had a plan going in South Carolina where nothing happened anywhere else over civil rights." And then, just a few years later, Lamar, South Carolina, happened. Stokes was there. The county was integrating the schools, and the U.S. marshal needed help making it happen. A crowd of angry whites was waiting for the first bus with black children to arrive. They attacked the bus. One man used a long, heavy chain to break the windows. Another popped the hood, took off the distributor cap, and threw it in the woods. Others were rocking the bus, trying to turn it over. While all this was going on, Stokes and others were at the back door of the bus, shepherding terrified children to safety. He told me they were able to arrest twenty-eight members of that white mob and convict them. After it was all over, he went down into those woods and found the distributor cap. He still has that distributor cap.

Many people in South Carolina's law-enforcement community, as well as citizens and business owners, believed there was a real possibility that students from State and Claflin College would join forces with local African Americans and riot. They had seen images from riots in many major American cities—including Watts (August 1965), Detroit (July 1967), and Washington, D.C. (August 1967)—and imagined the same could happen in Orangeburg. Mayor Pendarvis claimed that the marching permit was denied on Wednesday because of Tuesday night's violence. He and others were concerned that students might cause more damage to businesses. Pendarvis said, "I saw pictures. I read articles about Detroit, Los Angeles, Newark. We just don't want any part of that here. Some of these people have been indicating—not by finger shaking, not by mouth, but by their actions what we can expect." Add to this the belief that black power advocates were on the campus, a lack of real communication between races, and a few students throwing bricks at cars, and the recipe for rumors was complete. Many white people sincerely believed that Orangeburg would be the next Watts.

Yet, if a riot had broken out in Orangeburg, most members of the South Carolina Highway Patrol had undergone riot training in 1966 that should have prepared them for such circumstances. After the training, each district was given a copy of an FBI and Department of Justice produced booklet titled *Prevention and Control of Mobs and Riots,* which covers tactics of crowds. The authors noted that crowds often have goals and objectives and can be either leaderless or under the leadership of an "insurgent agitator." Either way crowds can become volatile and cause property damage and loss of life. The manual notes that controlling such errant crowds or mobs requires well-organized and executed tactics on the part of law enforcement: "In regular police training the officer is taught to act and react as an individual. For riot duty, this must be expanded to cause him to act as a member of a team." If possible, law enforcement should prevent a riot from ever happening through containment, isolation, and crowd dispersal. "The old adage

'An ounce of prevention is worth a pound of cure,' is applicable to distur-
bances and riots." If prevention doesn't work, police should "apply the cure."
The manual is clear, though, that "the cure" does not have to be, and should
not be, "brutal or inhumane." "The premature application of excessive force
will only contribute to the danger, aggravate the mob, and instill in the individual a deep-rooted hatred of police." To that end, each police force should
establish its own "sequence of force" protocol. This book offers the United
States military's sequence of force as a useful model: "1. Unload rifles with
bayonets fixed and sheathed. 2. Unload rifles with bare bayonets fixed. 3. Tear
Gas. 4. Loaded rifles with bare bayonets fixed." The manual makes it clear
that following such a sequence is one way to prevent the use of excessive force
and the provocation of further violence. Every possible action should be
taken before lethal force is used. "The most extreme action which a law-
enforcement officer can take in any situation is the use of firearms. Under no
circumstances should firearms be used until all other measures for controlling the violence have been exhausted. Above all, officers should never fire
indiscriminately into a crowd or mob."

*Prevention and Control of Mobs and Riots* is especially clear on one point:
prevention is key. The discussion of a "sequence of force" comes, tellingly, at
the end of the manual and after an exhaustive discussion of preventive measures. The manual stresses: "Prevention and control of civil disorders are a
community responsibility—not an exclusive function of the police. Actually,
police agencies function most effectively where there is mutual understanding of both community problems and police responsibilities." It notes that a
respect for individual rights is crucial in a democracy and reminds readers
that one of our country's founding documents acknowledges that all men are
created equal. "Any unjust denial, actual or imagined, of man's basic rights,
needs or aspirations can give rise to a feeling of frustration and desperation"
and perhaps to violence. Thus, the authors claimed, to prevent riots or mobs,
we must work "to eliminate conditions which could lead to friction and misunderstanding and ultimately to violence and lawlessness." This happens
when law-enforcement work closely with communities to understand problem situations, communicate with "key groups," and create ways for "release
of tension." Left unaddressed, such situations lead to anger and resentment
and "bitterness." When there's a spike in feelings of "bitterness" law enforcement should take warning. It's clear that law enforcement in South Carolina
took warning, but it's not clear that they or most of the white citizens of
Orangeburg tried to understand the roots of student complaints in February

1968. It's not clear that *anyone* took their complaints seriously or understood that this was more than just about going bowling.

James Charles Pace (or J.C.) was ninety-three years old when I interviewed him (just months before his death on November 9, 2009) and a retired captain of the South Carolina Highway Patrol. He was also my great-uncle. I always seemed to hold a special place in his heart and he in mine. I think this was in part because he had only one child, a daughter, who was much older than I. When I was growing up, J.C. always seemed delighted to see me and would slip me a Lincoln when my parents weren't looking. Back then he was silver-haired and in uniform. And he was rarely serious about anything in my presence except when extolling the virtues of hard work and obedience to the law. One night when I was seventeen and drinking a beer at a party, I joked with another nephew of his about this. "Uncle J.C. would be pissed if he saw us now!" We chuckled but then the thought of how he *really* would handle the situation crept in and chilled us to the bone.

Despite his reverence for the law, J.C. was not afraid to have a good time. He was a man about town, and his calendar was always full. He liked a free meal and a party and seemed to be either coming from one or going to one in his dark blue Crown Vic, filled to the gills with papers, cups, and random articles of clothing, the accumulations of his high-flying lifestyle. J.C. lived like this well into his early nineties. A series of health issues eventually led to an infection in and subsequent amputation of his right leg. Now he had a permanent seat in a wheelchair, where he sat among the folks at the Oaks nursing home in Orangeburg. And yet he still tried to get out, to go to this wedding or that awards banquet, this dinner or that reception. He wanted to be with people because it brought him joy. And this is the thing about J.C.: his love was palpable. A few days before our interview for this book, my wife and I took our three-month-old daughter to visit him. When I arrived, he was chatting up the receptionist in the lobby. I heard him as I walked up: "They're coming to see me. My nephew's coming to see me with his baby."

I wheeled him outside underneath a portico to shield him from the sun. Because he'd been in and out of the hospital, J.C. had contracted MRSA virus, and our pediatrician was none too keen on us taking our baby into an enclosed space with him. That was fine by him; he'd still get to meet baby Amelie and didn't care that it was a typical Orangeburg July day, ninety-five degrees with equal humidity. At first glance of Amelie he threw his hands up in the air like his beloved Clemson Tigers had just scored a touchdown. "All right!" he shouted. He was overjoyed at the sight of my sleeping baby and shared his delight with everyone who exited or entered the home. Everyone seemed to know him, and they all called him "Captain."

As we were leaving, J.C. whispered to me, "I spoke with your mother about your project. I'd be happy to talk with you. Let's meet on Thursday." This was said with a directness and coherence that belied his illness and age. The gesture of reaching out to him to talk about what happened on February 8, 1968, clearly meant something to him.

When we met, J.C. was all business and solemn; this was not to be fun and games and slipping me five-dollar bills. He got the preliminaries out of the way—"I was born in Sumter, South Carolina, and moved to Orangeburg when I was two years old"—and cut to the chase. "I was second in command in this district the time that happened. I was a senior lieutenant and stationed in Orangeburg." He knew something was up, that something was going to happen. The college students were angry, and the whole town seemed on edge. He remembered one time that week when some students were marching over to the bowling alley. He got out of his car and started walking with them, trying to figure out what was going on, what it was all about. They talked, the highway patrolman and the students. The students told him they were just having fun. "They had no intention of creating trouble; they just thought it was something fun. And that's the way it was. But people don't realize how much hell *we* caught."

He remembered having good, honest conversations with those students, faculty from the college, and others in the community. But it was such a violent incident; he still wondered if it had to happen at all. "I just remember thinking, this is a serious thing that's happening." And it did get serious. On Tuesday night he was right there when the glass window at the bowling alley shattered and the melee ensued.

"My commanding officer assigned me to go into the bowling alley and make a telephone call. And I went in and I was standing at the door when they broke in. I was lucky I wasn't hurt or something, but I wasn't. It was a bad situation. All types of officers from every division, every agency that you can think of, were involved. And some of them were running after the students after the break in and trying to stop 'em." He was never sure who did it, but several businesses had their windows smashed. He was not sure why the students were acting out in this way and wondered if they were caught up in the moment. "I hated that the situation was like it was because there were a lot of good students who were just doing it for a lark. It's like kids coming along and they'll say, 'That man has a football in his yard. I bet you won't go take it and run with it?!' Crazy little things, you know."

"But don't you think they were frustrated that the bowling alley and many other places in Orangeburg were still segregated? That they couldn't go places if they wanted to because of the way they looked?"

"Well, that's true," he said, and his voice trailed off. There was a silence for about five beats and then, "I didn't like it. I never did!" He clenched his fist and banged on the armrest of his wheelchair. "Listen, your family and my family—it's right poignant—but both families have never been racial in the sense that we ever looked down on anybody. I saw my daddy, I tell you what right now, he wouldn't stand for anybody being mistreated. No black. No white. One time two fellas were takin' advantage of one of his black employees and charging him an unbelievable amount of interest on a loan. He'd never be able to pay that little debt off. And they said, 'We'll take you to court.' And my father said to them, 'You try to take him to court, but right now you get the hell off my property!'"

I ask J.C. if he knew about the civil rights movement in Orangeburg prior to what happened in 1968. "Yeah, we knew; we had a group working on it. You can't hold that against them. They had a right to work for their rights. If a black man was to walk in a store, and he paid his money for goods, and the proprietor says, 'You can't come in here.' 'Why can't I come in?' 'Well, I don't want a black in here.' Well that's bad business, first of all. But I don't like it. Our families didn't like it. And that's it. That's just a matter of fact, Jack."

To that end, he thought Harry Floyd was taking too hard a line on the issue of his bowling alley, that he should have opened it up; it wasn't worth the struggle he went through to keep it segregated. Then J.C. allowed, "I knew him well. I knew his daddy. I went on a fishing trip out on the ocean with him once. . . . I just think he took it too far. Something ticked him off, I reckon." And there were a lot of folks in Orangeburg applying heavy pressure on him to not integrate. There were all kinds of people and groups telling Floyd all kinds of things. Some of these people who opposed integration were "friends of your family and my family." But he wouldn't say who, won't give names.

As things got more intense that week, J.C. found himself out on the street even more. On Thursday evening, he was out on Highway 601. There was a buzz in the air. I tried to walk him through the events that led up to the shooting, but we kept getting sidetracked. He focused on gunfire he said he heard coming from the campus, telling me he "could hear the pellets hit that warehouse, the W. A. Livingston Warehouse."

"Why didn't anyone go and try to find the gunfire and stop the person shooting?"

"Why didn't they? They did. Tried to track them down. It was just one of those unfortunate things."

"So where do you think they were shooting from?"

"Well, they'd moved over to the Claflin area which made it close to the warehouse."

"Why do you think it happened?"

"It happened because of that fella, and I tell you he was an instigator. But I want to stay away from that. He's still active. Ain't no question about that. He was a professor at Carolina and now he's president at Voorhees."

"You mean Cleveland Sellers. But why did it happen at that moment? The story most people tell is that an officer, Officer Shealy, was hit in the head by a board and then later the patrolmen fired." J.C. was quiet for a moment. One of the highway patrolmen who fired, Sidney C. Taylor, mentioned J.C. by name in testimony to the FBI. Taylor claimed that, after the fire was getting out of hand, "Lt. Pace of District 7 came to our group and told us a fire truck was being sent to put out the fire in the street. Pace told [deleted] to move the District 6 riot squad up so as to protect the fire truck."

"Well, I had two fellows with me, subofficers. They needed to go to the office and to gas up their cars. I had just authorized them to do so when that thing broke out. We had the alarm that one of our men had been shot, and actually he had been hit and was bloody, real bloody. And word got out just like that, and they had the confrontation with the firing of the rifles and pistols or whatever."

In the hallway, just outside the door, almost as if on cue, a woman began screaming unintelligibly, disrupting my train of thought.

"Was the shooting a mistake?" I asked.

"Well, the shooting, it just happened. They thought he was shot."

"Do you feel regret? Do you feel sad that it happened?"

The screaming intensified. I wanted to get up and shut the door.

"I certainly do. Because you take the three that were killed, they might have just been there. . . . You had some people involved in serious things, but what led to it was nothing, nothing. And then they get involved in something serious. Still happens."

The screaming in the hallway continued, so I shut the door.

"I had some friends out at State College," he said, "and I had 'em well on down the line, but they caught the devil from all sides."

"Can you remember some of them? Do you remember the names?"

"I won't give any names. I was close to them. Close friends. . . . But at the time Maceo Nance was president, and he caught it from both sides right on down the line trying to get the two groups together, trying to get blacks and whites together, to get over that incident, that unfortunate action that had taken place, and try to work together and have peace." As he said this the screaming woman in the hallway bumped into his door, and I could hear nurses and orderlies trying to calm her down and take her back to her room.

J.C. told me he was also interested in the community coming together after the shooting, but allowed that there is still much work to do. "We're still battling it," he said, "still battling this thing. Some individuals don't have God in their heart. How can you judge a poor black here in such a manner and say he's not pleasant to be around? Well in Orangeburg you got a lot of poor, poor blacks, and they can only do so much. But they're going to have to be treated right before it's all over."

There has been some progress, he said, some change, but there's still so much segregation—socially, culturally, geographically. "Not all whites like that they live in a place where 75 percent of the population is black. Well the blacks might not want to live in a place where 75 percent of the population is white. And that's the way it is. And sometimes real-estate folks push people to live here or there." He looked down for a moment. I could tell he was getting tired from our talk.

"Do you think about that night a lot?"

"I've given it too much thought. It's aggravating. I'll never get over that because there were so many good people involved. And those three could have been innocent people."

"Do you think mistakes were made that night? Is there something that could have happened that would have changed the outcome?"

"No, that fella had 'em keyed up. It's like them cheerleaders out there that have him cheering and hollering for their team. They were keyed up to that point. He wasn't the only one, there were others, but I do believe he was the principal one. I do believe it. And anybody who was involved to any extent would have to believe it. And he had 'em keyed up to the point where it exploded."

He paused, looking stressed. "You know, I wish I could tell you more. I can tell you right now that pressure was put for that to develop. It could have been avoided so easy, so easy. And it's caused us to suffer in this area and it makes me sad. I believe in equality. I believe that people should have their rights—firmly believe that."

"But weren't there things that the city could have done?" I asked. "That the white community could have done to respond to the demands from the black community?"

"Yes," he answered, there were things that whites could have done. "They had a complaint. Sure, they had a complaint."

And then, as I was leaving, he stopped me and looked me in the eye, warning me, "Jack, I just want you to be careful with this." And then he followed me in his wheelchair and stopped at the television room for his wing of the nursing home, a spartan place, all white walls, ceilings, and floor, a hospital not in name but in style and purpose. A game show blared from the set in the front of the room and fifteen or so patients and nurses faced forward in rapture. Black and white faces content with *The Price Is Right* and the quiet release that informed consumerism brings one on a hot summer morning. I left J.C. to the television and walked out, passing a painting of Jesus Christ, his arms up in the air as if he were about to slam dunk a basketball.

I remember something J.C. once said to me. Shortly after I began teaching in Ohio, I was telling him about life there versus life in South Carolina. The conversation turned to college football, and he said, "You know, I always liked Ohio State football. And I still respect Woody Hayes, despite what he did." That is a loaded statement coming from a man whose blood runs Clemson orange. Indeed a Clemson fan will never forget that moment at the 1978 Gator Bowl when Ohio State coach Woody Hayes punched Clemson nose guard Charlie Bauman after he intercepted an Ohio State pass. Hayes landed a direct hit to Bauman's throat. Then one of his own players tried to step in, and Hayes had to be restrained. It was a moment of wild rage, a moment of violence that has entered college football mythology. But when J.C. talked about the story, he had left his anger in the past. "You know," he said, "I forgive him for that. I do."

The conventional narrative is that there was limited media coverage of the shootings at South Carolina State. In their recent history of South Carolina, Jack Bass and W. Scott Poole wrote: "Unlike Kent State, national media barely covered what happened at Orangeburg. The shooting occurred at night with no vivid TV images, the students were black, and press attention had shifted to growing protests against the war in Vietnam and from civil rights to urban riots outside the South." While there may have been little television coverage, there was significant newspaper coverage in the immediate aftermath. Much of that coverage is and was problematic. Most notably the

Associated Press (AP) circulated reports of the events that appeared in major newspapers and claimed there was an "exchange of gunfire" and that students in the crowd had fired at police and firemen. An AP photographer named Dozier Mobley was cited as having made this claim, but he later stated that he had been misquoted.

The state government perpetuated the "exchange of gunfire" story wherever and whenever possible. In a press conference shortly after the shooting, Governor McNair claimed that the violence in Orangeburg was "sparked by black power advocates who represent only a small minority of a total student body at South Carolina State College and Claflin College." McNair said that the shooting occurred after "a long period of sniper fire from the campus 'and not until an officer had been felled during his efforts to protect life and property.'" This statement, of course, refers to Officer Shealy being hit in the head by a piece of wood, though it reads as if he'd been shot. The governor's representative in Orangeburg, Henry Lake, went so far as to claim Cleveland Sellers threw that object. Other stories went a step further in portraying the students as aggressive instigators. On February 9, 1968, a story based on AP reports ran in the *New York Times* claiming that there was a "blast of gunfire between students and law enforcement officers" and asserting that Shealy was "struck in the head by a bullet." This wasn't the first exaggerated claim in the pages of the *New York Times* about the events in Orangeburg. An article about the melee at the bowling alley claimed that students overturned "several cars" on their way back to campus.

Reports also surfaced in major African American newspapers such as the *Chicago Daily Defender,* and the difference in the amount and perspectives of that coverage is revealing. What was a "Carolina Riot" in the *New York Times* was a "Carolina Slaughter" in the *Defender.* But so pervasive was the "exchange of gunfire" story that even the *Defender* reported on February 13 that students were involved in "firebomb throwing and sniping." The *Baltimore Afro-American* reported on February 10 that three were dead and fifty shot and that it was the result of a "melee to halt firebomb throwing." This report was from Mike Davis, a reporter for the paper who was arrested by law enforcement just prior to the shooting. Prophetically the *Defender* wrote: "Even if a Klansman should be the undisputed cause of a racial flareup, black power will be the scapegoat." The *Defender* and the *Baltimore Afro-American* explored the many responses of the black community throughout the United States—responses that ranged from anger to grief with every stop in between. The *Defender* reported the response of H. Rap Brown, who called the incident "The Orangeburg Massacre" and added "if we are going to be murdered for acting peacefully, we might as well be murdered while trying to kill a few white honkies." Brown claimed that the tone that led to the shootings was set by those at the top, namely President Lyndon Johnson, but that that reckless attitude began with John F. Kennedy. He told reporters: "Let white America know that the name of the game is tit for tat, an eye for an eye, a tooth for a tooth, and a life for a life." Brown and SNCC wanted to take the Orangeburg case to the United Nations. In the same edition of the *Defender,* there's a photo of Rev. Jesse Jackson, who gave a sermon at Chicago's New Friendship Baptist Church in which he spoke at length about Orangeburg. Jackson also called the event the "Orangeburg Massacre" and said "those were our children who died"; they weren't just names but "symbols of oppression." He concluded, "The bullets that pierced those bodies were designated for all persons who express the desire for freedom." Martin Luther King Jr. called it "the largest armed assault undertaken under color of law in recent Southern history."

In addition to black leaders, black college students made their feelings known. The Black Student Alliance of the University of Chicago held a Requiem for a Black Trinity at Rockefeller Chapel on February 18. At Crane Junior College (now Malcolm X College) in Chicago, 125 students marched carrying an empty casket. Another empty casket, labeled "Orangeburg Massacre," was carried in front of Madison Square Garden. Students at Benedict College and Allen University in Columbia, South Carolina, held a memorial service and passed a resolution calling for Governor McNair to dismiss and prosecute the highway patrolmen. Nine black people and a dozen white people "paraded in protest in front of the Federal Building" in Greenville, South Carolina, on Monday, February 12. Most were students from predominantly white Furman University. On Thursday, February 15, about three hundred students from Johnson C. Smith University in Charlotte marched to the city's main post office and burned an effigy of Governor McNair. There were at least nine student protests that day across the South, including demonstrations in Durham and Greensboro, North Carolina; Denmark, South Carolina (Sellers's hometown); and Petersburg, Virginia. For good measure, the group from Johnson C. Smith did it again the next day.

What happened at South Carolina State College shocked faculty, administrators, and students at colleges and universities throughout the nation. The *Chronicle of Higher Education* followed events in Orangeburg for several weeks. They too confused the story, claiming that the patrolmen were trying to clear the way for firemen to put out a fire in a nearby house and that there was an "extended period of sniper fire" before the firemen went in. A few weeks later the *Chronicle* reported on responses from colleges. The presidents of six historically black colleges in Atlanta wrote a letter to Attorney General Ramsey Clark and President Johnson demanding an investigation. Meanwhile white college students at a regional meeting of the National Student Association made plans to organize "white alert teams" to "stand between black students and law enforcement."

Locally residents of Orangeburg awoke on February 9, 1968, to a newspaper headline in the *Times and Democrat* that read: "All Hell Breaks Loose—Three Killed, Many Wounded in College Nightmare." Tensions were high in the community for weeks after the shooting, and the town was under a curfew. Perhaps, for good reason—some were out for revenge. The *Los Angeles Times* reported that *Washington Post* reporter "James Hoagland was attacked and beaten by a Negro wielding a lead-weighted club and wearing a 'Mau-Mau' necklace popular with black power advocates." His assailant was, in fact, neither a college student nor from the local community. Other outsiders were trying to get a piece of the action. The United Klans of America tried to hold a rally in Orangeburg the Saturday after the shootings, but their request was quickly denied by city officials.

Reporting for the *Charlotte Observer*, Jack Bass covered the shooting and aftermath extensively—his reports underscore the complicated emotions of the community and the college students involved. For one article Bass interviewed Bobby Poole (a twenty-one-year-old senior at State), who disagreed with McNair's accusations that the students were under the influence of black power activists and claimed that there were no more than fifteen or twenty radicals at State. "If the governor could have been here for the meeting Wednesday, he would have seen that black power didn't play as big a part in shaping student resentment as he thought." In many and important ways, Bass was giving voice to opinions and evidence that countered what was coming from the office of the governor. His reporting may have led to many of the nuanced editorials that the *Charlotte Observer* published. In one the editors wrote, "There was reckless and senseless provocation and action from the student side, to be sure. But South Carolina was repeatedly shown that legitimate grievances were creating a dangerous hostility among Negroes at the college and among other Negroes interested in the institution. Like traditionally Negro colleges in other states South Carolina State is woefully shortchanged. Yet South Carolina continued to dawdle in answering just demands for improvements." The bowling alley, they claimed, only fanned the flames of an ongoing issue that needed to be addressed.

And yet despite the best efforts of a few persistent journalists, what happened in Orangeburg, South Carolina, unlike what happened in Kent, Ohio, never truly caught the nation's attention. Perhaps—as the *Charlotte Observer* editors noted—State's status as a historically black college is the primary reason why. After Kent State there was a massive boycott by college students across the nation—at least 450 campuses participated. Neil Young famously sang about the "four dead in Ohio"; many books were written; seven documentaries were produced; a thorough investigation took place. There's no famous tune about Orangeburg that resonates, that gets stuck in your head—that makes you pause for a moment to think about the *three* dead in South Carolina. There's no Pulitzer Prize–winning photograph like the one taken by Kent State student John Paul Filo of Mary Ann Vecchio crying out in horror as she knelt over the body of Jeffrey Miller. She cried for help. She cried in anger. She cried in wonder—what had happened? What was happening? Indeed the other students around her appear dumbstruck, confused, helpless, almost nonchalant—the violence of Vietnam had arrived in the Midwest and in the middle of the day. The image speaks to that moment when nonviolent resistance became a thing of the past and the United States was hurtling down an uncertain path. It is a prescient and prophetic image. It is the one image anyone who knows anything about Kent State remembers.

Another image, an image from the aftermath of the shootings at South Carolina State, shapes our public memory in a more complicated way. Three highway patrolmen stand over the wounded bodies of Henry Smith and Delano Middleton in the wake of a nighttime shooting. The two young men are barely visible because of the legs of the highway patrolmen. One can just make out the pained face of Smith. In the foreground, a blood-splattered sidewalk. Off-center, a tense hand gripping a billy club. The three faceless white men stand over the wounded black men. This photograph has been taken before, the brutal aftermath, the white men, the black men. This photograph has been taken before. The bodies of black men, limp and broken, strung up next to a tree. Years before, this photograph has been taken.

# 7  THE STRUGGLE

In the wake of the deaths of Samuel Hammond, Delano Middleton, and Henry Smith, the United States Department of Justice, pursuant to the Civil Rights Act of 1964, sued for the desegregation of the bowling alley and the hospital and was successful on both counts. The Orangeburg hospital had been placed under court order to desegregate in 1965; yet the government asserted that, as of October 1967, "Negroes were still being put in a different part of the hospital than whites and cared for mostly by Negro personnel." The court finally agreed that the hospital was in compliance with the Civil Rights Act in late March 1968.

On Sunday, February 11, 1968, the NAACP organized a meeting in Orangeburg and called for the removal of the National Guard from the city. They also used the meeting to plan a boycott of white businesses. Rev. I. DeQuincey Newman, the South Carolina field director for the NAACP, asked that the boycott begin immediately. He also called for more black people to be employed in city and county jobs and for full integration of public schools. Newman was pointing to the underlying structural problems that led to the initial bowling alley protest. He claimed that state officials created the climate in which the events in Orangeburg had taken place.

Investigations were launched by the Department of Justice, SLED, the South Carolina Advisory Committee to the United States Commission on

Facing: The bridge in Edisto Memorial Gardens where Confederate troops mounted their last defense of Orangeburg

Civil Rights, and the Southern Regional Council, a civil rights organization based in Atlanta. Many prominent academics and civil rights leaders made it known publicly that all eyes were on Orangeburg and on the investigations. Indeed Martin Luther King Jr. sent a message about the investigation to Attorney General Ramsey Clark on April 4, 1968, asking the Justice Department not to let the shootings "go unpunished." In 1970 Jack Bass and Jack Nelson published their book, famously (or infamously, depending on who you ask) titled *The Orangeburg Massacre.*

Bass and Nelson paid particular attention to the most important post-shooting investigation—that of the FBI. Their research uncovered a few holes in this investigation, holes that some believe warrant a new investigation. In particular they questioned the close relationships between law-enforcement officers and the bureau. For example Charles DeFord (agent in charge of the Columbia FBI office) shared a hotel room in Orangeburg with Chief Strom from SLED. Special Agent Nelson Phillips, who had been in the state for eleven years, had a longstanding relationship with the South Carolina Highway Patrol; he testified that he heard shooting coming from the students right before the officers opened fire. More important, the Department of Justice did not learn of these relationships and that three FBI agents—DeFord, Bill Danielson, and Phillips—were on the scene of the shooting until April 1968. They had previously told Deputy Assistant Attorney General Robert Owen that they were in Orangeburg but not on the scene. Why the secrecy, Bass and Nelson asked? FBI director J. Edgar Hoover and Attorney General Clark rarely saw eye to eye on anything, to put it lightly. Can it be boiled down to that? Or, considering the historical moment, was the FBI simply overwhelmed and incapable of a more thorough investigation? Bass and Nelson claimed that in general there was a "lack of enthusiasm for the case" at the FBI. Whatever the reason, there wasn't enough evidence to convince a grand jury comprising twenty-three white people and two black people) to indict the patrolmen. After the verdict on November 7, 1968, Governor McNair expressed his hope that everyone could move forward and "put aside any remaining bitterness and animosity." More than one hundred South Carolina State students were not about to "put aside" anything, however, and they marched on South Carolina Highway Patrol headquarters on November 25, 1968, with John Stroman leading the way. And the Department of Justice did not "put aside" the case, charging the shooters with imposing "summary punishment" on the victims, thereby violating their constitutional rights. This charge, of course, led to the May 1969 trial in Florence, South Carolina, in which the highway patrolmen who shot and killed

Hammond, Middleton, and Smith and wounded at least twenty-eight others, were cleared of all charges.

We were sitting in a corner booth in the IHOP on North Road in Orangeburg in February 2010. We could easily have been at any IHOP anywhere in America. The aromas of coffee, fried bacon, and pancakes. The shouts in the kitchen and the scampering waitstaff. Only a few tables were empty when we walked in, and I could sense that my companion was a bit nervous—where were we going to sit so that no one would hear what we were talking about? A smile and a suggestion to the waitress found us a corner booth, and the steady din of the Saturday lunch crowd drowned out most of what we were saying. Nonetheless he leaned forward and spoke in hushed tones. When someone walked up to our table to greet him, he cut off quickly. Chatted it up with his friend. Waited until he left and cut back to our conversation.

This was a big deal for Clyde Jeffcoat. Outside his circle of friends, he had never really talked to anyone about what he experienced that night. There was a lot at stake for him. He's from this community, and he lives and works here. He knew what people would think if he told his story, if he explained how far he had come in his own thinking about race, if he said what he wanted to say: that what happened at South Carolina State College on February 8, 1968, shouldn't have happened.

His story begins on a farm in rural Orangeburg County. Like most folks from his generation, he remembers playing with black children as a child, but he also remembers obvious and apparent separation: "We had several black men who worked on the farm year 'round," he remembers. "When we would butcher a hog or something, they would eat in the house but at a separate table. You didn't ask, but I would say I was very much a segregationist. I believed in segregation at the time. It was the only thing I knew. We were taught it and that was the way that we understood fairness. And of course we didn't have anything to do with the system—we were born in it."

He was aware of the fact that "the system" was crumbling. He knew there were protests in Orangeburg and elsewhere. "My thing with black people was never any hatred. I always wanted to be fair to a guy—white, black, whatever. I just believed in segregation." Back then he didn't think black students should be making such a big deal about the bowling alley, but at the same time he didn't think they should be shot for it. He doesn't think any of the violence connected to the civil rights movement was necessary. "I don't think that it was necessary for those kids to get bombed in that church in Alabama. That was always despicable to me. Even those people in Alabama now who knew about and covered it up is still a sore spot to me on that state." But that violence always seemed distant to him; the water hoses and German shepherds weren't a part of his world.

But when he was called up on Tuesday night, February 6, his views changed. His memories from that first night are blurry; things got more precise when he remembered being out there by the railroad tracks between Boulevard and Magnolia on the evening of February 8. "Right where the crossover is," he said. He wasn't far from the students, but he couldn't see them that well. "But we could hear. We could hear everything very well." Jeffcoat knew this part of Orangeburg like the back of his hand. At the time he worked for an insurance agency. "And my debit route was Russell Street. Maxcy Street. Dickson Street. Directly across from the college. And I worked almost five years for the same company, and most of the time I was right there across from the college. And most of the time I'd collect at night 'cause that's when people were home. As soon as we were off duty that week, I was back out there on Maxcy and Dickson Street. I would park my car on Maxcy or Dickson and walk all through there. And I'm talking 8:00 at night. Directly after going off duty from the Guard, I was back out there where we'd been. And I never felt threatened even then. I knew a lot of the people there."

Standing out there, a soldier on the streets where he worked as a civilian, felt strange for twenty-five-year-old Jeffcoat. He was a squad leader, and the situation was intense. They had been warned about a two-story house across from where they were stationed. Rumor had it that Cleveland Sellers was in that house, and they were to keep an eye on it. He recalled that one light was on in an upstairs room, but that was it. The action, he said, was happening in the opposite direction. Jeffcoat and the other men in his squad could hear what sounded like gunshots, but they couldn't pinpoint exactly where the sounds were coming from. Every once and a while they would hear it. "They didn't even sound like they were in close proximity the few shots that we heard. I couldn't tell if they was from a firecracker or a gun. I thought it was a gun. But again, it was very sporadic." His men asked him how they should respond. Many were concerned about their duties and the repercussions of those duties. They didn't have any orders except to assist law enforcement, which never gave the guardsmen specific orders. How far did things have to go before they should or could act? They asked him. Jeffcoat told them, "If we're fired upon, we'll return fire. That's the only case. We don't return fire if we just *hear* a gunshot. If we know that we're fired upon, we'll return fire. But we never was." This is the part of his story that he was so hesitant to tell. This is the part of his story that still bothers him.

"I can tell you this: where we were, we never felt threatened. Now when I say we didn't feel threatened, obviously when you're in the area where tensions are as high as they were, there's got to be a certain amount of anxiety. But I never felt enough of a threat to allow the guys to lock and load." They had full-clip ammo at hand, but Jeffcoat never felt—the whole time they were out there—any need to distribute it. "We didn't ever feel the threat," he said.

Time has erased some of Jeffcoat's memories from that night; he was honest about that. But his memories of what he heard and what he felt while standing near the train tracks in the cold and darkness remained clear. "I didn't hear any shooting before the round of shots [from the highway patrolmen] and I got a very clear memory of those shots. I mean it did sound like—I mean you've heard a whole pack of fireworks set off at the same time—that's what brings the memory of it. It was scary. I knew what it was. I'd shot guns my whole life. And I do recollect this: it was not like they went 'pow' and then stopped. It was like you had less than ten seconds and it was like you fired off as many shots as you could. And they were started together."

But, he said, even then he didn't distribute the ammo to his men, even after hearing all those rounds go off. There was no immediate and clear danger. They were too cautious. They had all been around guns their whole lives and knew the possibilities they represented. Somebody could get excited and fire off a shot. And then, he said, you're in a mess of trouble.

"No one ever interviewed you," I asked, "or talked to you about what you saw and heard?"

"Never. It was almost like we wasn't out there. I wasn't even interviewed by my company commander, first sergeant, or my platoon sergeant. And here I am, with all this information, in close proximity, and you're the first person that's ever called me. I've never wanted to get into a courtroom over this stuff, but I haven't done anything to stay out. I've just never picked up the phone and called the Justice Department. But back then I thought there would be a court case, and I thought I'd have to move or something 'cause I couldn't answer questions the way a lot of people would have wanted to hear 'em answered. I was worried that I might do some damage to somebody when there was some strong justification that I didn't know about. And there still could be."

Jeffcoat told me he'll never forget that night. It's his albatross to think about what he heard and to know that so many people were shot down as they were. He's thought this thing through many times over. He's thought about the movement of the students, the weapons used, why the patrolmen fired when they did. He's thought about it all. "I can tell you," he said; "if you're moving forward toward those gunshots and only three guys died, they must have immediately fallen on the ground or turned."

I asked, "Do you mean if they were charging at the time they were shooting?"

"It would have been really a slaughter."

Jeffcoat's mind wandered and he speculated about what would have happened if some of the students had pulled out guns after that volley of shots, about the patrolmen's orders and who was in charge. "I could understand how some of it happened from fear. Somebody fired a shot from fear, and the other guys just jumped, piled in from fear. They had to be mentally prepared to react. It couldn't have all been spontaneous. You're not going to shoot down a human being just from a spontaneous thing. Something's got to be built up to a point for that to happen."

He paused and thought about what he was about to say. "This is one reason why I've never wanted this interview before. I think that it was a terrible mistake in judgment. I don't know why it ever came up in their mind that they needed that much firepower and force for what was going on in campus. When the students came to the bowling alley or other places, they were never armed, to my knowledge; they never told us that the students were armed. My belief has always been that they wanted to stop them and not let them off campus. But why they came to that conclusion at that particular time unless they were rushed. . . . I've dealt with guns my whole life and it doesn't take long to load." If he had been on that jury, he said, he wouldn't have been a bit of help. The whole thing was senseless. They didn't need to shoot as much as they did to get things under control. Bricks and bottles didn't warrant a volley of buckshot, he said.

Then Jeffcoat came full circle back to the problem of race. He wondered if that was what caused the shooting. And he wondered if the shooting has had, in the end, a positive effect on race relations in Orangeburg. But he shook his head, eyes looking down at the table, "To say that it turned things around will never justify it." He continued, "I wouldn't want to be one of those highway patrolmen that fired those shots. Even though they will never be prosecuted, I wouldn't want to have to live with it. I'm a Christian, and I think they can get forgiven for it from the Lord. If they are 100 percent wrong, they can get forgiven for it, and they won't have to answer for it."

"Did it shift *your* thinking?"

"Oh, yeah. But most people haven't changed as much as I have. I wasn't ever comfortable with the shooting up on campus, and I stayed away from it.

I didn't talk about it for years. But I've changed a lot, and now I have a lot of questions." Some of those questions are slowly being answered. He met John Stroman recently and was surprised by their connections—the student and the soldier who had been wrapped up in that whole mess but never knew each other. Jeffcoat felt comfortable talking to Stroman, almost as if they were somehow supposed to have met. And a lot of what Jeffcoat said corroborated what many students had been saying for years. "Some of the stuff he knew and I knew lined up. A lot of it lined up."

Jeffcoat added that John Stroman could hardly believe what he was hearing. "He said I was the first guy he'd heard say it from the other side. Then he asked me, 'How do you know the students weren't shooting at you guys or the law enforcement?' I said, ''Cause nobody ever got hit. We were an easy target! And if the students had weapons and the highway patrolmen fired like that, it seems to me [the students] would have fired back.'" If he'd been on that hill with his men, Jeffcoat assured me, there never would have been a book written about this stuff. It never would have happened. And then he asked me why I think they shot at the students, what's my theory? I told him I really don't have an answer. He nodded and said, "I don't think there is one. I don't think there is one."

But things have changed. Jeffcoat has changed. This community has changed. "Let me give you an example. I seen the guys harass George Dean, the first black man in South Carolina to join the guard. Not hurt him. I seen 'em harass him. If he had anger in him, he didn't show it. I've seen George Dean come in a mess hall, and white guys would be sitting down at the table, and they would get up and move and leave him sitting there by himself. I also saw that before George Dean got out of the guard, he was respected by a lot of guys, and they might go sit down by him instead of getting up and leaving."

George Dean told me it went like this: first of all, he was no gung ho soldier by any stretch of the imagination. Joining the National Guard was a good way to avoid a one-way ticket to Vietnam, and he knew it. Didn't care that there weren't any black men in the South Carolina National Guard. Didn't care that his friends might think he was crazy for joining up. He just wasn't interested in going to Vietnam. And his parents sure as hell weren't going to pay his way to Canada. It was that simple. Join the guard. Avoid 'Nam. Lots of folks were joining it for the same reason.

Dean got the idea from a fellow named Marty Green. Dean was working as a salesperson in an Orangeburg appliance store when he met Green. Marty was from Illinois and worked for WORG, the local radio station. One day Marty came into the store and said he'd joined the National Guard. Dean had been moving from state to state in order to change his status and stay ahead of the draft board, but he was getting tired of that game. Green's plan sounded more reasonable. Join the guard. Do your six years. Stay out of Vietnam. There was nothing terribly heroic about this move, he'll admit, but nonetheless he did integrate the South Carolina National Guard in 1965.

"And I caught hell for at least three of those six years. But I learned a lot about the South and the southern white man's mentality. I'm the lone black man in the whole damn South Carolina National Guard. And I'm with farmers, lawyers, everybody. And then I'm just with human nature. I find out that it ain't about no vocation, it's about the person now." Peer pressure, he told me, shaped the way many people interacted with him. "Now it's not just that he don't like Dean. It's just that if he is seen by his peers talking to Dean." Case in point: word spread that Marty Green was friends with George Dean. "And they'd say 'Green Dean the nigger lover.'"

Dean wasn't necessarily looking for a helping hand, and based on how he was treated, he didn't even expect it. He said that when he'd walk through the chow line, the cooks would slam food so hard on his tray, they'd knock it out of his hands. The first time he went on a bivouac, nobody would share a tent with him. "I'm not talking about what I heard—when I sat on one end of a table, they would move to the other end. I'm not talking about what I heard; I'm talking about what I experienced. But I hold no malice for no man." And yet, he said, the National Guard was hell. "I'm dodging Vietnam, and I get caught on the other side of the fence in the civil unrest of the South. That was hell."

George Dean comes from a long line of tough-nosed, boundary-crossing, erudite, and persistent dissenters. His family has deep ties to South Carolina and Orangeburg. Rev. A. J. Townsend, his grandmother's brother, was a graduate of the University of South Carolina right after slavery. His grandfather, Rev. I. H. Fullerton, was pastor at Trinity United Methodist Church, where Martin Luther King Jr. once preached. At one time the church stood where the county courthouse is today. Local officials, Dean said, wanted to use the spot for the courthouse and seized the land. For years church members worshipped in a tent while constructing the current building, which is located across the street from State and Claflin.

"My history is a part of this fabric, you understand, and when I think of my hometown, I think of it different than just 1968. I don't define Orangeburg as so many people do, by the Orangeburg Massacre. You know, this is my hometown. And this is my heritage. My grandmother is a graduate of Claflin. My mother is a graduate of Claflin. My father, he's class of '31 at South Carolina State."

Dean grew up in his grandfather's house on the corner of Highway 601 and Dutton Street, not far from South Carolina State. His father worked for Clemson College Extension Service and his mother was a schoolteacher. He doesn't have a "typical African American rags to riches story." That wasn't his life. His people were middle-class black Americans. They were proud and hardworking. "My perspective of things in this community, and my experiences, might be a little bit different than some because I was in a certain setting. But when I grew up here, in the fifties, the South was the South. And everybody knows the history of the South."

Dean was never afraid to confront that South. In 1956, for example, when he had just started high school, a young and brash George Dean was driving around town with some friends. They decided to stage their own little protest and drove their car up to the window at the A&W Drive-In by the Edisto River on Highway 301. They asked for four hot dogs and four sodas. "And the reply was that 'we don't serve niggers.' And so we said, 'We didn't ask for niggers. We asked for four hot dogs and four drinks.'" Despite their wit, they didn't get served. But they were young and persistent. They hatched a new plan. This time they decided to get the entire football team to ride along with them to the A&W and take up all the spaces in the parking lot. Someone exposed their plan to the assistant principal and then to their parents, who were petrified, thinking, "The Klan's gonna throw our children in the Edisto River!" He chuckled when he told me about it, but said that incident taught him to be a bit more covert, to work behind the scenes: "There are so many people in Orangeburg and all over the South and all over America who were heroes who never shined. People in the background who kept things going— who kept stability within the movement. Back then this was referred to in print as 'the civil rights movement.' We who were in the struggle called it just what it was—'the struggle.' And it was a struggle."

What people don't understand, Dean said, is that because of the two colleges, Orangeburg was a mecca for civil rights activism. This is too often glossed over because of what happened in 1968. Not that what happened then isn't important, but it wasn't the first time students had protested. "A lot of my peer group," he said, "who were the children of college professors, for example, became activists. Because, you know, we had seen the passiveness of our parents and the results of their passiveness in the South. A lot of the activists of the sixties were coming out of college and university settings.

They weren't rabble-rousers. They were intelligent and could interpret the inequities of the system."

As he matured, though, Dean gained some perspective on Jim Crow and what it did to his parents. He started to understand what he then thought was simply accumulated passiveness. His father, for example, was a state employee and, therefore, was in a particularly difficult position. Speaking out too forcefully might have meant losing his job. And losing a job is a big deal when you have seven children to feed. Years later Dean discovered that, in the wake of the shootings, his father had served on a biracial committee whose goal it was to ease tensions in the community. He learned again that sometimes subtle efforts to foster change can be as effective as direct ones. Maybe both are necessary.

There's no question, however, that racial tensions were out in the open and on the table in 1968. When those students showed up at that bowling alley, Dean said, it wasn't just about having more options for recreation. "In 1968 every community was fighting in some way. You know, they took ten years after *Brown v. Board of Education* to desegregate." And the schools in Orangeburg were still virtually segregated on that cold day in February 1968 when he was called up for duty. Dean counts himself lucky because he had a commanding officer who respected him as a human being. His name was John A. Shuler (no relation to me), and he was from Bowman, South Carolina. Shuler first made Dean his Jeep driver, not a bad gig if you weren't an officer. But that didn't last long because the white community started talking. They didn't like having a black man driving the commanding officer around town—especially in that moment. Dean was quickly given a job at the armory, out of the public eye. He wasn't down by the railroad tracks, but he still saw and heard a hell of a lot. "And I never said a word. I never said a word."

From his position inside the armory, Dean could tell that tensions were mounting at an alarming rate. Some folks were taking things out of proportion and were afraid of what a bunch of college students might do to Orangeburg. The first chance he got to leave the armory he went home, took off his uniform, showered and shaved, hopped on his bicycle and made a beeline for State's campus. "And I told the powers-to-be that if there was any way possible to keep the children off the street tonight, do so. Because if not, they're gonna kill 'em. And they did. They did. They shot 'em in the backs, retreating."

On the night of the shooting Dean witnessed something that disturbs him to this day: Pete Strom, the head of SLED, walking into the National

Guard Armory, grabbing a box of ammo, and walking out. Dean couldn't believe it then and doesn't believe it now. "And his words were, on the way out of that armory, 'I'm tired of playing with these niggers now.' I don't know what Strom did with that box of ammunition when he walked out of the armory with it. But I tell you one thing I do know: less than an hour afterwards, twenty-seven children was wounded in the back, and three were dead. I know that. And I don't need nobody to tell me that."

Today Dean still rides around Orangeburg seeing and reliving that week. He sees his fellow guardsmen in combat gear and the tanks in the streets blocking intersections, and he relives the fear and tension. These are his battle scars, his own deep and festering wounds. And he wonders whether or not others who saw those tanks and those soldiers feel the same way. What did the *children* of Orangeburg think when they saw those tanks and soldiers? "I don't think the southern white man realizes the scars he has left on generations of people. It still bothers me a lot as I walk my walk, day to day. You know, all a man wants is just to be respected as a human being, wherever he lives."

Dean stopped and told me he didn't want to talk about '68 anymore. "You know. Jack, you don't keep eating things that you don't like. You don't keep talking about things that hurt. You know? One day you realize that you're eating off a plate of apples and the apples are bigger than you." But he would talk about the hospital workers' strike in Charleston in 1969 and when he was called up for duty for that. In some ways, he said, *that* was the most difficult experience, the most transformative experience. In Charleston he had to patrol the streets with another guardsman, a white guy named Jim who stood about 6'4" and weighed somewhere around 250 pounds. Dean is well shy of 6 feet and says the heaviest he ever weighed was 154, just out of basic training. They were Mutt and Jeff, strolling the streets of Charleston in full combat gear, M-16s in arm. One evening as they were walking their walk, somewhere on Calhoun Street near the hospital, an old African American woman walked up to George Dean. She stopped, put her arms on her hips, and said, "You ought to be ashamed of yourself." Dean shook his head and told me, "A lot of people don't know the things that a black person has to endure that have nothing to do with the content of their character, just with their skin color."

If you were to perform the events of that week in February 1968, the cast would be complicated and large. First start with students at a woefully underfunded historically black state university and their historically black private-college neighbors. Students frustrated by the pace of change, offended by the status quo. Typical college students in some ways, but in others not. Students who knew about the violence of racism. Add administrators, also frustrated but knowing that confrontation might take the students nowhere except the hospital or the morgue. Put these groups on a stage with a white community for the most part resistant to change and fed on the pap of a news media and state government that misunderstands the black power movement, that sells them images of violence in northern cities, conditions unlike Orangeburg in some ways though alike in others. And where is the governor in all of this? Governor McNair, who a year before handled a student protest at State with level-headedness and an attentive ear, earning the respect of many students, faculty, and administrators? Why didn't he do what he did in the spring of 1967? What had changed? Was it the fear of a Newark-style riot in South Carolina happening on his watch?

Bring out the National Guardsmen. Some are soldiers through and through; others are just doing their best to avoid Vietnam. All are from the area. They know the community. They may not be professionals, but they do their best to act professionally given the circumstances and where they are. They know the people. Hustle in the South Carolina Highway Patrol, some from the town, others not. Professionals. This is what they do. Someone has been telling them that black power advocates are in town. They think they know what that means. And they feel—so they say afterward—threatened by the students. But no weapons are ever found that can be directly linked to the young people standing around the bonfire. Many eyewitnesses note that there was sporadic gunfire throughout the night, but all indications are that the gunfire was coming from a .22 fired from the vicinity of dormitories on the edge of the Claflin campus. That weapon is never found.

There's no clear reason why the patrolmen loaded their guns with buck-shot, none that makes sense to me. And there's no clear evidence to prove that an order to shoot was given or that there was some sort of conspiracy. And in some ways, this makes what happened that night all the more tragic, all the more resonant. If no one gave an order to shoot—it becomes a last gasp, a movement of the collective unconsciousness of the white community to shore up the final vestiges of a three-hundred-year reign. The white patrol-men felt threatened by a group of students who were throwing bricks and bottles, not shooting guns. They were threatened by a crowd of black college students, young black men and women. They were threatened by an idea, by a potentiality, by a possibility. They had heard reports of violence from cities in the North the summer before. They had heard that black power was in town. They had heard about or participated in the melee at the bowling alley two nights before. Because there was no true communication between parties after Tuesday, there was no real way for them to understand each other and the situation—that Cleveland Sellers was more or less a local, that the bowling alley wasn't the real issue, and that no one wanted violence.

For all intents and purposes, the white men standing out on the streets that night did not understand what was going through the minds of the students, who in turn didn't understand the possibilities that those men envisioned. So it was that nine men opened fire on a group of unarmed students over what can best be described as a fiction. On February 8, 1968, Alabama and Mississippi came to South Carolina.

In April 1969 and again in February 1970, when students occupied Voorhees College in Denmark, South Carolina (hometown of Sellers), and demanded a majority black board of trustees and faculty, the campus was shut down. And in both instances students were arrested, but no one was killed or injured as National Guard troops occupied the campus. In those moments the guard proved that violence wasn't necessary—there was another way, another possibility.

Walking home from the Brooklyn Public Library in November 2001, a checked out copy of *The Orangeburg Massacre* under my arm, I felt the wind shift a touch and I thought I could smell the smoke from Ground Zero, the smell of burning building, office equipment, and human being. That was the last time I remember smelling that smell, and I hope I'm never reminded of it again. It is a horrible stench that reeks of violence and sorrow and trauma. It is all the more horrible, in part, because of what came next—more violence, more sorrow, and more trauma, proof that there is a tacit approval in our world for violent responses to those things we don't understand. Destruction first, then understanding. There must be another way.

# PART TWO

History, as nearly no one seems to know, is not merely something to be read. And it does not refer merely, or even principally, to the past. On the contrary, the great force of history comes from the fact that we carry it with us, are unconsciously controlled by it in many ways, and history is literally *present* in all we do.

James Baldwin, "The White Man's Guilt" (1965)

# 8 "THAT THING HURT ME"

John Stroman is a Muslim and lives in Orangeburg, South Carolina. That makes him unusual for two reasons. One, he made the personal choice to stay in the place that caused him so much pain. And two, he made the choice to convert to Islam in the Bible Belt, a choice he made a while ago after an unfortunate encounter and an even more unfortunate comment. Some years after the shooting, he was waiting for a friend at a bar and time was passing. His friend hadn't showed up yet; he wondered if he'd missed him. So he asked the guys sitting next to him if they'd seen him. Guy #1 looked surprised when Stroman spoke to him and turned to guy #2 and said, "Can you believe it? That's John Stroman." Guy #2 said, "Who's that?" Guy #1 replied, "You know, Stroman! The fellow that got those students killed on campus." Stroman told me that's one of the hardest things he's ever heard in his life. The white hair in his beard and on top of his head indicated that maybe he'd thought long and hard about that comment and the history and feelings behind it.

"That thing hurt me. And it bothered me and it bothered me and it got the best of me." Until one day he was walking by a small mosque near State College. He surprised himself and went inside. His normal response when he encountered Muslims was to turn and walk the other way. This day, though, he stopped. He listened. And he liked what he heard, but also what he observed—something that resonated with him in a way that Christianity

Facing: Fountain at the entrance to Edisto Memorial Gardens

never did. "Muslims stick together. Christians don't stick together. They've got too many differences." Loyalty is a big issue for John Stroman. He grew up in Savannah, where black folks were extremely loyal to each other. It was necessary for survival in a hostile world. As a child he learned to take pride in himself, in his family, in his race, and he learned to be loyal to other black people. His grandmother, who had dark skin, repeated self-respect truisms again and again: "The blacker the berry the sweeter the juice"; "God loves us better than he loves you, because he took time to paint us; he didn't color you." Those axioms stuck with him, and he heard echoes of them in that mosque.

"Orangeburg taught me one thing: my life ain't mine. But, see, they can take it anytime they want as long as I'm right with God. I'm not going to say, 'Go ahead and kill me.' But I don't mind; if I die I die. I don't fear death." Islam has relaxed his mind. He's content in a way that he wasn't before devoting his life to his new religion. He doesn't drink and never did. He doesn't use drugs and never did. And he loves his wife and always has. The only thing he had to give up when he became a Muslim was Jesus Christ.

Stroman's faith makes him a bit of an anomaly, but he's at peace with that fact. He's always been an outsider in Orangeburg. Stroman was born in Orangeburg, but after his father passed away, the three-year-old Stroman was taken to live in Savannah, where he was raised. That's where he learned to be proud of himself. In Savannah the social stratification was clear-cut: "Here's what we say about Savannah. We say the Jews own it; the white man run it; and the nigger's in charge. Now, when I grew up, we had problems with white folks but nobody got shot." But Orangeburg is and was different. There's a class system, he told me, and this troubles him. In his mind Savannah was an ideal place where the village raised the child. There was more than an ounce of disappointment in his tone. Stroman is a bit of an idealist, and the ways he sees blacks treating each other frustrates him. "I mean, every time a door has been closed on my face for a job or some help, it hasn't been a white man." He thinks some of this has to do with the fact that he is vocal about a few things connected to the events and aftermath of February 8, 1968.

According to Stroman, he has a different story that some folks don't want to hear: Cleveland Sellers had nothing to do with what happened. Yes, he had been on the campus, had been an organizer for SNCC, but he was not involved in what the students were doing the week before the shooting. He shook his head when I mentioned that many whites still believe that Cleveland Sellers was an outside agitator who came to State College to organize students. "I'm going to say this," he said. "Cleveland didn't rile up John Stroman. He didn't rile anybody up because when Cleveland spoke the students told him to go hide." On the one hand they knew Sellers had a target on his back, but on the other, Stroman told me, they wanted to run the show. This was *their* protest. Ultimately, Stroman said, South Carolina made Sellers the scapegoat. And because they made him the scapegoat, he eventually became the exonerated hero. This rubs and rubs and rubs Stroman the wrong way, and it's hard for him to talk about it. Our conversation was a roller coaster that went up and down and bent and always returned to this thing, this one thing—his truth.

For Stroman, the events of that week so many years ago still feel too raw, too real, and he's yet to come to terms with what happened. When the truth, as he understands it, comes to light, he might begin to be at peace, he told me. "My greatest anger is not with the highway patrolmen. I don't like with what they did, but when I write my book it's going to be more about the aftereffect. What I went through and what I've seen happen to other people who were a part of it. You know, I felt sorry for Cleveland because he was in jail for something that he was not part of." Stroman is upset in part because he doesn't feel as though all the people involved in the protest have gotten credit for their work. The story is about Cleveland Sellers: former SNCC organizer, unjustly arrested, exonerated, and now a college president.

Why does Cleveland Sellers get all the attention? One response is quite simply that he was the one who the state fingered; he was the scapegoat. A more complex response is the idea that if there were many black student leaders, many black people with legitimate claims; recognizing that fact would be an admission of guilt and would require a complicated accounting not only for one's history but for one's role in the ongoing narrative of racism in this country. It's easy to blame Cleveland Sellers, an outside agitator with connections to advocates of black power, which at the time conjured images of the Black Panthers and their guns, of urban rioters and their Molotov cocktails. It's more difficult to recognize that many students at South Carolina State College, some of them born and raised in Orangeburg, were willing to put their bodies in harm's way because they were fed up with the community's quiet approval of racism. Jim Crow had stuck around too long, and he was ruining the party.

Cleveland Sellers acknowledged at the time that he was in Orangeburg as an observer rather than a leader, and in his memoir he admitted that he wasn't interested in the bowling alley issue; he had other plans for organizing on the campus. But that's not what Governor McNair was saying and not what some in the press were saying. Sellers explained to me that people often said to him after the shooting "that they [the patrolmen] thought that Henry Smith was me." One can imagine how this makes Sellers feel—to hear that this young man was shot because people thought he was radical activist Cleveland Sellers. Sellers must be carrying that around with him to this day. But he doesn't want to talk about himself, he told me. "The thing that most people leave out of this, and we talk about the period up to the shooting and the victims of the shooting, the victims are much more massive than anybody gives credit." There are many people, he said—students and parents—who were never able to get back on track after that night. Nobody ever addresses their trauma. But even though he has said all this, Sellers continues to be the key figure in the Orangeburg Massacre narrative, and this troubles John Stroman.

"Is this something that you think about a lot?" I asked Stroman.

"Well, I get angry on and off, but it's not like it used to be because I figure the truth got a way of surfacing."

"Are you upset partially because of the—I mean, the families of the victims of this event have never really received any restitution. Would that make you feel better?"

"No, the state can't make me feel better. Like when Governor Sanford made that statement, it didn't mean anything to me. Now if Governor McNair would have made it at the time it happened, it would have meant something. Or like the mayor here in Orangeburg, he came up and apologized. That don't mean anything to me. It could have been a black governor. He's a young fellow, Mark Sanford. He wasn't here when it happened. So why is he going to tell me how he feels? He apologized, and it doesn't mean anything to me. Obama could apologize, and it wouldn't mean anything to me."

Yet Stroman is convinced that all the protests and even the shootings did a lot for the community of Orangeburg. Things have changed. Doors have been opened. But then again, those young men didn't have to die. "It shouldn't have happened because it didn't happen other places. Now what really p's me off, when I pick up a newspaper, and it's not as bad as it used to be, but during that time when the kids at Kent State got killed, they didn't talk about what happened in Orangeburg. When it happened they kept it quiet." There are white and black people who lived in Orangeburg then that have no idea of what was really going on at State College, Stroman said. "And this is our history, not 'his' story but *our* history, black history. This day should have been taught and should be taught in all schools."

Stroman's own struggles with this history are part mental and part physical. The physical struggles have taken a lot out of him—they make the mental struggles much worse. Shortly after the shooting, Stroman left Orangeburg. It was hard for him to find work; his reputation preceded him everywhere he went. Then the U.S. Department of Justice came knocking in January 1970. They were looking to hire young students to visit colleges on the East Coast and help ease tensions between students and administrations. Stroman was perfect for the job; university student-administration relations was his bailiwick.

He was six months into the job when it first happened. He's not sure of all the details, but he was working at the University of Miami, and one day he started acting strange, almost as if he were drunk. The guys he was working with took him back to his hotel room and asked him if he had his medication with him; he wasn't sure what they were talking about. What medication? They told him he needed to get home and go to a doctor. He went home, but he didn't go to a doctor. Whatever it was, it wasn't a big deal. No need to worry. But then it happened again. This time he was back on the State College campus. This time he started saying things to the campus police, to people he knew and liked. That night he got someone to drive him down to Savannah, and the next day he saw a doctor. The doctor told him he had epilepsy. Stroman thought the doctor was crazy. So he flew up to New York to visit a doctor he knew in Queens—a doctor he trusted. That doctor gave him the same diagnosis.

He was confused. There wasn't a lot of information about the disorder back then. What would happen to him? And what if it happened again? What would people think of him? He couldn't find work in Orangeburg and mostly kept to himself. "I'm from a big family of eleven kids, and I just forgot about my family then. My mother worried about me, and she would always check on me. I would always lie to her because I didn't have a penny in my pocket. She'd ask, 'You got money?' I'd lie and say, 'Yeah, I got money.'"

These days his seizures are mostly under control. But he told me, "It depends on me. I don't care what medication I'm on, but if I get angry I'm going to have problems." Stroman never had a seizure until after the campus unrest in Orangeburg. He believes that his seizures are the result of having been hit on the head several times during the Tuesday night melee.

He tried to change the subject. "I was the first black person to bowl at All Star, me and Jim Davis, officially. And I bowled a 206 that night."

"You ever bowl a 300?"

"No, a 276 was the best I got."

"But you continued to go there after that?"

"I went a little after that. One night I had a seizure when I was bowling, and when I came back to my senses, everybody was looking at me so I felt like a freak. I finished that game, and then I just stopped."

Argentine poet Alicia Partnoy described the complications of a traumatic experience in her poem "Survivor." The speaker, the survivor, explains, "I carry my rage like a dead fish, / limp and stinking in my arms." When people see this survivor they flee from her. She wonders why this is. Why do people shy away from her? The speaker wonders "is it the smell of death / that makes them flee / or is it the fear / that my body's warmth / might bring rage back to life?" Stroman carries February 8, 1968, around in his arms like that dead fish, and its smell is hard to escape. He is ready to talk, to tell his version of the story at the drop of the hat. He said that this, in part, has made it hard for him to keep some jobs. Most people are ready to move on, not willing to listen to John Stroman's side of things and perhaps not willing to acknowledge what he represents: the rage and the trauma of a survivor. Perhaps it is guilt; perhaps it is sorrow; perhaps it is anger; whatever it is, Stroman struggles. The past is in and of his body.

Ernest Shuler also walks around with the past in his body. He, too, has yet to heal. Sometimes he'll put weight on his foot as he's getting out of the shower or carrying something heavy, and the pain is so intense he's scared he's going to fall down. He's had several doctors examine his foot, but it's a tricky procedure—one of the reasons the bullet wasn't removed in the first place. So he's left with the pain in his foot and memories from that night. "I can remember that night standing out there yelling to the police, 'Y'all can't shoot me, y'all can't shoot me.' Some of the students was probably cursing at them, but they weren't doing anything that should have caused them to fire on them like that." But the police did fire at the students. To this day Shuler can hardly believe that those highway patrolmen would do such a thing. It happened so fast. Yelling. Shooting. Chaos. He can't even remember what the patrolmen looked like, but when it was all said and done, the suede jacket he was wearing had seven or eight holes in it. "My coat was flying up 'cause I was running and didn't have it buttoned up."

Things could have been much worse for Ernest Shuler, but he doesn't regret his decision to stop by the campus that night of all nights. Shuler thinks that what happened that night was a turning point for Orangeburg. It changed *his* reality at the very least. Before that night, it was impossible for a black person to travel about white neighborhoods if they weren't yard workers. Prior to his being shot, Shuler's previous encounters with the law were for being in the wrong space in a segregated community. After that night, he thinks, white people began to ease up, perhaps out of guilt or perhaps out some real transformation.

"I think a lot of folks felt like it wasn't necessary. And they felt sorry for black people. We still got prejudice, but not as much as it used to be."

"But do you think Orangeburg is still racist?" I wondered aloud.

"Some white people don't want us to be equal to them. They feel that we're beneath them, some of them. It's an older generation. But today you see so many black kids and white kids together. But the older generation . . . some my age, that was instilled in them from their parents."

"Are you still angry?"

"In a way I am. I'm hurt and angry about the way it happened. And I don't blame white people as a whole, I blame the individuals that did that to us."

"Could you forgive the people that did it?"

"Nah," he said. "It wasn't necessary. But then if someone does wrong I can forgive. I'm a Christian person, and I *can* forgive. Maybe the patrolmen were ordered to do it; maybe they thought they were doing their job. After a while, I think maybe I could forgive them."

"But you don't feel like you have yet?"

"No, but maybe some time in the future I'll be ready. Maybe they can take this bullet out . . . and give me some money to pay for it. It's bothering me more and more."

Shuler was at the memorial service in 2001 when Governor Jim Hodges said, "We deeply regret what happened here. The Orangeburg Massacre was a great tragedy for our state." Shuler thinks Hodges was sincere. It's important, he told me, when someone in that position apologizes. On the one hand, they represent the government, but on the other they're speaking for themselves. Hodges spoke for himself first and his government second, Shuler said. It was genuine. After Hodges spoke, Shuler went up and shook his hand. Shuler doesn't know what to make of the more recent apology by Governor Mark Sanford. Actually, he laughed, he's not sure what to make of Sanford at all.

Before I got up to leave, I asked Shuler an obvious question.

"What do you think about the fact that we share the same last name?"

"I worked for a man once—his name was same as mine: Ernest Shuler. When he wrote out the check he said, 'What's your name?' I said, 'Ernest Shuler.' He thought I was kidding and said, 'You and me might be relatives then.' I said, 'Maybe so.' I met a couple of kids named Shuler at Orangeburg Prep. You know the slaveholders gave 'em their last names at times." But he said he doesn't know too much about his family history, though he's sure some of his ancestors were mixed. Today a few of his relatives have very light-colored skin. "You know how black and white get together and they have features of both." With a grin he added, "Might be some connection between you and me back a ways. Hah! I gotta tell my sister about this, 'Guess what, one of our white cousins came to see me.'"

Of the three who died that night, two—Samuel Hammond and Delano Middleton—have last names that recall South Carolina's slaving past. Indeed, Middleton and Hammond have deep roots in that past. Arthur Middleton was a signer of the Declaration of Independence and onetime master of Middleton Place plantation, just outside Charleston. And the Hammond family's most famous descendant was James Henry Hammond—planter, governor, and United States senator. Best known for a speech in which he declared "cotton is king!," Hammond was a staunch defender of slavery and state's rights. Later a private school in Columbia, South Carolina, was named in his honor.

Names reverberate across the centuries. Growing up in a small town means carrying the burden of a name everywhere you go. In my hometown having a good one is a badge of honor. I was and am a Shuler, which "means" I'm hardworking, as are my parents. Perhaps I'm a bit conservative financially, but I'm from a family with a long history in the community. People would use this to keep me in check when I got out of line. I heard, "Would your parents want to see you acting like this?" on more than one occasion, including once when a police car rolled up to the end of a road where I was drinking with some friends.

Waiting for some books in the History and Genealogy Room of the New York Public Library one day, I began to browse the oldest census records for South Carolina, from the year 1790. I flipped to the pages for Orangeburg and went down the list until I came to the handful of Shulers. I discovered something that I'd always been aware of unconsciously, but never really had proof of—my ancestors owned slaves.

I pulled "an Edward Ball" and ran a background check on my ancestors. One of those ancestors, my great-great-great-grandfather, Alfred Shuler (June 19, 1812–March 28, 1879), was the last slave owner in my immediate lineage. His farm was located near Holly Hill, South Carolina, about thirty miles southeast of Orangeburg. According to census records, in 1860 Alfred Shuler owned 175 acres of improved land and 1,450 acres of unimproved land.

The cash value of his farm was about five thousand dollars with another fifteen hundred in livestock. Shuler also owned nine human beings—the oldest, Anthony Robinson, was fifty years old and the youngest, nine months. Toward the end of the Civil War, Shuler served the Confederates as a major in the South Carolina militia. While away, the story goes, he left his farm in the hands of his wife, Julia, and Robinson, who with the other slaves would soon be free. Another startling figure came to my attention when investigating my own family: in 1860 Orangeburg County's total population was 24,896—8,313 free and 16,583 enslaved.

Perhaps there are no clear answers about what happened on February 8, 1968, because there are so many narratives floating around Orangeburg—narratives about that night, about the past, narratives shaped by deep and complicated feelings and histories, narratives deep in the blood and bone of the community. For that reason apologies from government officials aren't always enough to change the facts on the ground and in people's lives. Oscar Butler knows he can't prove it, but he thinks that a decision was made to shoot before that night. "I think somebody got tired of the niggers and the unrest and they wanted to stop it." So when Hodges and Sanford offer their regrets and apologies, Butler hears only the siren sounds of politics. And when the mayor of Orangeburg apologizes, is it because he wants the *town* to move on? Because the Orangeburg Massacre "hurts the image" of the community?

Butler agrees with those who call for another investigation though he's not sure anything new will be discovered—anything that hasn't already been said by victims. "So what?" he asked. "Will an investigation into the shootings make the banks really reinvest in Orangeburg to wipe out blighted neighborhoods?" That would change a lot of things. Blocks away from city hall and the county courthouse, he points out, there is housing that doesn't belong in the twenty-first century. And a lot of folks in Orangeburg would rather ignore that problem than address its roots. The banks can't change that history, but the leadership in the community could address it and effect change. The same goes for schools, Butler told me—there needs to be a commitment from the entire community to better the schools rather than ship kids off to private schools. He's talking about a shift in attitudes, a shift in focus.

"There's not a lot of interest in the Orangeburg Massacre or the event that happened in Orangeburg and ended up being called 'the Orangeburg Massacre' because some things have changed. The bowling alley is closed, sure, but some attitudes have not died. We are still treated the same way.

That's the way I feel about it. Yes, Belk's department store is no longer down-town with its separate water fountains. Sure, you have blacks on city council and county council. But the city of Orangeburg is still about seventeen thou-sand people, and within a five-mile radius you have maybe ninety thousand people, the majority black. And we're still talking about the schools, which aren't adequate. Come on—if you're serious about providing for all the citi-zens of the county. . . ."

Butler reminded me that many of the folks who seek change in Orange-burg are not native. "I'm from Tennessee; I came here on an athletic scholar-ship. The state of South Carolina has been good to me because it has paid for me to attend programs at the Catholic University of America and Har-vard Business School. It put me in a position to prepare myself and to do a lot of things for my family." For these things he's grateful. But he under-stands the hopelessness that many feel. "If you really want to see how much Orangeburg has *not* changed just go down to municipal court one morning when they're in session. When you look around the room you'll say, 'The only people here are black?' That's not just an accident; it's a design that's a part of American society."

I asked him what in Orangeburg gives him hope.

"The fact that you're a product of Orangeburg. You are the first white product of Orangeburg that I've known that's ever talked about this. And I will be just as honest with you as I can. The only reason I'm sitting here talk-ing with you is because of my opinion of your father. It's people like your father that have given some hope to changing some of it, but there's only so much that he can do. I'm only talking to you out of respect for your father. I mean, I've always known him to be a fair person and a person that if he gave you his word you could sleep on it. Otherwise, when you called me, I would have just flat told you 'No.'" In a way I knew this going into the project—that some people in Orangeburg would speak to me before speak-ing to other journalists or documentarians. Being a native, someone with roots, would allow folks to trust me in ways that they might not trust out-siders. But that that trust began with the good will and relationships my father and mother had cultivated in the community since before I breathed air—that was a revelation. Now, perhaps, I can better understand what was going through my head when I lost my cool in that high-school classroom so many years before. I was reacting to my classmates' comments in part because of something my parents had taught me, perhaps indirectly, many years ago—some attitude, some sense of injustice, some understanding that the way things were, were not the way they had to be.

Butler believes that there have always been a few white people in the town who have worked toward equality: Mary Williams, for example. "But they were in the minority. They did what they could and many of them still do what they can, but until recently I had no idea that so many whites are under the same kind of pressure that we are under." Pressure to toe the line. To send their kids to private schools rather than public ones. Pressure to segregate. Pressure my own parents must have felt. "I'll say it again," Butler reminded me, "I'm glad you told me who you were. Otherwise, I would have told you, 'No.' Because I just don't see the sincerity in just continuing to talk about it and talk about it. You know, we've already beaten that dead horse; let's try something different."

# 9 "A DIFFERENT LIGHT THAN BITTERNESS"

The telephone was on Johnalee Nelson's side of the bed, so when it rang around 1:00 A.M., she was the one who had to answer it. On the other end was a family friend, a local funeral home director. He had to talk to her husband, James Herbert. Awake in the darkness of her room she was thinking to herself that any news that came at 1:00 A.M. couldn't be good. And as she listened to the whispered replies of her husband, what happened became clear—some students had been shot at State College, and some may have died. And to think James Herbert had just been there that evening and had talked to students and college officials. Everything seemed calm and quiet. Everything seemed okay.

James Herbert, or Rev. James Herbert Nelson, was pastor at St. Luke Presbyterian Church, Orangeburg's historically black Presbyterian church. Originally from Sumter, South Carolina, Reverend Nelson was a long-time civil rights activist and had become actively involved with the student struggles at State College when he was called to work in Orangeburg. One part of his weekly duties was to meet with students of the Westminster Foundation, a student group supported by the Atlantic Presbytery based in Charleston. Early in the morning on February 9, 1968, Reverend Nelson and his wife Johnalee must have been deeply concerned about those students. But Johnalee Nelson won't discuss those emotions. When I talked to her, she was

Facing: First Presbyterian Church on Summers Avenue in Orangeburg careful not to make too much of it. To do so would be to lose sight of the bigger picture of life, love, and her faith.

She is thin and stately; her deep-honey-colored skin reveals her age, and her methodical language reveals her wisdom. She had me pegged from the moment I walked through her door. Not one to accuse, she merely noted, first thing, her concerns with the ways most writers have depicted what happened in Orangeburg on that night her sleep was abruptly disturbed. With a permanent smile and with southern subtleties flowing from her lips, she pointed out that they were writing about one single incident, "But sometimes the writer enlarges what he or she is talking about and you really don't get a true picture. It was something that was unusual, and I'm aware of that." But don't go reading much into this, she seemed to say. If you want to write about this, write about the bigger picture. That's the real story. That's her story.

Johnalee Nelson was born in Beaufort, South Carolina, about an hour and a half down Highway 21 from Orangeburg, through the dense swamps and farmland of the South Carolina lowcountry. She left the South when she was in the second grade and moved with her family to Portsmouth, New Hampshire, where she stayed until she finished high school. Race was not an issue for her southern ex-pat family. There were few black people in Portsmouth. Perhaps this is why they met such limited resistance. She was the only African American in her school and has vague memories of one classroom incident: a white student was just about to make a derogatory remark about black people when the teacher nipped it in the bud. Maybe there were others, she said, but nothing stands out. She chalks up the fact that she can't remember such incidents to her strong faith, to the intercession of the Lord's spirit preventing her from focusing on past wrongs.

Mrs. Nelson's first experiences with Orangeburg were as a nursing student at State College. It was supposed to be a temporary thing—only for the fall semester and then she would start school in New York City. On her trip south on the way to college she encountered Jim Crow. When the train stopped in Washington, D.C., the conductors came through and made all the black passengers move to a car reserved for blacks. She told me that this first conscious encounter didn't bother her too much. When she got to State College she began to understand the situation a bit more—most noticeably that there were no white students. What she did find, though, were friends, in particular a group of young women from her old Beaufort neighborhood.

After leaving Portsmouth, New Hampshire, where you could count the number of black families on the fingers of one hand, Johnalee Nelson had entered a wonderful new world: a historically black college with black students and black faculty. I prodded a bit and asked her what it was like on that campus. Did folks talk about race, about the white-run world outside of the college gates? "Let me just be honest with you," she replied, "because I was so excited and motivated and inspired and every adjective that you can think of to be there. It was a matter of associating with individuals of the same color every single day and it was a new thing to me." She was living a dream, surrounded by people she felt comfortable with and doing what her grandmother had always wished for her granddaughter—that she would move to the South and help her people. She remembers hearing that a lot from her grandmother as a child, but it never meant much to her until she was at State. She heard the stories, and she saw firsthand the many manifestations of Jim Crow—what it did to people and what it did to institutions.

Because her immediate family was still in Portsmouth, she wasn't able to go home for Christmas while she was a student. She remembers little from Christmas breaks during her first few years of college but remembers everything about the Christmas break during her senior year—and for good reason. That year she was staying with a friend in Sumter, South Carolina. At a send-off party for all the students going back to college, she met a charming young man who later became her husband.

James Herbert Nelson was tall, and pastoring ran through his veins; his father was a minister as were three of his brothers. Clad in the uniform of civil rights movement pastors—dark suit and tie with a white, ironed dress shirt, and a fetching pair of horn-rimmed glasses—Nelson stood about a half foot taller than anyone around him. He was a striking presence in any room both visually and morally. George Dean remembers Nelson as someone who "stood in the gap," someone unafraid to act as well as speak.

Reverend Nelson began "speaking" as pastor at both Westminster Presbyterian in Clarendon County and Congruity Presbyterian in Sumter, South Carolina, before receiving the call to St. Luke Presbyterian in Orangeburg in 1961. Johnalee was delighted to be moving back to her college town with James Herbert and their two children, but Orangeburg had become a hotbed of protest. The NAACP was meeting regularly, and there were frequent marches. Because of his position at an important black church, she knew her husband would be in the thick of community controversies from the get-go. Because he was working at State College as director of the Westminster Foundation, he would also understand the mood among students. Black people in Orangeburg were fed up with Jim Crow and wanted action. Reverend Nelson was in the right place at the right time with a theology of hope and deliverance predicated on the actions of individuals and institutions. Change will come, he believed, but we can't wait for it to come to us—we have to act.

Reverend Nelson preached a social gospel and believed fundamentally that the church was supposed to set an example, and in order to do so, the church had to seek social justice. On his résumé from the 1960s is a statement about his personal theological understanding of the church's role in social and economic matters: "The church is playing catch up with secular organizations; the church will certainly be in a bad state of affairs if she does not take longer strides and run a little faster." Underscoring his belief in a socially active church was his understanding of Jesus as a man who desired social justice. In a sermon to his Omega Psi Phi fraternity in 1955, he noted that central to Jesus's message of social justice was the idea that we must all care for one another no matter who or where we are. "When the whole globe is a big neighborhood," he noted, "no individual, group or institution can isolate itself from crime, disease and social blight." We must all address social problems by finding their roots.

The roots of the central social problem of his day—Jim Crow segregation—stretched deep into the ground of Orangeburg, and Reverend Nelson understood that pulling up those roots would take a lot of hard work. He prayed, he marched, and he spoke out whenever possible. He did something else too, something basic. Something obvious. He sought out the *other* Presbyterian minister in Orangeburg—the white Presbyterian minister, Rev. McLeod Frampton at the all-white First Presbyterian Church on Summers Avenue (the church I grew up in). Johnalee found that relationship particularly interesting: "I don't know exactly how or when he and Framp came together, but I do know it was because they were both interested in developing a community of oneness rather than of separatism. And they bonded together as individuals, as clergy helping people who needed help."

Dr. McLeod Frampton was nervous that one day a black person would show up for church on Sunday. How would folks react? What would he do? Frampton was not a civil rights minister. He didn't go to marches. He didn't sit in at lunch counters. He even voted for Barry Goldwater over L.B.J. Frampton had been born on James Island in 1908, and, in the words of his son Don, the pastor carried a bit of the paternalist attitude left over from his ancestors. So Frampton wasn't exactly hoping for this day to come. First Presbyterian itself was no champion of radical change either. In February of 1961 and October of 1964, the leadership of the church sent messages to their local presbytery asking them to advocate a resolution to dissolve connections with the National Council of Churches of Christ (NCCC). At the time the NCCC was cooperating with efforts to advocate civil rights in the South; the 1964 resolution noted that the NCCC was training people "for the purposes of invading the South and particularly Mississippi and thereby has interfered with their right to settle these problems locally in a peaceful manner."

But things were changing in the community of Orangeburg and in Frampton's church. On October 3, 1965, at a joint meeting of the church session and diaconate, church member Dan Roberts advised everyone present (including J. C. Pace) that there had been an amendment to the Presbyterian Book of Church Order. This amendment stated: "No one shall be excluded from participation in public worship in the Lord's house on the grounds of race, color, or class." Ushers were told to implement this amendment by ushering any black person who wished to worship into the sanctuary. No questions asked. Church leaders noted their approval of the amendment and the new plan of action in that meeting's notes. When the day came for them to execute this plan, things went off without a hitch. Some folks looked around. Looked at each other. Looked at Dr. Frampton. But nothing happened. The ushers ushered two black people to a pew. They sat down. The service started. Hymns were sung. Prayers were prayed. An offering was collected. A sermon was delivered. And the world shifted (ever so slightly) that Sunday morning.

McLeod Frampton was no radical. He just believed Jesus Christ taught that everyone was a part of the family of God and that they should be treated as such. Frampton was no radical. He just had hope that things would change. He was not naive or idealistic. He understood the reality that we're all in the same boat, that we're all sinners in need of God's grace. Most of all he understood that he was a sinner too. This theological belief—coupled with his self-deprecating nature—won him many friends. Frampton had a noble mien and a deep sonorous voice. He always wore a coat and tie and didn't drink a drop until he retired (and even then he'd stop after one glass of wine). Like Reverend Nelson he was a presence when he walked into a room. He was a people person, but he was no radical. He wasn't political by choice, but there he was in Orangeburg in a position of power and leadership. There he was in Orangeburg in the wake of the shooting deaths of three young black men at State College and the wounding of thirty or more others. Frampton was no radical, and yet there he was—involved and working to bridge the divide in his community's most crucial moment. His friend Reverend Nelson was standing right beside him. Both men were standing in the gap.

In the wake of the shootings, a biracial human-relations committee was formed to address what happened and explore possible avenues for reconciliation. This group had been one of the students' initial demands. The committee, which comprised twenty whites and twenty blacks, elected Frampton chair and Nelson vice chair. At the time an article in the *New York Times* quoted Frampton as saying: "Unrest and violence, hatred, prejudice and even revolution will engulf us unless somehow we are willing to establish effective and effectual lines of communication, so that we may understand the needs and problems of one another. We must bear in mind that no individual, no home, no community will be safe until every home and every individual is safe and that no one is as strong as us all." He concluded, "We appeal to all our citizens of all races to put away hatred, animosity and racial strife in a solid attempt to find peaceful and permanent solutions to our problems."

One of those problems, however, was the persistent structural racism represented in part by the committee itself, which was appointed by the white mayor and the all-white city council. No doubt the appointments were met with suspicion by many African Americans in the community. In fact on February 13, 1968, only a few days after the committee had been formed, the NAACP lodged a complaint because "it did not approve of the Negroes named to the organization" and should have had some input in the groups' formation. (It seems, however, that the NAACP later gave its blessing to the committee. On February 23 the *Charlotte Observer* reported that "all of the Negroes have been recommended by the Orangeburg chapter of the NAACP.") Mary and Sumter Williams, George Dean's father, George Dean Sr., and many other important community members, took part in this endeavor.

Frampton was well known for his ability to defuse anger on both sides of an issue and get people to begin relating to one another again. This was perhaps his moment to shine. At sixty years old, he had the experience, the wisdom, and the credentials. He had been involved in the struggle from the beginning and carried with him the respect of many blacks and whites. He and Nelson were called on to react in a moment of crisis. There are few records of these meetings, only hearsay. The group met for a while but eventually ran out of steam; its agenda was picked up by later generations and some of its concerns remain unaddressed. But some things had shifted since the shootings. Things had changed at both St. Luke and First Presbyterian—

to a certain degree. On April 7, 1968, Frampton asked First Presbyterian's leadership if he could preach at Reverend Nelson's church on April 28. All present at the meeting were in favor—except for one single church member.

Johnalee's husband was shocked by the phone call on February 8. It didn't make sense. He had been on the campus that evening, and things were fairly quiet. He'd spoken with students. He'd spoken with SLED. The storm appeared to have blown over. So the fact that the highway patrolmen had opened fire on a crowd of students was almost unbelievable to him. Johnalee couldn't believe it either. The campus, she told me, had "quieted down for the night and then all of the sudden, boom, and the Middleton boy . . . I had him as a student at one point. I was just utterly in horror." Like most folks in Orangeburg, she knew something had been happening that week. Her nephew had been at All Star on Tuesday. But she wasn't worked up about it. The students who were trying to go to the bowling alley knew that they weren't wanted there, but they were young and cocky and willing to give it a go, to keep trying until they found a way in. The Lord was on their side, she believes, giving them the persistence and intuition to do what they did, despite the odds. And yet while she respected what they were doing, she also saw the events of that week from the perspective of a parent worried about what might happen to those young people testing the limits. Many parents were irritated, not out of anger at what their children were doing, but out of concern. They had been down this road before and were well aware of the treacherous territory into which the young people were headed.

"So you felt like they were testing the limits in the way that young people like to do."

"Yeah. And of course, when you have that frame of mind and you're black—and there were things that we, as blacks, wanted to do. And in Orangeburg, Sumter, Columbia, or wherever you had whites who were against that."

She paused.

"It really concerns me that the media gets into the situation as much as it does because I know that they want to make money, and I know that's the way they make money, but then the media can give you a really bad impression of what really went on. You know Sellers, Cleveland Sellers was not the person. He looked like the person to them." The police and the FBI were looking for someone—a tall black man with an Afro. It happens all the time, she said, a vague description is put on the wire, and fingers start pointing, and somebody becomes the scapegoat.

"You know," she mused, "Orangeburg is not an unusual place. If you stay anywhere long enough you are going to learn that everything is not apple pie and ice cream. I have not regretted a day that I have been here. I say that with love, eyeball to eyeball. I have not regretted a day. Yes, there were some things that probably went on that I didn't like, but after all if there are not things that you don't like, something is wrong."

I pressed on and asked again about those things that were wrong. If things happened, how do you work toward reconciliation?

"That has to be done between the individual and his or her God. You or I or anyone else can't make anyone do what they don't want to do. We can't make them think. We can talk until we're talked out of breath to get individuals to do right. And you know that's the same thing that happens to individuals who are alcoholics or addicts. We can't help them unless they are willing to be helped themselves. And if people don't come out and say that they have asked for forgiveness or that they are ready to forgive, then we will never know if they will ever get over that deep feeling or not."

"You don't seem like the kind of person who would hold anger, but did you feel angry about the shootings or about being told you had to ride in a certain train car?"

"No, I've never had an angry feeling. I've probably had a dislike, but not anger." For Johnalee Nelson, conflict resolution ultimately comes down to forgiveness, about asking for it or giving it. There is no other path. "The thing is, we all sin every single day," she said. "No one is free from sinning. But when you know that wrong has been done, you've got to work through that whether it's something that someone else did or it's something that you have done. In many instances some people are not willing to work through whatever has taken place." But some folks will carry it deep inside them, she said; they hang on to that thing.

"So they don't ever have to deal with it? The sin? The past? The trauma?" I asked.

"Yes," she replied and addressed the elephant in the room, "and then when you ask them about it they'll tell you very frankly, and I think this happens with both races, black or white, they'll say, 'That happened so long along, how foolish of you to bring that up.'"

Nelson said it's not about dredging up the past, but rather that we have to move forward, always must move forward because "time and tide wait for no man," as they say. "But where wrong has been done, wrong needs to be righted." With that she returned to the need to forgive. "You know the passage in Mark about the man who wanted to know how many times to forgive a person? Jesus says, 'Seventy times seven.' So it's a matter of forgiving a person each time someone has done wrong or you have done someone wrong, black or white. And we're not prone to do that. If you haven't been taught to say 'thank you' or 'I'm sorry,' which means to forgive me, then you feel like you don't ever have to use that. There must be a coming together, sitting down and putting all the cards on the table and really looking at those cards. It's not a compromise; it's an understanding."

No one needs to tell Johnalee Nelson about struggle or sorrow. She knows what it looks like, and yet she won't let it confound her. Her husband passed away in 1981, and her oldest child, Jemella, died from complications of sickle-cell anemia, leaving behind her own husband and two children. Johnalee knows about loss, but she doesn't let it get the best of her. To every question or concern, she responded with some positive assessment or reply. Digging for a story of struggle and sorrow, she talked only of grace and redemption. Johnalee Nelson is an uncommon human being.

But she *is* a human being, and lives in the real world. She'll be the first to admit that not everyone is hardwired to forgive. It's a process; it must be learned; it must be cultivated. In her mind that's the real struggle, the spiritual one. All other struggles are material. "Everyone doesn't grow spiritually in the same way. There are many, many persons who never get to that spiritual growth and that's up to them. They're the ones who have to face the Master, not me. But you pray for them, and you try to be a friend to them. And you try to get them to look at whatever has taken place in a different light than bitterness."

There's a joke that South Carolinians like to tell visitors and newcomers to explain the various cultures of the Palmetto State. It goes something like this: When you're in the upstate, Greenville for example, and you meet someone, they'll ask you what church you go to. If you're in Columbia, in the midlands, they'll ask you where you work. And if you're in lowcountry Charleston, they'll ask you what you want to drink. It's no surprise then for South Carolinians to learn that Rev. Nate McMillan heard the call of God in a church in the upstate—in Greenville, South Carolina. It is surprising, however, that he heard that call while sitting in a white Southern Baptist Church, just about the most unlikely place in the state that one could imagine for a black man not only to get religion but to begin his journey down the path to ordination. The upstate in general is the historical hotbed of social and religious conservatism in South Carolina. Bob Jones University calls it home. Back in the day, this was populist Pitchfork Ben Tillman territory. Willie

Earle was lynched there in 1947. But McMillan thinks that he had to see the light in that most incongruous of locales because it fueled him and shaped his mission—to build bridges between whites and blacks through his Christian faith.

McMillan found himself in Greenville because the insurance agency he worked for gave him a promotion. While he was still new to the area, one of his colleagues invited him to church one Sunday. McMillan accepted the offer but just before attending, he found out that the several thousand members of this church, Southside Baptist (now called Southside Fellowship) were all lily white. Despite that knowledge, McMillan went anyway and continued going to the church for some time; something kept drawing him back, though he was unsure what it was. McMillan prayed about it and began looking for other churches, black churches, but God, he says, gave him no peace. He listened more closely, and one Sunday morning heard a message from the pulpit that explained everything and awakened him to his true mission in life.

The pastor told how his daughter had phoned him frantically the other day. She had been vacationing at a fancy hotel in Alabama. She was enjoying the hotel's swimming pool with her child and her husband when an African American couple came in and put their belongings on some chairs by the pool. As they did so she found herself thinking, "You mean they let black folks in here?" She caught herself. She'd never realized how prejudiced she was. The pastor explained that until you react to some experience, you might not even know who you really are. And then, as soon as she was thinking this, her son fell as he was running outside the pool. She hadn't been paying attention. No one went to his aid except those two African Americans. The pastor paused. And then he spoke to that church audience and said something that McMillan could not believe: "We need to be dealing with the racism inside our own selves if we're going to really live out the commandment that God gave us to be Christians." When he said, "we," he clearly meant white people. The pastor continued, "Every time I see Nate McMillan in the audience my heart is blessed because of the fact that he has braved the challenge of being here in this particular church with all of us white folks."

Nate McMillan finally understood why he was there in that particular church. He told me that "God wanted reconciliation to come through what he was doing in my life." This is Nate McMillan's testimony, his conversion narrative. And he was sweating from the telling. He pulled a handkerchief out from his coat pocket and wiped his brow. Despite his suit and tie, glasses, receding hairline, and neatly trimmed moustache, Nate McMillan has the joie de vivre of a teenager. He's bright and alive—smart, sharp, and sanguine.

In 1985, about a year after his moment of recognition, McMillan was promoted again, and this time he was slated to be the first black district manager for his company in Orangeburg. He believes that God was again moving in his life. "I began to see that reconciliation was taking place even in the business world." McMillan also believed that there was a particular reason for his being moved back to Orangeburg, a place that he knew from firsthand experience needed racial reconciliation. McMillan had graduated from Wilkinson High School in a class that would have included Delano Middleton. On the night of February 8, 1968, McMillan had been working the night shift at Smith-Corona while his classmate was gunned down in front of State College.

McMillan's family had moved to Orangeburg from Brooklyn in 1965, and it was quite a transition. In Brooklyn, he told me, "You had so many different groups: Hispanics, Jews, an amalgamation of folk. And so racism wasn't part of our conversations at home." He said that he wasn't even really conscious of his own racial identity until his family was back in South Carolina. Suddenly he was a black American, and he began to hear stories about what had happened in the past and what was happening in the present. He also began to experience overt racism firsthand. There were places where he didn't feel welcomed, and there were places he simply couldn't enter—restaurants, the drugstore, the bowling alley. His high school, Wilkinson, was all black and the other high school, Orangeburg High School, was all white. Race, he learned, was a lived reality in Orangeburg.

But he didn't pay much attention to protests over these things. He didn't have time to. His parents kept him busy working part-time jobs when he wasn't in school or at home studying. The shootings at State College, however, forced his attention on the problem. Whereas before he had felt disconnected from the civil rights movement, after that night he was aware and awake to it. He knew Delano Middleton. He was the same age as Delano. And like Delano he was excited about graduating, about the future. So he was angry that Delano had been killed, but he was even more angry because there seemed to be little conversation in the community about what had happened and why it had happened. "There was a low rumble and then all of a sudden it was almost a hush. We just wanted to put this to bed."

McMillan said he was not talking about the community—though that could be implied—he was talking about his family, his peers. There was a sense that nothing could be done because there was no effort to truly address the issue at its roots. The leadership had made their decision. The patrolmen were exonerated. It was time to move on. Many felt there was nothing else they could do. "It happened and everybody just kind of sighed."

In the early 1990s, though, he began to notice and take part in groups that were seeking to address the racial divide in Orangeburg. Things seemed to be moving in the right direction. There was a feasibility study, an assessment of the community in order to think about how the community could grow and develop. The study showed that in order for Orangeburg to move in any new direction and to attract young people, it would have to address the racial divide. "The situation in Orangeburg, motivated by the '68 massacre, is ingrained so deep. And it's going to take a lot for us to be able to come up out of this. It's a tremendous task here because we're dealing with some real issues." He knows there are plenty of places in the Deep South with issues, but that doesn't exempt Orangeburg from addressing its own. "Until we deal with these ingrained issues, we only think we're in a different place but we're really not. And it takes these kinds of major episodes to bring it up out of us so we can deal with it. The Orangeburg Massacre brings things on the table that are ingrained."

I asked him what he says to those who want to let bygones be bygones. He replied, "My response to them would be, 'Well, how are we going to move forward?' Yes, we've got to move forward; we can't live here. If we live here, we'll die here." He said he feels a sense of responsibility to address racism, both personal and institutional, for the benefit of future generations. "Things are happening to them that they can't explain. They need to know that we've had this history, but that we're improving from it."

McMillan senses a lack of respect all around. The white community must recognize the significance of having two universities in their midst. And everyone needs to understand that in a community, for better or worse, each person's successes and failures are interconnected. "I think it's possible as we begin working together to form a whole new relationship, a whole new individual that's created because of working together. Where you were before and where I was before, that was one thing, but as we begin to work together we form something new."

Working together, living together, and being social together. These are important first steps, he told me. Events such as annual "prayer breakfasts" which bring a cross-section of the community together are significant. McMillan also pointed to the community ministerial alliance, which started in the early 1990s, as an important effort for community reconciliation. McMillan sensed that if the community was going to change, those in positions of leadership, including the clergy, would have to show the way. "I called the Reverend Bill Coates, who was the pastor of First Baptist Church here in Orangeburg, and I shared with him my heart. I wasn't even an ordained pastor of a church at that particular time. He met with me at Shoney's one morning, and we talked about it." Coates liked McMillan, and he liked what he was saying. They planned a breakfast meeting and invited all the pastors in Orangeburg. The meetings were held on Saturday mornings and provided a space for clergy to talk about their differences and the steps they could take together to foster change. The group met once a month for several years, at times meeting only in pairs or "prayer partners" so that people could build closer relationships. McMillan said this lasted for several years but died out as pastors retired or moved to different churches. But recently, he told me, it has started up again. And again the conversation is about reconciliation, about "two opposing sides coming together for synergistic purposes. Understanding each other's value, giving up some things for the greater good."

"And what about forgiveness? Isn't that even harder than reconciliation?" I asked.

"That's why I fully adhere to the biblical view of how you have to do it. Forgiveness is about love. First Corinthians, chapter 13, talks about how love doesn't make a laundry list; [love] doesn't hold on to stuff." Love is about not putting yourself first; that's why it's so hard. "That's why you can't do this except with the assistance and the power of God." Jesus offers a good model for how to forgive because he forgave those who crucified him.

Like Johnalee Nelson, McMillan views the problem of racism in terms of sin and sinning, straying from the path. It is a common and shared language in this community. But for him it's not only about having a language of faith; it's about demonstrating faith through action. "Faith without works is dead," he said. "It's got to be more than just reformation. The ultimate end to this thing is not reformation; it's transformation. That's what's got to really take place—a transformation from where we are to where we need to be."

As Nate McMillan tells it, the Orangeburg area Southern Baptist Association had been praying for years about the problem of race relations and the church. They decided they wanted to start a new congregation, one that was integrated from the get-go. And then they found Nate McMillan in their midst. In August of 1999 they started a Southern Baptist Church called Petra Community Church, and he was ordained as its minister.

"What sort of messages were you getting when you decided you wanted to join this traditionally white Southern Baptist Association?"

"Well, you know, the first inclination was, 'Why are you doing this? Why are you alienating us and going over there with white folks, those Southern Baptists?' There's a major history with Southern Baptists; a lot of them supported slavery. But I began to see what level this assignment was on. Thinking about Orangeburg, the '68 massacre and all the circumstances and all this stuff and people not saying anything—we just kind of buried it alive. And see when you bury something alive, when you ever resurrect it, it's grown, it's got larger because you haven't dealt with it at all." So McMillan began his ministry in Orangeburg with his eyes wide open. He was ordained by the local association at an event attended by fifty or so pastors, black and white, many of whom, he said, couldn't believe that the Southern Baptist Association was going to ordain a black preacher. "They wanted to see it for themselves!" he chuckled. "So my first official event as a minister with this association was about reconciliation. The congregation was packed with black and white folk. It was just amazing. This tells me it was more than just me— God was ordaining the whole thing for all of us to be agents of change."

But it may take more than an ordination service and a heap of good feelings to move Orangeburg down the path to reconciliation. It may take a lot more. As Jerome Anderson, pastor at Orangeburg's New Mount Zion Baptist Church, put it, the problem, is that it's difficult to reach common ground when we all come from a different point of departure, when we all have had different experiences. And when race is the issue, things get even more complicated. "W. E. B. Du Bois talks about a double-consciousness. There has to be the ability to see it from two perspectives. One is that I live in the culture as an African American and the other is that I've been exposed to the white culture and therefore can understand that perspective. It would be harder for a white person to understand my perspective because they never have to enter into my experience."

It's a process that begins, he said, with storytelling. "Oftentimes we want to tell our stories but not listen to each other's stories, to incorporate them into our lives to understand what exactly it is they're experiencing. So I think we have to listen to the other's story and to incorporate their story so that you don't have competing stories, so that you have your story and my story to develop *a story*. That should be the truth and reconciliation—that the truth is not just my story, but the truth is when I include your story with my story and that's truth for both of us."

Stories do only part of the work of reconciliation, Anderson explained. The other part must include some understanding of the experiential. Learning about the legacy of slavery and how it lingers in American institutions is one thing, but understanding how people experience that legacy in their daily lives is another. Jerome Anderson is a successful man with a doctorate—and yet in certain situations he feels as though he's still in the 1950s. In a sense, he told me, we have to be mindful of the ways in which history reverberates in the lived experiences of many African Americans every day—in the way they are looked at and talked to by people every day. A true project of reconciliation would be mindful of this. "It has to be something that breaks down my defenses to judge you based on you being white and my experience of white oppression. It has to be something that breaks down those defenses and that allows me to perceive Jack Shuler for who he is. Not just as a white person, but perceive him for his personhood, the spiritual dynamic."

Anderson underscored the need for outside help. Humans are flawed, and we can't be expected to do this heavy lifting on our own. "Nobody will sit down and honestly talk about racism without emotions taking it in a whole different direction. But there has to be an honest discussion about stories. Sharing your story. I share my story. And your story doesn't come off as offensive to me. And my story doesn't come off as offensive to you. Also learning how to create a broader story. Until we come to grips with the stuff that's in us because it's very easy for me to see your problem but reconciliation and healing can't take place until I look at my problem. When people get together what they talk about is the blame game—why it's your fault or why it's my fault. And we never take a look at ourselves to see what we're contributing to the division. What it is that's allowed me to continue the cycle. That takes inner reflection."

Anderson grew up in St. Matthews, just north of Orangeburg in Calhoun County. He was extremely aware of what happened in Orangeburg in 1968. And now he's the minister of a church across the street from State's campus. Things have changed, a bit, but some people have a hard time visualizing progress—both social and economic. He thinks there's so much potential for a community such as Orangeburg to become a major metropolitan area, located as it is between Columbia and Charleston and close to I-95, and it can draw on the resources of two universities. Orangeburg could be a model for growth, but the community is permeated with a "spirit of division," which came out of the Orangeburg Massacre.

There have been efforts to talk about what happened, he claimed, but to little avail. Programs have been proposed and initiated, but no one really wants to discuss the real issues: racism and its stepchildren distrust, fear, and anger. He told me we're in a situation in which white people and black people essentially speak different languages. On the one hand, black people often speak in code—something he believes has roots in slave culture—and this language tends to exclude white people. On the other hand, whites often feel a sense of racial superiority whether they are conscious of it or not, and this can come off in conversations as condescension and at times passive aggression. What happens when these things collide is no communication at all and a pervasive sense of distrust. "White folk are saying one thing and black folk are saying another thing. The language is different but they could be saying the same thing. God sends certain people to speak both languages in order to bring people together on a common understanding."

Like Nate McMillan, Anderson thinks this is his role. And so do other ministers in Orangeburg. In the past few years, several of the town's most active white churches have brought in new ministers in their midthirties: Mike Smith at St. Andrews United Methodist, Kristen Richardson-Frick at St. Paul's Methodist, Cary Hilliard at First Baptist, Shane Stutzman at Northside Baptist, and Judson Jordan at First Presbyterian, McLeod Frampton's old church. This turnover has brought new blood from out of town.

Anderson is excited about this new group; he thinks they have a shared vision: "To be able to produce and promote an awareness in Orangeburg of its potential, of its ability to promote reconciliation and to bring about what we call a 'One Orangeburg.' Right now we have a divided Orangeburg." In fall 2009 some of these black and white ministers came together for a week-long revival. "Whites, blacks came together and worshipped in whatever style they were accustomed to," Anderson explained. "I've never been in a situation where you had a lot of whites and blacks coming together, and there was no concern about race. There was no concept of race—everybody knew why they were coming. The preaching and the environment and the spirit of oneness was just so prevalent that I think God allowed us to see a model of what Orangeburg could become."

There's a movement afoot right now, said Anderson. "You're not here by accident. And all of those ministers weren't sent in the last three or four years by accident. My belief is Orangeburg is going to be the model of how to do it. I think God has a plan for everything we go through and puts us in a place of purpose." God, he said, puts us where we need to be.

Mike Smith was in the right place, so to speak. When Mike was a young child, his grandfather took him to see a Klan rally just outside Ware Shoals, near Greenwood, South Carolina. Because he was Cherokee, the Klan had made his own childhood pretty miserable. He wanted his grandson to see the rally so that he could know what ignorance and hatred looked like. So he took Smith to get ice cream at the Twirl, a local dairy bar. Little Mike Smith ordered a chocolate cone and was reveling in its deliciousness when his grandfather turned to him and said, "Come on, get back in the car. I want to show you something." They drove down Highway 25 in the heat and darkness of a summer night. All of a sudden, his grandfather turned off his lights and made an abrupt turn off the road. He quickly swung the car around so they'd be able to look out across the highway. The engine was still running. Little Mike was stunned by what he saw. He'd heard the Klan existed but thought of them like the boogeyman—a story made up to scare little kids. But there they were. "These are pitiful people," his grandfather said. "They're ignorant and they hate people. Don't ever be like that." Across a cow pasture Mike saw people in white robes walking around and shouting by a fire. He can't remember if it was a bonfire or a burning cross, but he can remember being afraid. He can remember looking down at his melting ice cream and wanting to get out of there. "These are pitiful people," his grandfather repeated. And with that, he turned the car back onto Highway 25, and they went home. For young Mike Smith, it was surprising to see such virulent racism. He doesn't remember his childhood in Ware Shoals as some postra-cial utopia, but there was only one school, and it was integrated. He had black friends, and they played together, ate together, had sleepovers. The res-idents of Ware Shoals weren't somehow more enlightened than other South Carolinians, it's just that these were the kinds of experiences he had growing up—and they shaped his racial consciousness. Key to that consciousness are the images from that evening drive with his grandfather. They have never left him and never will.

Smith brought all of this—these memories and experiences—with him to Orangeburg when, a few years ago, he was asked to be pastor of St. Andrew's United Methodist Church, one of Orangeburg's largest white congregations. The church building itself is a community landmark. St. Andrew's enormous white steeple rests atop a white brick structure that stands like a beacon amid a sea of grass just off Highway 21 and Chestnut, one of the town's busiest intersections. Leading a church that many Orange-burgers drive past every single day takes energy. Leading a church in a com-munity with a complicated history, as McMillan and Anderson have noted, takes persistence. But Smith knew what he was signing up for. For five years he had preached at a church in Branchville, about fifteen miles south of Orangeburg. When I talked to him on February 8, 2010, he explained, "You know Orangeburg has a reputation that precedes it. And I think that the

Orangeburg Massacre has something to do with it. But I don't think Orangeburg is particularly unique in its racial makeup, I just think Orangeburg is unique in its reputation." And that reputation, he said, is sometimes unfair and sometimes not. Throughout South Carolina, the town has a reputation as being a divided, crime-ridden community. This is hogwash, he told me. "I'm the chaplain for Orangeburg Public Safety, and it would surprise a lot of people to know that Orangeburg isn't even in the top five cities in South Carolina in terms of crime." But the persistence of this myth, he said, might prevent industry from coming here.

The 2008 Uniform Crime Report statistics for Orangeburg give it a crime index of 878, which is lower than Greenville, Cayce, Beaufort, Chester, Darlington, Florence, Georgetown, Greenville, Greenwood, Lancaster, Myrtle Beach, Rock Hill, Spartanburg, Union, Walhalla, West Columbia, and York, among many other cities and towns across South Carolina. But public perception of the community, a veiled racism if there ever was one, is that Orangeburg is an incredibly dangerous place to live in. In May 2010 a Columbia television station aired a story about the opening of a new Greyhound Bus Station in Orangeburg. (The old one was a block from All Star Bowling Lanes.) The comments on the station Web site reveal a deep prejudice toward the community. One person wrote, "There is no way I would go to Orangeburg and wait for a bus. I value my life too much." Another person sneered, "Reality—new homeless shelter." Perhaps this is an example of Internet trolls—as they are wont to do—running amok in cyberspace, saying whatever they like behind the veil of anonymity. Or maybe it's just another example of the problem Smith speaks of.

But the racial divide, Smith will admit, is real. And it will take a lot of work to overcome it, but he senses a movement, the same movement that McMillan and Anderson spoke of: a younger generation of white pastors who are starting to see what older African American ministers have understood for years. Many of these new white pastors are not from Orangeburg. One is from Oklahoma, and another is from Florida. They understand race differently from their predecessors. "Our generation sees things differently. So, we've been more intentional and proactive in our interactions. We've had worship services with all of our churches and New Mount Zion, Trinity, Edisto Fork, North Orangeburg, Life Cathedral, and some of the other African American churches in town. The pulpits have suddenly opened up to one another. I have preached at North Orangeburg and Edisto Fork, both African American churches." Black and white pastors, Smith said, have been trading pulpits all around the community.

It's a long process, but they have to start somewhere; they have to challenge Martin Luther King Jr.'s comment that eleven o'clock on a Sunday morning is the most segregated hour in the nation. One of the reasons things haven't changed more rapidly, Smith told me, is because the church hasn't done enough. Sounding a lot like James Herbert Nelson, he claimed that the church must be prophetic. "The church should not be like the culture, the society, the church should instead try to transform the society, the culture. And so if our city isn't being transformed it's because the church isn't doing its job."

One obstacle these young ministers must overcome, Smith said, is the reality that people don't automatically respect the cloth in the way they used to. Preachers have to earn respect now by doing good and building trust. And when their congregants begin to respect them, then they trust that they are here to do God's work and that racial reconciliation is part of that work. According to Smith, they're not alone. God is on their side. "I do think that this has been God at work because I don't think you can get such a diverse group of people to converge on one spot at one time. And I'm not only talking about the new ones, I'm talking about the people who have been here—Nate McMillan, Jerome Anderson, Larry McCutcheon at Trinity, and many others who are already here—and all of us end up with the same mind-set about this situation? Nate McMillan has been here forever. And he's been praying for this thing since ages past, and he's been praying that God would put people here who'll be agents for change."

It seems that all these ministers believe Christianity is rooted in a language of action. You cannot just talk the talk; you have to walk the walk—in some situations quite literally. A few years ago the Southern Baptist Convention of South Carolina wanted to set up a ministry at a historically black college or university (HBCU) in South Carolina. So they chose South Carolina State, and they asked Nate McMillan to help them organize a search team. After a national search and many interviews, they found the person they were looking for—a young man named Lance Wright, who had been working at Southern University in Louisiana. Once again, McMillan noted, something remarkable was happening—the Southern Baptist Convention was supporting the campus ministry of an African American at a HBCU. And not just any HBCU, but South Carolina State University, home of the Bulldogs and site of the Orangeburg Massacre—ground zero for racial tensions in Orangeburg—and, some would say, South Carolina. McMillan saw this as an amazing moment of synergy, people coming together in ways he'd been praying for. "It's a God thing!" he told me. And it's also his church's mission statement: "to build bridges of communication and relationship to win this generation." People will never change, he said, if they are not shown what love is, what it looks like, and how it can change the world.

McMillan said he was delighted that this new ministry was starting at State, and he wanted to thank God and pray for its future as well as for improved race relations in Orangeburg. So he invited his friend and colleague Mike Smith to take a walk with him, a prayer walk around the campuses of State and Claflin. So one hot and sticky July morning, starting on Russell Street, they walked the whole way around, several miles, stopping occasionally to pray. They prayed in front of administrative buildings, dormitories, gymnasiums, and libraries. "It was good exercise!" Smith laughed. "But it was also a powerful experience." Their walk ended in front of State, right next to the hill where, decades before, a handful of South Carolina highway patrolmen opened fire on a crowd of students. "That's where we finished our prayers," Smith told me. And that's where they began their work of transforming hearts and minds.

# 10 EDITING THE STORY

Dean Livingston is an old-school newspaperman—cautious, concise, always looking for the right words and the best sources. He should be familiar with the newspaper business, given that he started working in it when he was nine, delivering newspapers. He eventually moved on to editing and publishing them. Livingston's first reporting gig was with the *Times and Democrat* right when the lunch-counter protests were starting. The Kress Store, target of many demonstrations, was next door to the newspaper's office on Russell Street. Protestors would walk down Amelia Street from State College, a block over from Russell, hang a left at Middleton, and walk to Kress's just across from the town square. At first, Livingston said, the protests were peaceful. But then more students came and the police turned hoses on them. When I interviewed him, he told me: "I took pictures of the whole thing. And it was something, and it was happening right here."

By 1968 Livingston was publisher, but because of the small staff he continued to report and write. Before the shooting happened on February 8, 1968, Livingston was out at dinner with friend Dozier Mobley, the AP photographer who was later misquoted as saying there was an "exchange of fire" between students and patrolmen. After dinner that evening, they drove over to State College to see what was happening. They walked around trying to get closer to the students. Livingston was standing near Officer Shealy when he got hit. This pushed tensions over the edge, Livingston told me; the tone

Facing: Live oaks on the road to the Oaks retirement community changed immediately. All the patrolmen standing there saw it. After Shealy was hit, they remained in a line and had not yet climbed the embankment up onto the campus. "I was in front of them; I was between the students and the patrolmen." And then the patrolmen moved forward and started climbing the embankment. That's when Livingston snapped a photograph of the highway patrolmen, guns raised, ready to shoot. And then they fired. "Thirty seconds maybe. I don't think there was any reloading or anything like that. It frightened me very much. I went all the way to the ground and stretched my body out." Stuck between the students and the patrolmen and with bullets flying over his body, he was petrified. After the shooting stopped, the first thing he saw was a lifeless body on the ground.

The shooting, Livingston told me, had a tremendous effect on Orangeburg. Not only on the community's conscience but also on its economy. Immediately afterward, "the entire community withdrew into itself, blacks and whites. Whenever you take an economy, such as the economy of Orangeburg as it was then, and slow it down one day, it takes a hell of a long time to overcome it." People weren't as much concerned about getting shot at or encountering more demonstrations as they were about where the community was heading.

For many years, according to Livingston, even prior to the passage of the Civil Rights Act, there had been people in Orangeburg working behind the scenes to bring about change—from the late 1950s onward, black and white folks who knew each other, who talked to each other, who had conversations and organized things together. People such as Lamar Dawkins, Jim Sulton, and Earl Middleton. "All these people are gone now and this worries me." Livingston is concerned about Orangeburg's economy because he knows it's inextricably tied up with the memories people have of February 8, 1968. He told me, "If we don't get some growth, economic growth, we're going to be in a hell of a fix in the next ten years. If you can go on national television and damn Orangeburg for this, and damn Orangeburg for that, you're not going to get industry." Livingston was referring perhaps to the release of a documentary called *Scarred Justice,* which explores the shootings and was aired on PBS stations across the country in February 2010. "If someone doesn't wake up and seek some moderation," he paused, "I mean, it's easy to whip up on the city of Orangeburg."

There have been several attempts by public figures to address what happened in Orangeburg in an effort to foster reconciliation in the community and the state. Most notably, on February 8, 2001, South Carolina governor Jim Hodges spoke at the annual memorial service for the three killed. On behalf of the state government, he announced that South Carolina "deeply regretted" what happened and added: "The Orangeburg Massacre was a great tragedy for our state. The state of South Carolina bends its knees and begins the search for reconciliation." That memorial service was also attended by six members of the South Carolina Highway Patrol. But true reconciliation requires a rather complicated series of acts—it cannot come, it would seem, from one statement, one gesture, or one event. First the parties must agree that there is a problem. They must agree that there is some tension. The parties then must air their grievances.

Orangeburg has had its share of airing of grievances. Another part of the process, a more complicated and tedious one is investigation and then storytelling. Storytelling—on an official and public level—has happened at various times. The Human Relations Committee, organized in the wake of the shootings, is one example. But, though many might disagree, according to Dean Livingston, it started in part for economic reasons rather than some lofty goal of peace and racial equality. A more recent effort to promote interracial dialogue was Project Hope, which started in the early 1990s after the Rodney King beating and verdict. Though no longer active, it was a welcome venture at the time. Lee Harter, current editor of the *Times and Democrat*, and Jim Sulton, a local businessman and a civil rights activist intimately involved in the boycott in the late 1950s, were tapped by the Palmetto Project (a statewide nonprofit) to organize the group. Harter explained to me that they held monthly meetings—sometimes sharing a meal, sometimes listening to a speaker. The purpose of the group was to foster conversation and friendships. It lasted for several years, but eventually interest waned. Harter told me that he and Sulton were hoping someone else would pick up the ball, but it never happened. "One of the reasons it gave out is because we were preaching to the choir, maybe. We were meeting with people who were very interested in racial reconciliation, and what we really needed was to find a way to reach other people." He wonders if members of Project Hope carried the group's momentum and goals into other places in the community. Maybe they did, but he'll never know for sure.

Orangeburg still wrestles with its past—how to understand it, how to remember it. "I'm sure people have told you," Harter said. "'Let me tell you what really happened because the people you're listening to don't know.' And the truth is that we're not going to ever know from this back and forth what the real story is. I remain unconvinced we could actually get to the truth anymore. I'm not a policeman or an investigator so I don't know, but I'm afraid we may end up no better off. The key players, at this point, are gone." But some things have happened in Orangeburg that were hardly imaginable once upon a time—for example the governor's apologies and the highway patrolmen attending the memorial service. Harter was quick to add, though, that there's still much work to do. "Goodness knows there are miles and miles to go before we can say there's been some sort of radical transformation in Orangeburg, but it's different. It's different. Blacks and whites are involved in things together now more than ever. That could be, in part, due to politics. Our politics are black and white. We're not fighting all the time over single-member districts and how blacks should be in political power and whites should not. It wasn't long ago that Orangeburg County Council was all white. It took decades for that to change." And the other day, he said, something remarkable happened that got very little attention in the community—Orangeburg Prep played Orangeburg-Wilkinson in basketball. It was the first time they'd done so. The newspaper called it the "Battle of Orangeburg." Harter mused, "It wasn't black versus white; it was a game." Reinforcing his sense of the many miles the community needs to go, he wondered aloud what the conversation about the game was like behind the scenes, off the pages of his newspaper.

South Carolina State history professor Bill Hine would agree with Lee Harter that Orangeburg has changed in some ways. Hine wonders where the community would be if the patrolmen had never fired their guns. The violence and its aftermath have been polarizing, but they have prompted many who might have avoided those topics otherwise to talk about race and racism. He wonders if this can be attributed to the event itself or to time. There's no way of knowing for sure. But he does know that whites who once may have quickly dismissed interpretations of the event that centered on the black experience, have begun to listen. When *Scarred Justice* was originally released in early 2009, Hine attended a private screening organized by State president Dr. George E. Cooper, who had invited prominent white community leaders—including Mayor Paul Miller, Cathy Hughes (publisher of the *Times and Democrat*) and James McGee (an ordained minister and director of a large retirement home in the area). Hine told me that some folks had expressed reservations about the film before they viewed it; they worried about how it would portray the Orangeburg community.

Directed by Bestor Cram and Judy Richardson, *Scarred Justice* offers a reflective visual and historical analysis of the events in Orangeburg leading up to and following the shootings, with a particular emphasis on the white community's general fear of black power, which fostered the violent response to the students. When the film was over, there was a worrisome silence among the viewing party. Finally the mayor spoke and said that the film felt like a rehash of Bass and Nelson's book, perennially unpopular among some local whites, and he wasn't sure what to think. Hine was concerned. He had no idea what would come next from the group. And then Cathy Hughes spoke up and said she thought it was quite powerful. And then James McGee responded the same way. The tone shifted. They talked. They listened to each other with respect and openness. And then, just a few days later, Mayor Paul Miller attended the Orangeburg Massacre memorial ceremony and apologized for the city's role in the event. A white mayor in this community saying these things was unprecedented. And James McGee gave the invocation. It was what Aristotle would have called a reversal, a moment of recognition.

Cathy Hughes started working for the *Times and Democrat* in 1972 and has been there ever since. She's never been bored, never wanted to move because there is always something new—some new story, some transformation. Down to the bone, she is a newspaperwoman. Today she is the paper's publisher, an important position in the vanishing industry that is the daily newspaper. Hughes grew up in North, South Carolina (about twenty miles up the road but still in Orangeburg County), hometown of Jack Bass. She told me she remembers Jim Crow—separate facilities, separate places to eat, separate swimming holes on the Edisto River. But she can't remember hearing much about State or Claflin—for most whites, she told me, these schools were far off the radar.

When Hughes was a senior at North High School in 1968, she heard rumors about things that were happening down in Orangeburg, but she didn't learn the details until she started working at the *Times and Democrat*. What she felt in the moment, when it happened in 1968, were—as with most folks in the community—complicated emotions. "I just hate to say it's the way things were, but you didn't know any different; you didn't know any better; you weren't being prejudiced; it was all you knew. If someone acts now like someone did in the sixties, then I think you would call it what it is—racism. But I'm not sure what it was when you didn't know any different." She admitted that it sounds like an excuse, but she can't imagine how she could have understood the world any differently in the South that she grew up in. That racism was, she believes, a learned behavior. Viewpoints were black and white. Today she hopes those lines are blurring.

Hughes has seen many changes in Orangeburg and in Orangeburg County. The economy has shifted from agriculture to industry. The population has grown with people moving in who weren't born in South Carolina—or the South for that matter. And, most notably, the position of State and Claflin in the greater community has changed. "For a long time people would say, 'Orangeburg is not a typical college town.' Well we should be, and I think [the universities have] reached out to the community, and the community has reached out to them; that's been a big change. But still in some ways, we live in as diverse a community as you could find anywhere, and yet we don't know each other."

Cathy Hughes paused and took a deep breath. She explained that how people live and understand race has changed because young people have moved out and come back. Thus there are more and more young people in each generation who take a stronger antiracist stance. "I honestly believe there has been tremendous progress in race relations in Orangeburg, in South Carolina, and I think it has taken generations for that to happen. After the Democrats' presidential debate, Congressman Clyburn said something like, 'Now South Carolina State can be known for something across the nation other than the Orangeburg Massacre.' I thought that was a big step and a big thing for him to say. He wasn't minimizing, it but it's almost like we turned the corner." Turned the corner, she said, and began walking in the direction of reconciliation.

The rest of the community, the state, the country, is missing the story, she told me, if all they know about Orangeburg, South Carolina, is the Orangeburg Massacre. Orangeburg's history is more complicated than that one incident, and its response to that incident is complicated but full of hope. In 1970 Cleveland Sellers was going to jail. In 2008 he became president of Voorhees College. But Hughes would be the first to admit that a lot of work has been done to get the community to where it is now. In 1998, coinciding with the thirtieth anniversary of the event, a battle raged on the editorial pages of the *Times and Democrat,* white and black, back and forth. It wasn't going anywhere, she said, "Things like, 'I was there, I know what happened, it's exactly opposite from what you're saying happened.' Well, months before the [thirty-first] anniversary in 1999, a group of leading citizens, black and white, started meeting privately and what came out of that was that was a full page ad with an essay about community reconciliation. We ran it in the paper on the thirty-first anniversary." If you wanted to sign on to it you had to come down to the newspaper, read it, and then sign it. More than 250 community leaders, black and white, signed the statement, which is cast in a language of faith shared by many in the community: "'Physician, heal thyself,' Jesus commanded to the Israelites in a time of broken covenants and spiritual unrest. . . . Bandaging those torn relationships, or healing themselves, was his cure that would lead to redemption. . . . Today, we must extrapolate Christ's proverbial command to the broken relationships in the Orangeburg community." The statement acknowledges that what happened at State was tragic and that the anniversary is a necessary reminder of that tragedy. Yet, the authors of the statement wrote, the memorial service and our collective memory of the event have become sites of racial discord. "As a group of people dedicated to racial harmony in Orangeburg, we ask that the curtain be drawn on the theatrics of this tragedy." The past, they noted, cannot be changed, but "it should be used to move forward." The memorial service should be an event for such forward movement and a platform on which to build new relationships. Racial divisiveness "leads to more negative publicity" and can only hinder the community's chances for social and economic growth. The authors concluded by returning to their initial text, asking others to join them as "physicians who bring healing to our broken community."

Some of the document's signatories are surprising while others are not: Dr. Roy C. Campbell, one of the doctors on duty at the hospital on the night of the shooting; former mayor Martin C. Cheatham; Dr. Henry Frierson; my old Orangeburg Prep principal Ann O. Glover; Cathy Hughes; Dean Livingston; artist and professor at State Leo Twiggs; former State football coach Willie Jeffries; former First Presbyterian pastor Barry L. Jenkins; Earl Middleton; Mayor Paul Miller; my uncle J. C. Pace; Mary Williams; state representative Gilda Cobb-Hunter; and my father, John F. Shuler. Many people from many different walks of life. But not everyone signed on. Not everyone, for whatever reason, was ready to sign such a document.

So I asked Hughes, "Do people really want reconciliation to happen?"

"I don't think everybody does. I wouldn't think everybody does on either side. But I think this community's leaders—and when I say its leaders I don't mean just the elected officials. I mean the people who do business here, the people who are involved in their communities and go to civic clubs, to church. I think they *do* want reconciliation." Not even a black president is going to change Orangeburg or this nation overnight. It takes time. This community, she said, has seen many changes; like the rest of the country, including major setbacks—job losses, crime waves, social shifts. Orangeburg is the United States of America in all its glory and sorrow. "We're really no different than any other community you pick out in this country. The demographics might be different, the income levels are a little different, but we're still just people struggling through day to day life experiences."

The man currently at the helm of this community of struggling people is a local businessman named Paul Miller. Mayor Miller's office is on the second floor of city hall in a room any dignitary could appreciate—several windows, awards and proclamations festooning the walls, an enormous desk with executive chair included. When I interviewed him, there seemed to be ten feet of desk between us, and the air reeked of officialdom. This is apt because Paul Miller comes off as a serious, brass-tacks kind of guy. And anything having to do with Orangeburg—or how it is perceived by the outside world—is serious to him. Miller cares deeply about this community even though he would be considered, by some, an outsider. He didn't move to Orangeburg until the mid-1970s, but he grew up in Alabama—Huntsville and Montgomery—so he knows all about segregated schools and lunch counters. He knows about Jim Crow.

From what he understands, there are still many folks who want justice, but he's not sure how that can happen now. He cannot control that, but what he can control is the tainted image of his office and his community. After watching the documentary, he decided to apologize on behalf of the city. Watching that film offered a new window into this event for Miller. He was able to see what was actually happening and not have it mediated through rumor or hearsay, through color or class. He couldn't argue with the footage. "I don't know what I'd have thought if I would have been over there and all these tanks and stuff and the National Guard and highway patrol," he told me. "It looked a lot like the state of South Carolina was being a little hot headed. The southern states were just doing as they jolly well pleased."

After watching the film and after the group discussion, Miller decided to follow in Governor Hodges's footsteps and speak at the memorial service. The time had come for the city to apologize. He wrote down exactly what he was going to say, something he rarely does. He wanted his words to be precise. One of the last mayors to speak at State on an important occasion was E. O. Pendarvis, whose attempt to smooth things over failed. "He was mayor when I moved here, and he was a household fixture, but I can only guess that he was trying to take the position of some of the business people in this community. I think his attitude was 'we're going to calm this thing down and we're going to move on.' And I'm sure that he had no clue that there was going to be anything of that nature."

Speaking on behalf of the City of Orangeburg, Miller apologized for the city's actions in connection with the bowling alley incidents, in particular what happened Tuesday night. He did it, he said, "as a means of reconciliation." His model was Governor Hodges, but he says he's now witnessed others apologizing as a way to promote reconciliation. The daughter of former Alabama governor and segregationist firebrand George Wallace, for example, recently apologized for her father's administration. Miller has taken some heat for his apology, but he's also heard some positive feedback. A lot of folks, he told me, think he did the right thing.

In some ways it is imperfect—he avoided apologizing for any community involvement with the shootings and stuck to the bowling alley and the incidents connected to it. And yet his apology has borne good fruit. Alonzo Middleton, the brother of Delano Middleton, called him the next day. He had refused to sign the 1999 statement, but, he told Miller, he would "be honored to sign the next document that had my name beside your name."

In his essay "On Forgiveness," French theorist Jacques Derrida lambasted such public apologies as hypocritical acts bound to religious faiths that can be exclusive. Such outings of the truth and movements for reconciliation, he wrote, are theatrical acts full of the "traits of a grand convulsion . . . a frenetic compulsion." He wondered if we can say that true "forgiveness" takes place in such moments when politicians apologize for the mistakes of the past. Forgiveness, he claimed, must come through human rather than institutional exchanges; the on-the-record statement of apology by a governmental representative is fundamentally insincere. Yet Miller wasn't necessarily asking for forgiveness. He could not truly speak for Mayor E. O. Pendarvis or Bob Stevenson or anyone else from Orangeburg. His words were a gesture, a beginning, a starting point for deeper work and more complicated conversations. Cathy Hughes said Mayor Miller surprised everyone with his comments. She wondered aloud, "Is an apology just words?" Answering her own question, she responded, "Yeah, but they were very meaningful words." Indeed Miller was accounting for the community's past in an effort to craft a new narrative for the future.

When James McGee says "I've been here a long time," it really sounds as if he means it. His words pour out slowly. And, despite how busy he is, he's a storyteller and always has time to talk. James McGee is CEO of the Oaks, a nursing home and assisted-living facility just south of Orangeburg. But he did a lot of things before he became a minister and before taking the reins of one of Orangeburg's largest nursing homes. From 1976 until 1980 he worked as administrator for the City of Orangeburg. A sign hanging in McGee's tiny, windowless office—amid family photos and images of churches—proclaims, "Give me enough coffee, I could rule the world." But he doesn't come off as the kind of person who would really want to rule the world. He's a big man, with a gray beard, deep-voiced with a thick, lowcountry drawl, not the twangy, tinny sound of eastern North Carolina, but the haughty yet respectful notes of a gentleman who somehow found himself in a powerful position in his community. McGee seemed almost embarrassed that I would be asking him what he thinks, what he feels.

He's an ordained United Methodist minister and served in several churches before taking on his role in the nursing home. The ministry came late in life; he spent years working for his family construction business, serving on county council, and working as a city administrator. McGee knows the community well. His father's construction business did a lot of work at both Claflin and State, so he knew a lot about both sides of Orangeburg's tracks before taking on the role of city administrator, but this job taught him about structural inequities in the community that couldn't be ignored. As city administrator, McGee spent a lot of time pounding the pavement and studying the history of city services by reading the minutes of the city council as far back as he could. What he read alarmed him: in general white neighborhoods received better city services than black neighborhoods. Most folks, he told me, will say that you're lying if you make that assertion. But, McGee said, "I walked the streets in areas where it was obvious that different levels of services were provided across the community."

What happened in 1968 was perhaps a result of some of those endemic inequities. Nonetheless it was still shocking to both blacks and whites, he said, and was something that everyone agreed should never happen again. He surmised that Orangeburg, like most places that experience some act of violence, was left with two options—destruction or renewal. But renewal doesn't mean moving on. "When you lose somebody, you go through a grieving process and everybody says, 'Oh, you have to get over it.' I'll never get over it; it's always there. It's part of your fabric that you cannot extract. Now, what you do with that part of your fabric is the decision that you *can* make. I cannot get over the fact that my younger brother was killed when he was twenty-five years old. I cannot get over the fact that there was a massacre or event which everybody calls a massacre. That event is not going away. That event is ingrained. Generations down the road it will be processed differently, but you got people that still talk about 'the War between the States,' 'the Civil War,' 'the War of Northern Aggression' and all that kind of stuff. You can talk to somebody who is my age and a little bit older in the African American community and say to them, 'Y'all move past this.' But they sat on the front porch and talked to their great grandmother who was a slave!" That can't be moved past.

"You know, despite all its frailties," he told me, "Orangeburg's still my home and I have great hopes for it."

"But, I asked, "what would you say to people who think Orangeburg hasn't changed much at all?"

Reminding me of my age, he said politely: "I got more experiences than you have time." He told me a story about my own father's work to integrate the local Kiwanis Club—verifying some of the things Oscar Butler had told me. It wasn't an accident, he said, it was hard work and it eventually led to Earl Middleton's becoming a member. Once he was voted in, McGee said, only one member dropped out. He pointed out the roles of African American church leaders, of public and private meetings between black and white community leaders, and, most important, of straight-up, human-to-human trust. It's imperative that folks trust one another, he noted; they don't have to agree with each other, but they should trust each other because, in the end, they have to. The reality of trying to live together with these different cultures, these different past experiences—it's not easy work and shouldn't be so quickly denigrated. "Are we there yet? We're a long way from there. What I think your generation is seeing, not having the benefit of these past experiences, is the reality that we're not where we need to get to one day."

Where we need to get to, McGee told me, is a place where things are okay. Orangeburg's past would still be present, but it wouldn't be a reason for distrust. It would be a starting point for a conversation. He explained what he means by applying concepts from the family-systems theories he uses in premarital counseling. Essentially he explained, you do a close reading of a person's family history and look for seminal events. "Did anybody die? What diseases? Anybody win the lottery? Anybody have a lot of jobs? Did they have cancer, diabetes, hypertension, all that kind of stuff? Were they married five times, one time, three times? Did they have six children, one child?" McGee noted that sometimes an event that happened in the past can show up in the present. Thus an accounting like this can be a useful learning process and useful for those about to get married. "It's about recognizing that we live in family systems and a marriage brings two complex systems together. If you have alcoholism, domestic violence, or multiple divorces in your family, it doesn't mean that those things are inevitable; it means you need to be careful and look for warning signs. Slow down and talk it through before you do anything rash."

Essentially he was saying to know your history before you move forward. And that history won't always be pretty to look at. "We grew up with a housekeeper and the housekeeper had a son named Harry. And Harry came over, and we all played and everything, and it was just kind of what we did." Fast forward a few years. A teenage James McGee was driving down a street in town and passed Harry on the sidewalk. McGee pulled over and got out to talk to Harry. By that time they were both in high school and cordoned off in their own little worlds. But they still knew each other and were happy to see each other. After shooting the breeze for a while, they parted. McGee got back in his car and drove down the road a ways when the lights of a police cruiser went on. He pulled over. A cop came up to his car window and told him in no uncertain terms that he was not to talk to any black "boys" in the street again. "I've never forgotten that," McGee said. It made him angry then, and it makes him angry now.

McGee's story of the cop and his friend is one of ugly racism. We see it coming from miles away. But he has other stories, more complicated, multifaceted stories with many entrances and exits, stories about reconciliation that are haltingly complex. On a business trip to Dallas, McGee called up a former Orangeburg High School classmate who he knew lived in that area. Her name was Laura, and she was one of the first black students at the school. She was apprehensive about talking to McGee, carrying as she did a burden of negative experiences for so many years. But they talked for hours, and it was instructive—if not for her, for McGee. She gave him a new perspective on her experience and her history. Turns out that she had come to the United States when she was six years old and that she was a dual citizen of the United States and Germany. But no one knew she was adopted, and no one knew that she wasn't readily accepted by the white community or black community in Orangeburg. No one knew the position she was in, and if they had, they wouldn't have understood.

# 11  BLACK, WHITE, AND GREEN

A gleaming glass and stucco building overlooks Interstate 26 as it races through Orangeburg County—in one direction, mountains; in the other, sea. This somewhat innocuous edifice just off exit 145 is in fact the future of Orangeburg. It is more or less a welcome center for investors. Headquartered within is the Orangeburg County Development Commission (OCDC), a group whose mission is to promote economic growth and bring jobs to the community. Waiting in the shiny lobby, display cases full of products manufactured in the area (ibuprofen, lawn mowers, ball bearings, tubing) support the claim that it is a "Great day in Orangeburg County!" Or at least this is how I'm greeted when I phone for an appointment as well as when I walk into the building. In a sense this building carries the hopes and dreams of those seeking to lure manufacturers to the community. There are many such commissions across this country—from the Rust Belt to the Bible Belt—all with the same ambitions.

But this one is different because this one has Gregg Robinson. He's a sharp businessman and community developer, and he has a pedigree that makes him perfect for this job. Born in Williamsburg, South Carolina, and raised in Hilton Head, he did similar development work in Springdale, South Carolina, and for the South Carolina Department of Commerce. But now he's Orangeburg's hired gun—recruiting companies and selling Orangeburg. When I asked him to give me his pitch, he literally rolled up his sleeves,

Facing: Welcome sign just off Highway 601 in Orangeburg

leaned forward on his desk, and preached the good news. His job, he said, is to introduce prospective businessmen to community resources and to help them solve problems. "So if they're making something, a widget, whatever it is, how do we help them to make more money here versus Georgia, Tennessee, or wherever? I bring all the resources to bear on this—South Carolina State, Claflin, Orangeburg County Technical College, and our county and city officials working together to bring water and sewer to property. You have to be able to show those resources." If he can help businesses reduce their costs related to labor, logistics and utilities, they'll make more money. And Orangeburg, he said, will benefit in the process.

Orangeburg and Orangeburg County are in a strategic location for the twenty-first century. "It's a linkage. If you look at the United States, about 280 million people are east of the Mississippi—that's the core of the United States." The Southeast is the fastest growing region, and South Carolina is one of the fastest growing states in that region—opportunities are on the horizon. Orangeburg's diverse and well-trained work force is prepared for these opportunities. "We're targeting good solid work related to logistics, distribution, and assembly. That's a proven commodity here. We're a blue-collar state; we don't have the concentration of universities that Boston or New York does, so we go with what our strengths are." Even more enticing for some companies is the fact that South Carolina is a "right-to-work" state. Although there have been a few moments of significant union activity in South Carolina (most notably efforts to organize upstate mill workers in the 1930s), today, according to OCDC, the state's union membership is the lowest in the nation.

A skilled and nonunionized labor force is an important selling point, but companies look to Orangeburg for a more specific reason: national and global logistics. Halfway between New York and Miami, Orangeburg County is strategically situated close to five interstates and eight major highways. Interstates 26 and 95 cross paths in Orangeburg and are crossed by U.S. Highway 301, forming what the development commission calls "South Carolina's Global Logistics Triangle." This strategic location, Robinson told me, is within four hours of Atlanta, Charlotte, and Jacksonville, three of the fastest growing cities in the South. Robinson said about sixty thousand cars pass through here every day. And the development commission has access to more than three thousand acres inside this triangle of commerce, within spitting distance of ports that will soon experience tremendous growth and transform Orangeburg in ways that community dialogue never could—for better or worse.

The big change that is coming to global commerce is what Robinson calls the "reversal of the route." More ships are reaching the Eastern Seaboard of the United States via the Suez. More important, a project to enlarge the Panama Canal will be completed by 2014, perhaps doubling shipments through that route. Robinson sees dollar signs as this trade between Asia and the East Coast grows. "Instead of having to bring that product all the way over from the West Coast, you now have the ability to come into Charleston, Jacksonville, or Savannah and therefore getting it to market faster." Little old Orangeburg, South Carolina, will be connected to Shanghai.

Robinson says OCDC is touting all these factors to potential investors: access to labor, logistics, and utilities. This sales pitch seems to be working. Orangeburg has been attracting some attention, most notably from a company called Jafza America, a subsidiary of Jafza International, a Dubai-based Economic Zones World company, has purchased thirteen hundred acres of land near the town of Santee (population 740) in the eastern part of Orangeburg County, half an hour from Orangeburg proper and adjacent to Lake Marion. Jafza initially planned to invest $600 million dollars to build a distribution center and hire between eight and ten thousand people. Now, after the economic downturn, the numbers may be lower. Robinson remains, hopeful. "Give me one percent of what they've got," he said. "They've got six thousand customers, including Heinz, Sony, Volvo, they're all there."

Robinson admitted that the slowdown in the economy has complicated this project somewhat, but the company remains committed to Orangeburg County. One indicator of that commitment, perhaps, was a 2010 report in the *Times and Democrat* that the ruling sheikh of Dubai purchased land in nearby Aiken County for his racing thoroughbreds. Such an article reveals that people are paying close attention to the Jafza deal. What's happening, Robinson told me, is that "[Jafza] is validating the work we've been doing. They chose this location based off of a very thorough investigation of the United States. They could have gone anywhere, could've purchased land anywhere in the country."

This is exactly the kind of employer Robinson has envisioned doing well in Orangeburg, and he's not alone. For years Congressman James Clyburn (arrested years ago while protesting segregation in Orangeburg) has advocated for infrastructure changes to help bring such distribution hubs to the area. Today the largest employers in the county are Husqvarna, Food Lion, Sara Lee Bakery, Zeus Industrial Products, Koyo Corporation, and Albermarle, and the median family income hovers around thirty-three thousand dollars. But unemployment is staggering—13.7 percent as of April 2010—

and there are pockets of rural Orangeburg County where people endure deplorable standards of living, poor housing, and food insecurity. That said, Robinson isn't sure (or wouldn't say) how many jobs will be created, what they will pay, and how soon the doors will open. But what he would tell me is that there will be jobs, and there's little doubt that Orangeburg County needs jobs.

This is heady stuff for what was once a strictly agrarian community, a place people drove through but rarely stopped. Gregg Robinson told me it's no pipe dream. Change is coming, and he wants Orangeburg to be ready for it. But what changes will come about if Jafza does follow through? What will Orangeburg and Orangeburg County look like twenty years from now? Today Jafza's future home, Santee, is a golfer and fisherman's paradise ("Orangeburg Is Bass Country" an old billboard on John C. Calhoun Drive once proclaimed), a favorite weekend destination, and a growing retirement community. Will this environment change because of the thousands of trucks that will pass through here daily? And how will the expected thousands of jobs change the culture, the community?

Robinson is a pragmatist. Families don't function well if there is unemployment, and if families don't work well then schools don't work well. We have to improve the economy before we can improve anything else. "What helps with test scores is money," he said. "No matter if you're black or white." More jobs will improve quality of life—the tax-base will expand and then crime will go down and so on and so forth. Jobs. Jobs. Jobs.

"But aren't there more challenges in this particular community? Like history, for example?" I asked.

"[History's] complicated everywhere," he responded. "We don't want to hide from it. It is what it is. But you know the Orangeburg Massacre and the things that have taken place—we've advanced the ball significantly. So, sure, from a historical perspective always pay attention to the past because it can guide your future. But we're so much more advanced in terms of diversity and our ability to bring in a Middle East company that's going to be building a logistics center over there in Santee. Unfortunately, whenever people Google us, a lot of that history comes up; I wish it didn't. But it's part of our past and we're not going to hide from it."

This isn't the first time outsiders have eyed Orangeburg's resources with envy and visions of dollar signs. The story is almost too good to be true—you might even think I'm making this one up. A group of investors representing a man named Walt Disney, arrived in Orangeburg County in the 1950s. They were looking for an enormous tract of land to build a theme park, an East Coast version of Disneyland to be called Walt Disney World. They had their eyes set on a swath of land in the eastern part of Orangeburg County, right where an interstate superhighway was about to be constructed linking the entire East Coast. The land was equidistant from New York and Miami. The climate was reasonable year round. There was little there except a beautiful lake and acres upon acres of farmland—land ready to build on and an open canvas for the master animator's wildest fantasy. The Disney speculators approached landowners, elected officials, and businessmen in the area. In the end the farmers put up a fierce resistance. They didn't want to sell. The Disney folks packed their bags and headed further south, down to Florida, and bought up about twenty-seven thousand acres of land near Orlando. True story.

So what is Orangeburg now? And what is the Orangeburg County Development ment Commission selling? The town of Orangeburg is roughly 137 churches, one for every ninety-five people. Orangeburg is a river, the Edisto, the longest black-water river in the world. Orangeburg is swamp on one side, coastal plains on the other. It is deer, foxes, coyotes, and rumors of black panthers. Orangeburg is 6.38 square miles and home to about fourteen thousand people, with about sixty-five thousand within a ten-mile radius of town. Orangeburg is a "majority minority" community in a nation that will be "majority minority" by 2050 or earlier. Orangeburg is a strip mall called Grove Park built on the site of a pecan grove, stores and cars replacing trees and nuts. Orangeburg is summer heat that sticks you to the earth and sends cats and dogs to suck wind in the shade. Orangeburg is hunting and fishing and farming and working outside. Orangeburg is high unemployment and poverty. But Orangeburg is also people living and working and trying. It is hope and home.

And this Orangeburg has transformed since my childhood. In the 1980s. Greenwood Mills, one of the largest employers in town, shut down and the community has since sought business after business willing to grow roots. It is not unusual in this sense. Cities and towns across the United States are still trying to find themselves in the wake of industry's swift southerly move. Orangeburg remains largely an agricultural community, but that too has changed. Large-scale agribusiness commands much of the attention now, and small farms are mostly a thing of the past. Yet cotton is planted every year, usually at the beginning of May and on into June. It grows quickly in the muggy summer days and nights and is harvested in late September, sometimes through late December. This wasn't always the case; cotton prices fell so dramatically in the 1970s that many gins closed, and most farmers planted only corn and soybeans, selling off their cotton-picking machines or simply letting them rust. About a decade later, cotton made a comeback as consumer demand for cotton increased. Folks were getting tired of synthetic products. Come to Orangeburg County in the fall now, and many of the fields shine white.

Much of the community has spread out from the old center, and a great deal of thought and attention has been put into revitalizing downtown Orangeburg. A new streetscape offers benches, lamps, a small corner park, and brick street crossings. These aesthetic changes downtown may reflect the potential for other kinds of changes as well. George Dean thinks that Orangeburg will change. Like Gregg Robinson, he's tired of people (black and white) who think only of 1968 when they think of Orangeburg. He told me, "There's more to my community than that, you know? The problem I have with '68, and I'll say it and be done with it, is that justice has never been served." But he's not going to hold his breath for that to happen. In the meantime, Orangeburg needs to start loving itself. He has to think this because, "if you are part of a community as long as we have been here, raising our children, me and my wife making a living here, you gotta believe in it. I've always believed that if you want to create serious, substantive change, then you must begin at your doorstep. This is why I try to be involved in my community."

Dean also believes in Orangeburg because he's a businessman and vice chair of the OCDC. He's owner of a downtown haberdashery called Dean's Limited, which has become somewhat of an institution. "See, the reason I chose the path I chose is because I figured the system out: that it wasn't about democracy. It ain't about the land of the free and the home of the brave where the white folks are free and the black folks brave. It's about capitalism." And so he went out to make his own way as a businessman because that was the only way, as far as he could tell, that a black person could move forward in this country. Dean has been successful, managing to carve out a middle-class existence—nice house, cars, and a rack of twenty, or more, classy fedoras hanging on a wall in his den.

His social position has allowed him to see things he might not have otherwise seen. He has been an active member of local business-community organizations, and he has been behind closed doors. Dean thinks Orangeburg needs to focus on the elephant in the room. If Orangeburg is going to set its sights on the global economy and stay in it to win it, then there needs to be a conversation about race and class issues—on a personal and structural level. "When we start trying to attract industry to our community, Jack, the basic things that they just want to know: How good are your schools? Not how good are your private schools. How good are your *public* schools?" Education is central, he believes, to create a sustainable community. When business prospects come to Orangeburg, good public schools (backed by the wallets and good will of the entire community) should await them.

According to Dean, Orangeburg can be beautiful; America can be beautiful. "What we could do!" he exclaimed. "We have to caress diversity. We got to. It's the only way we can grow. And we can't be phony about it. I figured that once they integrated the schools, and these kids start going to school together, aw man, we're going to see a change. Folks would learn that blacks don't have tails. Doors would start opening up at the university." But that never really happened and the community returned to where it started. We've had some economic growth in Orangeburg, he claimed, but we must focus on social growth—together as one community.

Dean has seen the churches and the new white ministers, and he thinks this will help. But he has also seen a brain drain—young people leaving as soon as they can for other parts. He pointed his finger at me but also at his own children, one working in publishing in New York and the other a professor of music in Philadelphia. "Could we use them here? Damn right. But not until we fix the plumbing. You got to change certain things and stop talking about changing them. Change! Straight. No chaser." Orangeburg needs to be appealing for young people. It needs to be appealing for businesses seeking to grow and expand. "The world is opening up" he said. "Orangeburg's got to open up. And now everybody's talking, 'We got Dubai coming in here! Blah. Blah. Blah.'" That's all well and good, Dean told me, but what will be waiting for them when they get here? What sort of community? Will they feel comfortable living here? If they're Muslim, where will they worship? Will Dubai coming to town challenge Orangeburg's own sense of diversity? This, maybe, is the next story.

When Gilda Cobb-Hunter and her husband, Terry, moved to Orangeburg from Columbus, Ohio, in 1977, the town's residents didn't exactly roll out the red carpet, load up the welcome wagon, or bake her a cake. She had a rough beginning in a community with complicated class and racial dynamics. Her first lesson about these dynamics came when her husband was interviewing at State for a position in the Art Department. While he was being interviewed, Cobb-Hunter visited the campus library and read through a week's worth of the *Times and Democrat* in order to find a place they might rent if her husband got a job offer. She told me that she called several places but to no avail. She called the Middleton Agency (owned by Earl Middleton), which was the black real-estate agency at the time. Again, nothing. By the time she met back up with her husband, she was beyond frustrated. They decided to drive around town to get a sense of the place. Driving past the town square, they noticed a sign for another real-estate agency and went in to see what they could find. They talked to a white realtor and told him they were moving to Orangeburg because Terry got a job at State, but they couldn't find any places to rent. "And he said, 'Well, have you tried the Middleton Agency?' I told him we had. So he kinda smiled and said, 'Well, let me call over there.' He calls over and talks to someone and tells them that we're going to be moving here and that my husband's teaching at State and we need a place to live. Do y'all have anything? They said, 'Oh, yes, we have this and that and so and so and so.'" Cobb-Hunter had failed to mention earlier that her husband would be teaching at State—meaning that she was somehow of "a better class." She laughed, "That was my first inkling of the stratification in this community." Maybe, she allowed, she's reading too much into that experience, but she thinks she understands exactly what was at play: "Race and class. Race and class."

On so many levels, Orangeburg was a culture shock. She went from urban Columbus, Ohio, with its freeways, enormous Big Ten University, and grocery stores that sold alcohol seven days a week, to conservative, largely agrarian, and church-going blue-law Orangeburg. She wasn't working when she first arrived and explained to me that her first year in town was essentially a year-long pity party. But Cobb-Hunter made her way in this community; indeed she held her own. When we met it was early morning on January 4, 2010, a time when one might think things would be calm. Not in her world. Her office phone rang. Her cell phone vibrated. The secretary entered every once in a while with a note. Cobb-Hunter is clearly connected and important in the lives of many people. Indeed people believe in her and are committed to her work. As I'm sitting there she shouted to her secretary, "Remind me to send this guy's family something; he just died." "This guy" was a man who lived a few blocks away from her office and who, for many years, sent her a dollar a month, despite his modest income. "Isn't that amazing?" she asks, knowing the answer to her question.

Gilda Cobb-Hunter exudes confidence and reminds me of a stern high-school teacher who'd never give the class an inch, but at the same time loves each student as if she or he were her own child. She's a bundle of care and action, of intelligence and badass. Because of these qualities, she has been cast in many roles in the play of her life and of her community. She is executive director of CASA/Family Systems—a family violence agency serving Bamberg, Orangeburg, and Calhoun counties. CASA has addressed domestic violence, sexual assault, men who batter, teen pregnancy, and family dysfunction in these communities for more than thirty-one years. She is also a state legislator who has represented the eastern portion of Orangeburg County (House District 66) for eighteen years. She's the ranking member on the Ways and Means Committee and a member of the Joint Bond Review Committee. She was once the Democratic leader of the South Carolina House—the first woman and the first African American to take on that role. On a national level she's chair of the Southern Caucus of the Democratic National Committee and, thus, a member of the DNC's executive committee. She has come a long way from her personal pity party.

Cobb-Hunter made her way by making waves. As she began to find her niche in the community, she started attending city and county council meetings. She was learning—educating herself about this place called Orangeburg. Even then she was met with resistance. At one meeting an older county-council member told her, "He said, 'You know Miss Cobb-Hunter, you know there's an old Gullah saying, '*Come Here* can't do like *Been Here*.' I asked him what it meant and he said, 'Well, folks say you come here from somewhere and here you come and try to do everything. And folks who've been here don't like that.' So I said, 'Well, when's *Been Here* gonna start doing something? 'Cause I don't care about that kind of thing.'" She didn't and she still doesn't. Cobb-Hunter got involved in the community and didn't look back. She began by working for the local Department of Social Services as a volunteer and was eventually hired. It was rocky, at times, she told me. She had the reputation of a troublemaker, someone who asked questions. She asked questions about the department, about the clients, about the community. And she began to figure some things out—especially about the workings of race and class in Orangeburg. She came to realize that the community she walked into, the Orangeburg of the late 1970s and early 1980s, comprised three classes in each race, and that there was no mixing across race or class. This realization helped her to understand the black community's tenacious affection for all things connected to State. And it helped her understand why there was no class consciousness between poor whites and poor blacks. Everyone had a place—by choice or otherwise. Coming into all of this as an outsider was even more difficult.

Time has given her a deeper understanding and perspective of why all this is. She remembers studying slavery and reconstruction at Florida A&M,

in particular how brutal the slave codes were in South Carolina. Of all the states that had slavery, South Carolina was one of the worst in the ways that it disrupted families and individual freedoms. That brutality lingered, she believes, well into the twentieth century and accounted for the reticence of many African Americans to speak out and stand up. That experience, she told me, "It's handed down, in a way. You know the poem, 'I stayed in my place and my place stayed in me.' That was a prevalent attitude at the time." One constituent told her a story that encapsulates this dynamic. He grew up with his sharecropper parents in the eastern part of the county in the late 1950s. The man who owned the land would come by every once and a while and rant and rave about Martin Luther King Jr. and how much trouble he was stirring up down in Alabama. The owner told everyone in earshot that King better not come stirring up trouble in his neck of the woods because his "blacks" would have hell to pay. This made every black man, woman, and child living on that land despise Martin Luther King Jr. If King didn't shut up, they surmised, they'd be out of house and home. It's a story of poor blacks siding with rich whites, the dirty work of old-school paternalism.

"Race is still important," she said, "but I maintain that the only important color in America is green. And if you're poor you're going to catch hell regardless of skin type." People, black and white, don't always understand that point. She mentioned history again, how the end of the Civil War opened up the possibility of poor whites and poor blacks coming together. That possibility was quickly crushed. "The rich planters saw that and were like, 'Oh, no. You don't wanna do that! You're white. You're better than them. You don't wanna go with them; they gonna wanna marry your daughter!' All that kind of stuff. They crushed it. And we are now, so many years later, suffering from that." A part of that legacy in South Carolina, she noted, is the general antiunion atmosphere.

Racial dynamics have changed quite a bit since 1977, she believes. "The Orangeburg of the twenty-first century is more open than it used to be; there's more interaction, more friendships, more understanding." But we're not where we need to be. It's a community that "seems to be willing to tackle issues of diversity and embracing diversity and that's because so many people have moved here from other places. The community has been forced to deal with issues of diversity." There are roadblocks. For example the fact that the private schools are still a vital part of the community bothers her; as others have noted, the fact that young people aren't learning together thwarts community cohesion. She pointed out that the initial purpose of the private schools—Wade Hampton and then Willington—was to prevent integration. Orangeburg still suffers from those efforts. "My biggest pet peeve with the private schools is this perception that one will get a better education at a private school than a public school and that the teachers are better. As a legislator I know we're comparing apples and oranges when comparing public and private schools." Private schools are governed by an independent association. Public schools are regulated by state legislature and the state education department. Public school teachers are certified, while some private school teachers are not. Students attending public schools frequently take a battery of exams, but private schools are exempted if they so chose. Public schools have to report crime and what happens on campus. Private schools don't. "We've got a dual system here, and it is reinforced in a lot of ways by prejudice and class." She'll allow that Orangeburg Prep (OP) is more diverse than it used to be. "They do have diversity from their perspective, but I certainly would hold off on the parade for OP until they really get diversity in terms of the teachers, the curriculum, and outreach." When OP opens the doors to some of her poorest constituents, then she'll think they're making a difference.

Race, class, and education—these are things that need to be on the table, things that need to be discussed honestly, especially if the changes that are in the offing actually do come to fruition, if Gregg Robinson and the OCDC's dreams come true. Cobb-Hunter would like to be optimistic about the Jafza deal, but she knows what happens when an economic boom comes to a small town. She grew up in a tiny South Florida hamlet called Gifford. There wasn't much going on, she remembers, besides the groves and the beaches. "When I go home now it is so paved over. So developed." When change comes, she claimed, it could transform Orangeburg and Santee into something unrecognizable. "I worry that it will look like any other place, any other strip along I-95." Also she's not gaga over the culture and capitalism of Dubai, citing human-rights abuses against workers and women. "I'm under no illusion that these nice people from Dubai are going to come in here with their boatload of money and transform the community in a positive way. I'm very prolabor, and when I look at the way workers are treated in Dubai—they're living in almost slave quarters. The breakup of families with people over there working so they can make money to send back; it's like indentured servitude." Indeed both Amnesty International and Human Rights Watch report ongoing issues with migrant workers—nonpayment of wages, poor working conditions, and no mechanisms for making complaints. The irony that Cobb-Hunter points to, I think, is that the United States developed because of the abuse of labor. Now, in another moment of rapid economic globalization, labor is again being abused. The old adage about not learning from history rears its ugly head.

One of Cobb-Hunter's Democratic colleagues, twenty-six-year-old Bakari Sellers (S.C. House District 90 representative and son of Cleveland Sellers), hopes that South Carolina can learn something from its past before launching into this bright and shining future. For the past several years, Sellers has proposed a joint resolution of the South Carolina House and Senate to establish a committee to examine the events of February 8, 1968. After a thorough examination, the committee would report back to the General Assembly on what actually happened as well as the "historical, social, and ethical ramifications of those events." The introduction to the text of the bill reads: "Whereas, on the night of February 8, 1968, three South Carolina State College students were killed on their campus by police gunfire and at least twenty-seven others were wounded; and Whereas, the people of the State of South Carolina have never been provided with an official account of what happened that night; and Whereas, several agencies of the State in recent years, including official statements by Governors Jim Hodges and Mark Sanford, have moved the State toward reconciliation regarding this tragic episode in our State's history; and Whereas, a comprehensive report can lead to a more complete understanding of this tragedy and the lessons that may be learned from it." Thus far, the resolution hasn't passed. It is doubtful that it will in the near future. And here South Carolina and Orangeburg stand in the path of a globalized superhighway, on the precipice of major transformation. Where will this history go?

Our history can, if we are inattentive, take us into a perilous future. Santee, the Orangeburg County town in closest proximity to the Jafza development, sits on the shores of Lake Marion. The lake, built in the 1930s as part of Roosevelt's New Deal, is a major source of hydroelectric power in the region. Thousands of drivers cross it every day as they drive through South Carolina on I-95 (running the gauntlet between South of the Border billboards that litter both sides of the road). As the 1930s wore on and the impending Second World War loomed large, the pace of the project was picked up and consequently many trees were not completely uprooted before the lake bed began to fill. Today the lake is peppered with the skeletons of trees past as well as living cypress. The presence of these stumps, half-trees, and living ones, makes the lake a fisherman's paradise. It is home to largemouth, white, and striped bass, bream, channel catfish, crappie, and a mess of alligators. Good fishing, but not always the best place for boating. You have to be careful, know where you're going, know what you're doing. Every once in a while, some careless boater drives straight into of those stumps, left over from the lake's hasty creation.

# 12  NEW NARRATIVES

It was a cold January day. State College history professor Bill Hine and I were standing on the sidewalk in front of the embankment that highway patrolmen climbed at about 10:30 P.M. on February 8, 1968, and opened fire on a group of unarmed students. Watson Street was between us and Highway 601 as we faced the railroad tracks and the open space where a warehouse once stood. As some witnesses claimed, a gunman somewhere on the edge of campus (closer to Claflin College) fired sporadically in the direction of that warehouse. The geography and architecture of this location have changed little over the years. A row of old businesses sits on the opposite side. The vacant house (the Brunson house) from which students took wood for their bonfire, is gone, replaced by a parking lot. Next to it is an open space with a few trees dotting the landscape; the trees are new. The first building from the field in 1968 was Lowman Hall, several hundred yards from the embankment. Hine pointed back to the embankment and told me that there used to be steps going up the small hill. And then he pointed to a manhole cover on the sidewalk we were standing on. "This is where Smith was, right here. He was right here. They replaced a few chunks of cement here last spring. I thought they were going to replace this. It's sort of my personal icon." This is the spot where the photo of the wounded was taken, just after the shooting. Standing on the sidewalk where those young men held on to what life they had left, humbled me. Time and history welled up inside of me, became palpable as

Facing: Rose in Edisto Memorial Gardens

I touched the metal manhole cover. Like Rainbow Row in Charleston (elegant homes built from a blood-stained economy), this simple manhole cover makes the abstract violence of the past very real. But this sensation is not uncommon in the Palmetto State, where 1670 was a few months ago, 1776 a few weeks, 1861 just yesterday morning, and February 8, 1968, last night.

Hine paused, "You know, I didn't hear the shooting here. The only shooting I ever heard was at Kent. I definitely heard that." Hine's nose was in the books when the shootings at Kent State occurred, busy working on his dissertation so he could get a more permanent position as a college professor. At the time, he said, he didn't even realize that the Ohio National Guard had opened fire on a crowd of student protestors. "I heard what I thought were loud firecrackers beyond my sight over the hill near Taylor Hall. But they had indeed shot into a not-very-well formed crowd of unarmed students." That he was in both places, just a few years apart, is uncanny, incomprehensible, and gives him a perspective on violence that few have. "Maybe I was or am naive, but it is incredible that people who are presumably trained—highway patrolmen and National Guardsmen—would use firearms on people who are not armed." Unthinkable until it happened and then happened again. The general inattention given to Orangeburg, compared to the other confrontation he encountered, doesn't surprise Bill Hine. The two state schools, Kent and South Carolina, might as well be on different planets.

Hine thinks that the ultimate blame for what happened in Orangeburg rests with the governor—communication between the state and campus administrators was weak at best. This lack of communication was fueled in part by the governor's fear of black power. McNair acted responsibly the year before when students had complaints against then-president Benner C. Turner, but his tune changed when it appeared to him that the students' complaints were against the state, not the college. In his mind and in the minds of many of McNair's white constituents, the students were rebelling against the authority of the government, and by default the community of Orangeburg was under threat. Hine chuckled at the thought of his students torching the buildings on Russell Street. It wasn't going to happen, he said. The students were upset, but the real issue was lack of communication, lack of leadership from the top, and lack of training.

Hine returned from Ohio in 1970 and began teaching at State College again. He's taught there every semester since and has watched interest in what happened in 1968 wax and wane. By the time he returned, many of the students who were involved in the protests had either left or graduated. The student body's collective memory of what happened declined precipitously throughout the 1970s despite the memorial service held every year. If not for Bass and Nelson's book, he thinks, we'd know very little. By the early 1990s, the *Times and Democrat* had begun to pay closer attention to the event, and more recently state and national media outlets have run stories about the event. More middle- and high-school students in South Carolina public schools study the Orangeburg Massacre. And every year he encounters more first-year students who know something about it. In general, he insisted, there's a growing awareness that this was an important moment in civil rights history.

Almost parallel with increased awareness of what happened in 1968 has been a community transformation, one that Hine considers striking. But, he said, he's not sure to what extent the massacre had anything to do with the changes. "I suspect that it did not have a profound effect. That is to say that Orangeburg would have remained two tightly knit parallel communities. Orangeburg was insular, defensive, felt put-upon. Maybe similar circumstances existed in other smaller southern communities as well." But Orangeburg has begun the process of freeing itself from all that baggage. It has taken a new generation, new ideas, and the influence of American popular culture. There are still some serious problems in Orangeburg, but it's in a much better place today.

This better place has been reached in part because of efforts to promote an interracial dialogue that has been at times fruitful and at others painful. "When you did get black and white people together early on you really got nowhere, it seemed to me. I would sometime be a part of these meetings. They'd sit down and express their pleasure of being in the company of the other race. And generally speaking these were better-educated people from the community, the colleges, local businesses, but very quickly it would deteriorate into accusations and recriminations and excuses. I didn't think it was very profitable. Often, people went away angrier than they came." At the time it didn't seem worth the trouble, but in hindsight, Hine realized that they had to start somewhere, and maybe getting it all out on the table was that place. Everything is not apple pie and ice cream, as Johnalee Nelson says. Orangeburg, like reconciliation, is a messy, ongoing, and constant work in progress. "Mistrust, suspicion, and racism still exist," Hine told me. "Ask Mayor Paul Miller how people responded to his apology delivered at the February eighth ceremony. Look at some of the vicious and nasty comments posted by a few people on media Web sites around February eighth." Yet, as

I left, Hine handed me a commemorative coin from the Orangeburg Massacre fortieth anniversary memorial service. About the size of a silver dollar, the bronze coin has inscribed on one side the words "Truth and Reconciliation."

Zach Middleton is the student government president at South Carolina State University, defensive lineman for the South Carolina State Bulldogs, and founder and head of a nonprofit organization called Changing the Perception. He's a native of Orangeburg, and he's also the great-nephew of Delano Middleton.

A product of Orangeburg-Wilkinson High School, Zach Middleton spent a year at the United States Naval Academy but decided it wasn't for him. When he returned home, he was rootless, directionless, and jobless. The experience humbled him. He scraped around for work and eventually found himself working at Popeye's, always smelling like chicken and biscuits, and working with folks who were also struggling but who were very negative about Orangeburg. This spurred him to go back to school and to get involved. "I was just wondering why we don't take our pride back in our community." So he started a nonprofit that tries to involve students from area colleges—State, Claflin, and Orangeburg-Calhoun Technical College—in community-focused projects such as voter-registration drives, a back-to-school "give back," and an annual talent show. Middleton told me his organization challenges apathy in the community by promoting the town's historical significance in the struggle for civil and human rights. Through this work, they're also working to change racial attitudes.

There needs to be a conversation in the community, Middleton said. Some things just don't feel right. "You know, what gives? Why don't blacks and whites interact?" At the Naval Academy he met and interacted with all kinds of people. "In Orangeburg we just don't have that. And because we don't have that I think people are. . . . It's not that we're racist, so to speak, but we're not free to step out of our comfort zone and that's what we have to do." And part of that stepping out must include a conversation about race. Race is such a taboo subject in the community, he told me, and sometimes when it's brought up, people claim the tension doesn't exist. "You know, but it's like, come on, let's just cut it."

He's tired of what happened in 1968 being a State thing: "It's an Orangeburg thing. So Orangeburg should embrace it, and they should use it as a tool to move forward. I want it to be something that will unite the city and engage people in dialogue." Middleton is an idealist, of course, but he's confident, and that confidence might work in his favor. He knows his history, knows how race relations were in the past, but he clearly is working from a new angle and is trying to reimagine the future while respecting the past. He's not going to forget it, by any means, but he won't let it slow him down.

Orangeburg's struggles around race weigh heavily on his mind, and it's not surprising given his family's history. Middleton attended the Orangeburg Massacre memorial service every year as a child; he has always known this history. In many ways he carries that history on and in his body. His relatives say he reminds them of his uncle. "From a personal standpoint I know his physical features. I know that when I walk up to one of my older relatives and they say, 'Boy, you look like Bump.' Bump was his nickname. I think he had acne at one time or something like that so they called him Bump!" The resemblance is uncanny, but Zach Middleton doesn't have acne; he's an athletic-looking young man, with a sparkle in his eyes that tells you he's up to something. He'd like to think he gets that from Delano. "I didn't know him of course, but I would assume that he was inquisitive by nature—just the fact that he went out there that night. And I'm also very inquisitive." He thinks about his uncle quite a bit. When he was running for student-government president, he saw it as a chance to fulfill his uncle's legacy.

There are some serious obstacles to overcome before perceptions can be changed in Orangeburg, he told me. "There's always going to be a little something. I think there's always going to be a little, maybe not animosity, but I just feel as though it's going to take time. Maybe not your kids, but maybe the kids after that." I wondered aloud if all the talk about "tolerance" and "diversity" is just talk. Do we really mean it? We're not that far removed from the civil rights era. Many people have dealt and still deal with overt and structural racism; those experiences are hard to wash away.

Maybe, he responded, but if we compare the world we live in today with the world of the 1960s or 1970s, "we're making progress. But I think until our kids go to the same schools, swim in the same pools, and just get together, it's going to fizzle out."

But, he said, there are many people who are still on the defensive. "I've heard each and every side. Just like you've heard a different side of whites versus blacks in the Orangeburg Massacre, I've heard blacks versus blacks in the Orangeburg Massacre. I'm sure there are whites versus whites in the Orangeburg Massacre where stories don't match up and facts don't match up. Bass and Nelson's book is not how I thought it was. And I don't know the answer to that one." And yet Middleton's interested in hearing all these stories—he'd like to see that happen, but what seems more important to him is how Orangeburg can think about launching itself forward as the racially diverse community that it is. "We have to engage in dialogue and we have to take necessary steps and come up with concrete 'measurables.' Like, okay, how do we know if we're better five years from now?"

Something that's started to happen could be considered a measuarable—political leaders have been apologizing. And Middleton is delighted that this has happened, but he would like to see some action behind those words. Not just "we're sorry," but "we're sorry, and we're going to do *x* and *y*." Middleton would like to see an investigation, and he'd like to see the state be the driving force behind it—that would leave a positive legacy. "That might be like a family incident where somebody did something wrong. Let's say, for example, I don't want to say domestic abuse or alcoholism to make light of it but if somebody said, 'I'm sorry' after such an incident, but then went right back to doing the same thing. Yeah, it's nice to say, but I want to see some action." Apologizing doesn't mean the issue has been resolved, he said, it means that the conversation, the action, should begin.

"One day," he told me, "I went to the Orangeburg County Library, and I told the librarian I was doing some research on Orangeburg. And the guy took me to the history section. He looks through everything and he said, 'Yeah, yeah, yeah and this is when General Sherman, this is when yadda yadda.' And when we got to Bass and Nelson's *The Orangeburg Massacre,* he says, 'It's a shame that most of America and most of the world, that's all they know about Orangeburg, South Carolina.' I said, 'How are you doing? My name is Zachary Delano Middleton and my great-uncle was killed in it.' And he turned red." And yet, there's something true and real about that librarian's comment, something that cuts to the core of what Zachary Middleton is trying to do.

He wants to change not only how people approach Orangeburg's history, but how *they* approach *him*. People are surprised by his positive attitude. People are surprised that he doesn't hold a grudge about the past. He told me, "If you're approachable and positive then it's like, 'Uh-oh, how do I respond to that?' I do believe we're going to change Orangeburg. I know we will, but forgiving, I think you have to do that, I think it's good for the soul. I think if you hold a grudge and you just hold onto something for years and years and years it's not going to serve any purpose." But you can't forget it either, he reminded me. When you do that, you lose the history and a part of yourself.

I was waiting for Zach Middleton. It was 7:00 P.M. It was cold and dark, and I was standing in front of MLK Auditorium at State, yards from where the shootings occurred. Zach was late, but I was in no rush. As I was waiting, a security guard slowed down as she drove by. "Can I help you?" she asked. Just waiting for someone, I told her. A few minutes passed, and a different security guard drove by. Same routine. Was I okay? Did I need any help? With all this attention, I couldn't help but chuckle to myself. It was, perhaps, unusual to see a white man standing alone in the darkness on this campus. Was I suspicious? Was I that much of an anomaly on State's campus? And yet, there was nothing funny about this encounter. Would it have gone differently if I were a *black* man standing alone in a parking lot on a majority white campus? Or a black man standing alone in the dark anywhere in the United States?

When Zach finally walked up, he looked as though he'd just stepped out of 1960s South Carolina State College—dark suit, shoes, and tie, white shirt. Tonight was the first practice after Christmas break for *Taking a Stand,* a play about the events of February 1968, which was written by a contemporary State student named Calhoun Cornwell and premiered at State on February 6, 2010. The play focuses on the experiences of the students in 1968—their friendships, their families, and their struggles with death and trauma. The main actors were members of State's Henderson-Davis Players, a student-centered acting company on campus, but these students had also reached out to the local community theater company, the Orangeburg Part-Time Players, for this production. Middleton was excited and had been working hard to publicize the play, talking to church groups and hanging up posters. "I want to promote everywhere, not just in the African American community, so there are no more Jack Shulers who grow up not knowing the whole story," he told me with a grin. But he had more pressing issues as well—such as learning his lines and his blocking. "I'm a flash card guy so I put my cue on the front of the card and my part on the back of the card. I hope it works." As he said this, more and more cast members filed into MLK Auditorium, site of the 2007 Democratic debate that launched Barack Obama's campaign. (A large banner at the back of the auditorium from the debate is still on display.) Eventually the actors all congregated on the stage. I sat ten or so rows back and took it all in.

They circled up and went through warm-ups and stretches led by acting coach and assistant director Wyleek Cummings, an intense young man dressed in baggy pants, a gray sweater, and black Nikes. After the warm-ups, Cummings welcomed everyone back from the long Christmas break. But then he quickly became fierce and demanding. He asked everyone to think about those who died that night in 1968: "think about all the Christmases that they did not get to spend with their families." After a seemingly interminable pause—the silence hanging—he said, "You think about the level of intensity." Again a long silence. "That you have to rise to." Silence. "To play these parts." Cummings had the dramatic pause down pat. His eyes were sharp, and his words came from some place beyond his age. He walked about in circles on the stage. "Now," he said, "I'm going to tap into some areas of your life that you are not going to want me to." They slipped into a method-acting exercise, an effort to force them into character. Some scenes were played out, and then Cummings got to the meat of it. He placed one black actor in the middle of the stage between a white actor (representing the police) and another actor (representing the students). Cummings told the actor representing the students that he had to get into the bowling alley—meaning get past the other black actor and at the white actor. Pushing. Punching. Shoving. Cursing. And eventually the actor between the "student" and the "policeman" had to wrestle the "student" to the ground. A few cast members were crying. It was so intense. All the while Cummings didn't allow anyone to break character. If he saw the smallest crack, he shouted, "This is not a joke!"

When the exercises were over, Cummings spoke to the cast again. He asked them, "How will you inspire those who come to see you perform? To so many, Smith, Hammond, and Middleton are just dead. And we are so close to joining them." His words clearly seemed to resonate with the students. For them, it seemed, practicing for this play was almost a spiritual encounter. I was getting goose bumps as he asked the cast to remember always that three young people died. "Remember those bodies," he said. For them, he said, "We have to resolve to leave this world better off than it was when we came in. We are one voice, one community, and our goal will be to resurrect these individuals for the purpose of taking a stand." He asked them to say it together: "Take a stand." Louder. "Take a stand!" Louder still. "Take a stand!" This play was more than a performance to these young people; it was a mission that carried great weight and mountains of meaning.

Playwright Calhoun Cornwell told me that he hopes the play will educate his fellow students, the Orangeburg community, and anyone else who'll listen. He's a student at State, so that's his focus in the play—what the students were thinking and doing. How they were reacting to the changing world around them, not only as activists but as human beings with emotions. This is a hard thing to do, he said, trying to get into the mind of a college student in 1968. Compounding that difficulty is the reality that each student involved in the protests was an individual with his or her own distinct personality. "Some react nonchalantly" to what happens, he told me. "Some character's buttons are easily pushed while other characters can take the sit-back role and try to meditate through the process." He wanted to get this right.

In order to get it right, he said, he looked to what has changed culturally and politically as well as what hasn't. He thinks that young people today are more likely to interact with people from other races, and that shows progress. But he gets the sense that Orangeburg and South Carolina haven't come to terms with their own history yet. "There's still a lot of tension because there wasn't a resolution." No one was held accountable. No government seemed to really care. "It was just shoot 'em up and walk away." In his play, he said, there's still an opening for one kind of justice. "At the end of the play the students are talking about how they are going to get reconciliation, how they are going to get justice," justice for what happened that night but also justice on a grander scale.

Cornwell told me he let some of his own experiences fuel the writing—for example the ways in which friends speak to each other and interact. But he also thought about injustices he's experienced. He's never seen the kind of gun violence his play depicts, but he has been profiled as a black man driving a car. He was pulled over for no apparent reason, and his car was searched; nothing was found, and the police went on their way. "It's really strange," he said, "that we're in the twenty-first century, and you can still experience things that happened in the '6os."

The violence of February 8, 1968, created a fissure in the community of Orangeburg to the extent that the event itself cannot be named—shooting, massacre, incident, riot. Violence is discordant; it ruptures humanity and language literally and figuratively. What shall we call that night? How shall we remember it? Whatever it was, it deserves our solemn reverence and reflection, and our modest attempts to transform it into something else, into a new story. This requires, I think, a newfound respect for history—not only in the classroom but in the streets. Writing about his experience as a foot soldier in the Iraq War, poet Brian Turner claimed, "History is a cloudy mirror made of dirt / and bone and ruin." We see ourselves in history's mirror, but what we see is often complicated and confusing and disrupts our personal narratives. It's much easier to offer pat responses to past atrocities—"it's time to move on"; "they need to get over it"; "live and let live"—than to address the dirt. And some things cannot be moved on from so easily. Reconciliation for Orangeburg means taking seriously what happened that night in February 1968. (Reconciliation must always be a place-specific phe-nomenon—in Sharpeville or in Selma—confronting the underlying causes of what happened in a particular place, with a particular history.) Reconcili-ation means recognizing the trauma that continues in the lives of some of the shootings victims and perpetrators. It also means taking seriously the under-lying issue—racism.

Orangeburg is a symptom for a larger problem, and it needs to be dis-cussed frankly. The bedrock of our national history is as much wrack and ruin, chattel slavery and native genocide, as it is the heroes of '76 and Lin-coln's benevolence. We have to look at this history closely. We have to ask why so many of our nation's schools and neighborhoods are so segregated. We have to ask why we are so obsessed with race. These are Orangeburg's issues, but they are also those of New York, Los Angeles, and Des Moines. South Carolinian James McBride Dabbs wrote in 1958 of the old plantations that were once spread out along the Carolina coast. The remoteness of some of these plantations gave their owners the sense that they were royalty, ruling over their tiny kingdoms. "Yet the river ran by the doorstep," linking these kingdoms to the rest of the world through networks of commerce. Never was this more true than today. We are dependent on each other because we are each other. We have to figure out how to live with each other—there's no alternative.

One way to begin again is by valuing each other's stories. We order our lives with stories. In *The City of Words,* Alberto Manguel argued, "Language is our common denominator." And stories, how we share them, how we understand them, can unite us. Manguel explored the work of German writer Alfred Döblin, who, Manguel wrote, believed that language tells us "why we are together. Most of our human functions are singular: we don't require others to breathe, walk, eat, or sleep. But we require others to speak and reflect back to us what we say." "Stories" Manguel claimed, "are our memory." They are meant to persist, they are meant to remind us that we are bound together. Writing after his tenure on the Truth and Reconciliation Commission in South Africa, Desmond Tutu said just that, noting that we must always remember that our "humanity is caught up, is inextricably bound up" together. For Tutu the experience of serving on the committee was emotionally fraught—horrific stories, the politics of granting amnesty to perpetrators, the public attention. But, he wrote, it showed him that a new narrative, a new way forward after atrocity, is entirely possible. And why not? What's the alternative? He wrote, "Somewhere deep inside us we seem to know that we are destined for something better. Now and again we catch a glimpse of the better thing for which we are meant . . . when for a little while we are bound together by bonds of a caring humanity." He continued, saying "we are created to live in a delicate network of interdependence." Retribution, entrenchment, and animosity do little to sustain this network of interdependence, instead such responses promote only disconnection.

In the margins of the 9/11 narrative, New Yorkers scribbled tales that speak to the inhumanity, to the horror of the three thousand human beings who were murdered. Indeed many New Yorkers acted in extraordinary ways in the days and weeks that followed. Blood banks overflowed; drugstores ran out of socks and toothbrushes for workers at Ground Zero; and people offered shoulders for others to cry on. At midmorning on September 13, I took the Q train into Manhattan. As the train came out of the tunnel to cross Manhattan Bridge, the few people on the train with me stood up, walked to the window, and stared in amazement at the smoke rising from that gaping wound in lower Manhattan, that cemetery. A skinny West Indian woman standing to the left of me said what everyone was thinking, "I just can't believe it. God bless." A Sikh man to my right said, "Yes, it's terrible." The smell of ash and smoke, of burnt flesh, was still so strong. The train lurched along.

I got off the train at Union Square and meandered south through the West Village occasionally looking skyward, staring off into the distance where the towers once stood. I made my way to the West Side Highway. I'm not sure what I was looking for that day, but when I reached the highway I found a woman standing by the road handing water to workers as they drove into and out of Ground Zero. "Wanna help?" she asked. For the next three hours, I handed out water until we ran out. The next day I went back and there were a few more people doing the same thing. Again I worked. By the third day the Red Cross had taken over.

Why did I keep going back into Manhattan? I had no real reason for being there. I was, I believe, compelled to confront the city. And I was also grieving and, through that confrontational process, trying to make some sense of what happened. By the simple act of standing there handing out water, I was trying to write a new narrative of building and creating, of grace in the wake of violence. Others held candlelight vigils, wrote poems, hugged neighbors, and prayed. At a shop down the street from my apartment, a group of Buddhist monks worked for several days constructing an intricate sand mandala, only to destroy it when they were done. I handed out water.

No big sacrifice. But I hold on to those days of volunteering and hold onto them still when I consider all the violence and hate that has come and continues to come in the wake of 9/11. Standing out there on the West Side Highway was my moment of stopping time, trying to understand what had happened so that I could move forward, building rather than destroying.

There are those calling on the State of South Carolina to take a similar pause and reopen the investigation of the Orangeburg Massacre (any federal investigation may result in double jeopardy, according to some legal experts). Bakari Sellers and others continue to present their legislation while some write letters to newspapers; still others wish to move forward out of concern that an investigation would perpetuate South Carolina's negative reputation. Recent events have not shed the best light on South Carolina—Mark Sanford's Argentine tryst, Joe Wilson's shouting out that the president is a liar, state senator Jake Knotts of Lexington's racist comment about Nikki Haley, and the ongoing conflict over the Confederate flag on the State House grounds, for example—have done little to improve the state's image. Bill Hine believes that an investigation should be about trying to understand what happened and not about pointing fingers. "The well intentioned attitude of many people is to sweep it under the rug because of the pain and anger such an investigation might unleash, especially in the short run. But many people also do not want an investigation because what transpired in Orangeburg is ugly—an ugly part of history. . . . But it's all history—like it or not. And all of us have a responsibility to try and understand that history." Unfortunately, history is never a clear statement of facts. It's an ongoing narrative always in flux—always open to exploration and interrogation.

A state-sanctioned investigation could open up a public conversation that has yet to happen and give South Carolina and Orangeburg a new redemptive story. It could also validate the claims of violence and the concerns the students had in 1968. But community leaders such as Zach Middleton and the students who organized the play are not dutifully waiting for the legislature or their elders to figure this one out. They are working now to effect change. And they are doing so by remembering their history. On Saturday, February 6, 2010, the Student March for Progress came up Russell Street past the remains of the All Star Bowling Lanes. Orangeburg policemen escorted a group of four or five dozen students and supporters, guarding intersections along the way, as they marched to Orangeburg City Hall. This is "the march that never happened"—the student march that was not allowed in 1968 when the city refused the students a permit, a march that might have eased tensions and allowed students to feel as though their demands were being heard and validated. Coincidently 2010 marked the fiftieth anniversary of a march in Orangeburg that led to hundreds of arrests. When Bill Hine reminded Zach Middleton of both of those facts, Middleton put the wheels in motion.

The march was about honoring those (like Middleton's great-uncle) who put their lives on the line during the civil rights movement, Middleton said, but it was also about changing the lived realities of State students in Orangeburg today. Like the students in 1968, Middleton has a list of demands. He wants Orangeburg to be more welcoming to students; he wants its businesses to demonstrate a greater willingness to hire students and its municipal government to ask them to serve on community committees; he wants zoning regulations that are advantageous not only for the North Road side of town but for the Whittaker Heights side, where many students live. He wants the community to recognize that his fellow students are a great resource. But he also has a list of demands for his fellow students. They need to register to vote in the community they are living in; they need to fill out the 2010 Census; they need to attend city and county council meetings; they need to lobby; they need to ask how they can be of help; they need to work to change the perception of Orangeburg for the better. Middleton doesn't want simply to point out what is wrong; he wants to find solutions.

There's a scene in *Taking a Stand* that made a deep impression on me. It comes after the shooting has taken place, back at the home of one of the law-enforcement officers involved. The officer, played by Bo McBratnie, is deeply disturbed by what he's seen. He comes home distraught and talking to himself. He grabs his telephone and slams it on the ground; anger and confusion have taken over. He can't believe he was involved in something so heinous. It's not what he signed up for. He pulls out his revolver and appears to be contemplating suicide. The audience gets quiet. There's a knock on the door, and the officer's wife wakes up and answers the door. It's the officer's superior, who tries to talk the officer out of shooting himself by telling him a story, one that he hopes he'll believe, one that will let him learn to live with himself. The superior says, "I heard these bullets whizzing by my head." The officer replies, "I didn't hear any shots. You didn't hear any shots. You need to leave."

Cleveland Sellers told me this scene moved him as well. The scene is fictional of course, but it speaks to the web of trauma and anger that violence can produce. Sellers said it makes sense that the play would include such a moment because it helps tell the hard truth of the Orangeburg Massacre: the dead and the injured weren't the only victims. "There were other victims," Sellers told me. "And for whatever reason, however they got involved and implicated, history has tied them together. They were trying to show that." Anytime something violent happens that disrupts the ordinary, it hurts us whether we are the perpetrators or the victims.

The scene in *Taking a Stand* continues, and again the officer's superior repeats, "They were armed. They had guns." The officer replies, "No, they didn't." The superior, as if trying to give the officer a story with which he can lie to himself, repeats, "*They had guns.*" On the night I went to the play, an audience member shouted out from the darkness of the auditorium in a voice that sounded a lot like John Stroman's: "*No, we didn't!*"

That voice crying out in the darkness is a reminder that those three— Smith, Hammond, and Middleton—are gone, but a bitterness remains, a taste of blood and bone. Because that past is so present in Orangeburg, because it is a lived reality for so many, writing this book was exceedingly difficult. In the first place, it was difficult because it was an encounter with violence. In the summer of 2009, after a week spent conducting interviews, I had a recurring dream, a nightmare really, over the course of three or four nights. In the dream I was walking down a hallway with many doors. Each time I opened a door I encountered one of the families of the three men who were killed. They were grieving and looking directly into my eyes. That dream reminded me that what happened in Orangeburg was also the tragedy of violent death—the violent deaths of three young people and the disruption of the lives of countless others. Whenever a young life is cut short anywhere, we should mourn. And yet we seem, as a culture, to be numb to violent acts when there are so many deaths around us.

My own ties to Orangeburg made this book difficult to research and write. It required me to speak to friends and family about something few wished to discuss, and it was even more difficult because it forced me to confront my own racism, my own prejudice, and my own history and privilege. It forced me to realize that we do have options when confronted with violence and racism, both structural and personal. Because of these hurdles, I have struggled throughout this book to make sense of the word "reconciliation." What does it really mean? One of the more unsettling ways to define the term is that it is a coming together, a restoration after a disagreement. And yet that would imply that there was some period of racial harmony in Orangeburg, in South Carolina, in the United States, prior to 1968.

We must, then, see that word from other angles. For me it means understanding how the tragedies and horrors, the massacres, of the past are present in all that we do, to borrow from James Baldwin. The past makes "the now," and we are all wrapped up in that "now" for better or worse. The next step, the work of reconciliation, is to account for that past and act positively in the present. We can move on and ignore the complications of the past; we can choose to persist in a state of paralysis; or we can make the choice to acknowledge the discord and work to understand from whence it comes. We can agree that the research, the learning, the conversation, will all be difficult (in part because we are learning about ourselves, our neighbors, our communities) but that the process is necessary for our survival. And this is the first step of that larger process. This is where we begin, where we begin a new narrative about how a community deals with loss, how a community responds to it, and how a community ultimately heals. This is where we start the work of reconciliation—by talking and listening, telling our different stories, writing them down together, learning and changing. This is how we write a new history. As Walt Whitman understood it, "reconciliation" requires patience and time and work. But in the end, he wrote, that word is as "beautiful as the sky," a sunrise across the horizon, a lone Carolina wren breaking the morning silence. In the distance another calls out. And then another. And another. And another.

# Orangeburg Massacre

Henry R. Smith          Samuel Hammond, Jr.          Delano B. Middleton

On February 8, 1968, 200 student protesters gathered on the campus of South Carolina State University. Students were protesting the segregation policies of the only bowling alley in town. The bowling alley refused admission to African Americans. After several days of escalating tension, students started a bonfire and held a vigil on the college's campus to protest.

In an effort to end the protest, State Trooper Officers fired live ammunition into the crowd of demonstrators, killing three unarmed students: Henry Smith, 20 yrs old; Samuel Hammond, 19 yrs old, both students at South Carolina State University; and Delano Middleton, a 17-year-old high school student. Twenty-seven other unarmed students were wounded.

The University's gymnasium, Smith-Hammond-Middleton Memorial Center, is named in memory of the three students, and a memorial square was erected on campus in their honor.

The Orangeburg Massacre was the first incident of its kind on an American university campus, but received relatively little media coverage. The shootings mark one of the least remembered chapters in U.S. Civil Rights history.

# EPILOGUE

I was careful about how I approached the people I interviewed for this book. Many of them were just as careful about talking with me, especially the first time we met. Even then, some didn't want me to use their names. One of them later changed his mind. That was Clyde Jeffcoat. After we'd established a level of trust, I asked him to reconsider his decision. He hesitated—it was a big request—and then agreed. He saw it as an opportunity, as did I, to model a way of addressing Orangeburg's past. He also saw it as a way to move forward in his own life.

When I mentioned Jeffcoat's decision to George Dean he wasn't surprised. Dean told me that he had recently noticed other white people beginning to "lay their burdens down." Dean, descendent of a minister, was referring to a line from a famous spiritual: "All my troubles will be over, / When I lay my burden down." By letting go of your troubles—either by claiming them or speaking them aloud, the song insists, you will be free. It's high time, Dean said. And it doesn't have to be a public affair. On the contrary sometimes these things happen privately and anonymously. For instance, he told me, one day a few years ago he was working at his haberdasher's store when a white man walked in. The man was wearing a nice suit, which is all, Dean told me, he could remember about the man's appearance. The man looked Dean in the eye and said, "George, we served in the Guard

Facing: S.C. State memorial to the young men killed on February 8, 1968 together. You might not remember me, but I remember you, and I remember that we didn't treat you fairly. And I'm here to tell you that I feel awful about that. And I'm also here to tell you that I thought you were so brave to endure what you endured." With that the man left, and Dean hasn't seen or heard from him since.

The serendipity of Dean's encounter mirrored one I had as I was finishing this project. Most of the people I interviewed came to me by way of suggestion, others were central figures, and I called or wrote to them myself, explained my project, and told them who I was. Several people, though, were contacted on my behalf by intermediaries—someone I'd already interviewed or in a few cases my parents. That's how I made contact with Angie Floyd Vaughn. I was visiting Orangeburg in early 2010, when my mother mentioned to me in passing that Angie Floyd Vaughn, Harry Floyd's daughter (or so she believed then), lived in our neighborhood. "I know her," she said, "and she's really a nice person. Just a neat person. I think you'd like her." My mother admitted that she'd been hesitant about telling me this, in part because she was hesitant about approaching Ms. Vaughn on my behalf—the only way, my mother thought, that Angie might consider speaking to me. I asked her if she'd be willing to do so now.

On one of her daily strolls through the neighborhood (maybe "stroll" isn't the right word because my mother walks fast), she was about to leave a note on Angie's front door when her husband opened it. My mother explained my project, and he said that she might speak with me; she might. I should call her, and he would give her fair warning. A week later, I called Angie. When we talked that evening on the phone, our conversation was awkward at first. After some hesitation, Angie suddenly let loose and in a rush of excitement, tried telling me everything she knew about what happened. First, she explained, she is not Harry Floyd's daughter. Too many people think that's the case, and it's been a thorn in her side most of her life. She is, however, Harry's niece. Her father, E. C. Floyd, owned the lunch counter at All Star Bowling Lanes, and her mother, Hannah, ran it. Angie spent a lot of time hanging around that lunch counter, she said. She used to ride her bike over there after school. When she paused to catch her breath, I suggested that we meet the next time I came to Orangeburg. I told her I don't do phone interviews—except when absolutely necessary—and that I prefer to see the person I'm talking to and get to know them a little. She liked that. We'd meet and go from there.

When Angie came over to my parent's house for our initial meeting, she was dressed casually, wearing sandals, a teal-green "Life is Good" T-shirt, and her birthstone hanging from a silver chain around her neck. She's thin, has straight brown hair, glasses, and a brilliant smile, which underscores her positive outlook. Indeed Angie came off as a bit crunchy, a bit hippy. Not at all what I expected, though I'm not sure what I expected. I offered her ice tea or water. She said she's fine. So we sat down on my parents' back porch and chat. I asked Angie if she would mind if I recorded our conversation. She clammed up a bit and said, "No, not yet." I told her that's fine. Let's just talk.

She told me that after 1968 her family stayed in Orangeburg. They never left. They worked here. Went to school here. Died here. Since then, no one has interviewed any members of the Floyd family about what happened, and the family hasn't gone out of their way to say anything either. She talked about her mother's declining health and how she had given up her own career to stay in Orangeburg and take care of her. She told me about her own struggles with what happened in 1968—how it was hard at times to be so connected to those events, how some people thought those three men were killed at the bowling alley. And she wondered whether or not it would be a good thing for me to talk to her mother—what good could come out of it? We kept talking. She mentioned other struggles, including her husband's injury that has prevented him from working. I could tell that she has a lot on her shoulders, but despite it all, she's not burdened by what life has thrown her way. My mother was right, I like Angie. I offered to write her mother a letter. Angie thought that was the best way to move forward.

The letter worked, and months later, on July 16, 2010, I was knocking on the backdoor of Hannah Floyd's modest ranch house. When the door opened, Angie greeted me with a smile and a hug. I walked into Hannah's kitchen. Angie introduced us. Hannah has well-coifed white hair. (She told me she'd just gotten her hair done.) She walked with a cane, not surprising given that she's eighty-seven years old. We shook hands and went into a living room with wood-paneled walls covered in family photographs. Angie suggested I sit close to Hannah so she could hear what I said.

We started by talking about her childhood, where she grew up and how she became connected to All Star Bowling Lanes. She grew up in Branchville and was working in a sewing room there when she met Harry Floyd, who eventually introduced her to his brother, Ernest Custeen, or E.C. They got married and moved to Orangeburg. In the late 1950s or early 1960s, Harry approached his brother about opening a lunch counter at All Star. Harry would run the lanes, and E.C. would be in charge of the lunch counter. The day-to-day management of the lunch counter eventually fell to Hannah, as E.C. also worked in beverage distribution.

For the most part, throughout the interview, Hannah's answers were short and sharp; at times she simply said, "No" or "I don't remember." She can't remember how the trouble began: she remembers that E.C. told Harry it would be good for business to integrate, but that Harry was resistant for some reason. She can't recall the details. But she can remember the night it all went down. "Two guys came in there one afternoon," Hannah said. "They were light-skinned, kind of. And they wanted to rent a lane. And the guy working over there, he rented the lane. And they were bowling and it wasn't too long before two black guys came in. And they wanted to bowl." They were told they couldn't bowl, that they had to be members. To which one of them replied while pointing at the "light-skinned" pair who'd entered just before them, "Well, those two down there aren't members. They go to State College."

The phone rang, interrupting Hannah's thought for a moment. I told her it was interesting that she told the story like that, because that's more or less what John Stroman says happened.

Angie jumped in, "You wanna hear something interesting? That call was for Harry Floyd."

"Do what?" Hannah asked.

"When I picked up the phone just now a message said, 'This call is for Harry Floyd. If he lives here, press 1. If he needs time to get to the phone, press whatever. If he doesn't live here, press 4.' Isn't that something?" Angie and I exchange glances from across the room—was that a coincidence, or was someone trying to tell us something?

Hannah resumed her story: that was the first night, Monday night, she said. The next night was the night of the melee. "The league started at seven," she explained. "And somebody called Harry and told him that they were forming at the end of the A&P and that they were going to come into the bowling alley." At that point, she said, Harry told his wife, Carolyn, to get the key and lock the front door. "Well she got the key and got to the door, but she couldn't lock it. They pushed the door and almost pushed her down, and they came in." At this point, Hannah was racing through her story. "Cleveland Sellers was the first one in," she said. "He was the main one. And he came to the counter. They lined the lunch counter and they beat on it."

"How did you know that was Cleveland Sellers?" I asked.

"I knew. . . . I had seen pictures of him."

Most of what happened next happened by the lanes or outside in the parking lot. When it was all said and done, she told me, the parking lot was a mess, and her car was all scratched up. But the car was the least of her worries.

Apparently rumors spread that her husband, E.C., was Harry. They received threatening phone calls and had strange cars parked in front of their house. The next day the police sent a car to their house and picked up her children from school. They all went to stay at her sister's house until things died down.

Hannah asked Angie to bring over several photos of Hannah and E.C. and Harry and Carolyn. Both Harry and E.C. had striking features—dark hair and angular faces. I can imagine how people might confuse the two men. But some people in Orangeburg assumed Hannah was Harry's wife for many years. "When I went to work at Belk's," Hannah said, "some people there thought I was the wife of the man that ran the bowling alley. And I said no."

"Was that hard?" I asked.

"Well, I didn't pay it that much attention because I knew I was innocent of it. I mean I had nothing against them." Despite her negative response to my question, I did get the feeling that Hannah Floyd thinks about what happened often. She seemed a bit nervous with all my questions at that point and wondered aloud if I'll use her name in my book. Angie pointed out that it would be difficult to disguise who she is given the nature of her story.

I asked, "Do y'all talk about this in your family at all?"

"Not really," Hannah said, "I just let it go."

"And do you think it bothered Harry?" I wondered.

Hannah was silent for a few seconds, pondering the question, and Angie jumped in. "He loved the bowling alley," she said, with an emphasis on "loved."

"Did he get beyond what happened there?" I asked.

"Yeah, I think he did," said Angie. "He had black friends and black people who worked for him. . . . The whole world just came to a different understanding."

I asked Hannah when Harry passed away, and she couldn't remember. Angie stood up and pulled down a weathered family Bible from bookshelf. Among its pages are obituaries clipped from the pages of the *Times and Democrat,* but Angie couldn't find Harry's. She suggested we take a trip to the cemetery just down the street. She could show me the family plot—that way I can get all of the dates I might need.

I followed Angie's Honda Civic down Broughton Street and through the cemetery gates. We parked, got out, and walked over to Harry's plot. We were both surprised to learn that his birthday was the next day—July 17. Again we exchanged looks. "That's strange," she said, "another sign?"

I laughed. "Maybe, maybe."

We walked over to stand in the shade of a scrawny dogwood—the only tree in this part of the cemetery. She brought up what her mother said about Cleveland Sellers, how she thought he was in the bowling alley that night because people said it must be him. I told her that a lot of whites at the time thought that he was the rabble rouser because that was one of the big stories in the press. Maybe, she said, but it seemed that a lot of whites believed exactly what they "heard" about black people. As she said this, out of the corner of my eye, I caught sight of a red-tail hawk swooping up and down with a couple of jays nipping at its wings. The hawk cried out. Angie noticed it too, and we both looked up for a moment as the birds rose and fell.

"Angie," I said, breaking the silence, "I want to ask you a question. I was wondering if you'd be interested in meeting someone who also has a close connection to the Orangeburg Massacre." I told her about Zachary Middleton, and she said, "Yes, I would." I told her I'll be in touch. "Thank you, thank you for doing this," she said. The hawk and jays continued their midair maneuvers.

We met at Four Moons, a new, sophisticated eatery in Orangeburg. The food is New American with a heaping dash of southern, and the decor is ultramodern, dark save for several elaborate blown-glass light fixtures. When I walked in, Zach was already sitting down and busy with his Blackberry. "How you doing Mr. Shuler?" he asked. He always calls me that, and it makes me feel like an old man.

"I'm only ten years older than you," I told him, laughing.

Bill Hine showed up shortly after me. He had asked if he could come along. The historian in him wanted to witness this event—the first time, as far as we know, that members from these two families have gotten together to talk about what happened in February 1968. Our waiter popped by. I ordered a sweet tea, Bill a beer, and Zach a water.

"You sure you don't want anything else," I asked.

"I'm fasting for nine days; it's part of a diet," he told us. "I want to lose some weight. It's harder for me now that I've graduated and I'm not playing football." (Zach's a determined guy and so I'm not surprised that he sat through the entire dinner without eating a bite.)

When Angie arrived, I could tell she was a little nervous; she had trouble pulling out her chair. When she finally sat down she repeatedly picked up

and put down her silverware. I suggested we go around the table and introduce ourselves. The routine was inelegant, awkward. It wasn't a good start. I
knew that this moment was bigger than me. I was nervous: what if we all got
into an argument? What if we didn't have anything to talk about? What if?
My mind raced.

But then we talked about the menu and food in general, and Zach shared
with Angie his plan to lose weight. Which led to a conversation about exer-
cising and how we all wish we could do more than we do. Zach asked Angie
about the stone hanging from the necklace she's wearing. Her birthstone, she
said. We told stories. Three of us ate. We talked about why we were there,
about what happened in 1968, about where Orangeburg is now, where the
world is now, and where it needs to go. We told stories. Angie shared what
she remembered from that week. She told us that she remembers being
scared. She told us that later on she learned how to do nails and worked in a
salon for many years. In fact, she said, "I used to go over to Maceo Nance's
house and do his wife's nails." Small world. Zach told us about how people
think he looks like his great-uncle. "Well you do," I said. He grinned. We
told stories.

When we left the restaurant and stepped out into the August heat, we all
shook hands. Zach and Angie started walking toward their cars, while Bill
asked me a question about my writing timeline. We were lost in our conversation when I noticed, about twenty feet away, Zach and Angie standing
close together, talking. I'm not sure what they were speaking about, but there
was a lot of nodding and gesturing. They were clearly listening to and responding to one another. They looked comfortable, content, in the glow of
the parking-lot light.

## WHO'S WHO

ANDERSON, JEROME. Pastor of New Mount Zion Baptist Church in Orangeburg.

BASS, JACK. Journalist and coauthor with Jack Nelson of *The Orangeburg Massacre* (1970); born in North, South Carolina.

BUTLER, DR. OSCAR. S.C. State dean of men at the time of the shootings.

CAMPBELL, DR. ROY. Orangeburg surgeon on call the night of the shootings.

COBB-HUNTER, GILDA. State representative from Orangeburg and executive director of CASA/Family Systems.

CORNWELL, CALHOUN. Author and director of *Taking a Stand*, a play about student involvement in the 1968 bowling alley protest and Orangeburg Massacre, premiered at S.C. State in February 2010.

DEAN, GEORGE. Orangeburg businessman and community leader, first African American in the South Carolina National Guard.

FLOYD, HARRY. Owner and manager of lanes at All Star Bowling Lane; passed away on July 12, 2002.

FRAMPTON, McLEOD. Minister at the traditionally white First Presbyterian Church during the 1960s and chair of the Orangeburg Human Relations Committee after the 1968 shootings.

FRIERSON, DR. HENRY. Surgeon called in to work at the Orangeburg hospital on the night of the shootings.

HAMMOND, SAMUEL. Eighteen-year-old South Carolina State College student, who died from gunshot wounds in his back.

HARTER, LEE. Current editor of the *Orangeburg Times and Democrat;* one of the organizers of Project Hope in the early 1990s.

HINE, WILLIAM C. "BILL." South Carolina State University professor of history, at South Carolina State and Kent State during the shootings at both college.

HODGES, JIM. South Carolina governor (1999–2003), expressed "regret" on behalf of the State of South Carolina for the events of February 1968.

HUGHES, CATHY. Current publisher of the *Orangeburg Times and Democrat.*

JEFFCOAT, CLYDE. One of the National Guardsmen on duty the night of the 1968 shootings.

LIVINGSTON, DEAN. Editor and publisher of the *Orangeburg Times and Democrat* in 1968 and an eyewitness to the shootings.

MARTIN, ROBERT. Judge who presided over the trial of the nine patrolmen in 1969 and the trial of the mob that lynched Willie Earle in 1947.

McGEE, JAMES. CEO of the Oaks retirement community and an ordained Methodist minister.

McMILLAN, NATE. Pastor of Petra Community Church in Orangeburg.

McNAIR, ROBERT E. South Carolina governor (1965–71) at the time of the shootings.

MIDDLETON, DELANO. High-school student shot in spine, thigh, wrist, and forearm; died in the Orangeburg Hospital after an intense effort to save his life.

MIDDLETON, EARL M. Long-time Orangeburg-area businessman, community organizer, politician; the first African American from Orangeburg to serve in the South Carolina House of Representatives (1975–85) post-Reconstruction; ran for the State Senate against Marshall Williams in 1984 and lost.

MIDDLETON, ZACHARY. Great-nephew of Delano Middleton and S.C. State University student body president in 2009–10.

MILLER, PAUL. Mayor of Orangeburg who issued an apology on behalf of the city of Orangeburg.

NANCE, M. MACEO, JR. Interim president at S.C. State in at the time of the shootings in February 1968, became president in June of that year and served until 1986.

NELSON, JACK. Journalist and coauthor with Jack Bass of *The Orangeburg Massacre* (1970).

NELSON, JAMES HERBERT. Pastor of St. Luke Presbyterian Church and noted civil rights activist.

NELSON, JOHNALEE. Wife of civil rights activist minister, James Herbert Nelson, and active community member.

PACE, J. C. Second in command of Seventh District of the South Carolina Highway Patrol on the night of the shooting, and my great-uncle.

PIERCE, HAZEL. Mother of Geraldyne Zimmerman and long-time Orangeburg-area civil rights activist.

SELLERS, CLEVELAND. Civil rights activist, historian, and current president of Voorhees College in Denmark, South Carolina. The only person convicted of any charges from the events that occurred in Orangeburg during February 5–8, 1968.

SHEALY, DAVID. Highway patrolman hit in the head by a board or banister thrown by students; an incident some witnesses claim may have triggered the confusion and subsequent shootings.

SHULER, ERNEST. A high school student who stopped the S.C. State College campus on the way home from work the night of February 8 and was shot in the foot.

SMITH, HENRY. A sophomore from Marion, South Carolina, killed from shots to his right torso and the left side of his neck.

SMITH, MIKE. Pastor of Orangeburg's St. Andrews United Methodist Church.

STOKES, CARL. An agent for SLED (State Law Enforcement Division) during the civil rights era and witness to the shootings.

STROM, J. P. Head of SLED during the civil rights era, worked directly under South Carolina governor Robert McNair.

STROMAN, JOHN. S.C. State College student and leader of the bowling alley protest.

SULTON, JIM. Orangeburg-area businessman and civil rights activist.

TILL, ASHLEY. Librarian in charge of S.C. State University archives.

TURNER, BENNER C. President of South Carolina State College (1950–67).

WILLIAMS, MARSHALL. Orangeburg lawyer and South Carolina state senator (1952–95).

WILLIAMS, MARY. Community activist and member of Orangeburg Human Relations Committee.

ZIMMERMAN, GERALDYNE. Community activist and instructor at S.C. State College.

# NOTES

## Introduction

4   *"A More Perfect Union"*   Obama speech, March 18, 2008.

5   *"Orangeburg Massacre"*   E-mail from Bass, May 15, 2010.

6   *"While Orangeburg"*   *Orangeburg Times and Democrat*, February 8, 2009.

7   *"It is ordinary people"*   Krog, *Country of My Skull*, 59.

    *"restorative justice"*   Tutu, *No Future without Forgiveness*, 55.

8   *"Y'all see"*   Bass and Nelson, *The Orangeburg Massacre*, 76.

9   *"Word over all"*   Whitman, "Reconciliation," *Poetry and Prose*, 453.

## Chapter 1. The Archive and the Archivist

After visiting the archives at South Carolina State, I submitted a Freedom of Information Act request to get my own copy of the FBI files. Three Denison University students—Ayesha Venkataraman, Gail Martineau, and Holly Burdorff—helped me to sort and organize them by date. The citations identify these files by report date.

14   *FBI reports from the immediate*   U.S. Department of Justice, Federal Bureau of Investigation report, February 9–10, 1968.

15   *"Pop! Pop!"*   Ibid., February 20, 1968.

    *"the sound of shots"*   Ibid., February 21, 1968.

    *"small arms fire or fireworks"*   Ibid., February 18, 1968.

    *Indeed one fireman*   Ibid., February 19, 1968.

16   *"explosions made by"*   Ibid., August 14–28, 1968.

    *A State security guard reported*   Ibid.

    *He went into the arms room*   Ibid., February 21, 1968.

    *Black Awareness Coordinate Committee (BACC)*   During the late 1960s, black power emerged as a political and social movement advocating black solidarity and community empowerment. Stokely Carmichael used the term after James Meredith was shot during the 1966 March against Fear. Black power emphasized the need for African Americans to develop their own communities and recognize their potential as a political force. Many white people believed "black power" to be a call for violent resistance. (Lauren Araiza helped me with language for this brief description.)

17  *"confidential source"* FBI report, September 21, 1970.

*One fourth of the National Guardsmen* Ibid., April 26–May 8, 1968.

*Weather records from that day* Ibid., August 14–28, 1968.

*a reporter from the* Baltimore Afro-American Ibid., August 27–30, 1968.

*If so, the patrolmen* Ibid., August 27–30, 1968.

*"acting under color"* FBI transcript of the trial of the highway patrolmen, May 19–27, 1969. All quotations from the trial come from this transcript unless attributed to another source.

19  *In all about thirty-six witnesses* Bass and Nelson, *The Orangeburg Massacre*, 171.

*"FBI crime lab expert"* Ibid., 144–45.

20  *A local photographer* Ibid., 144.

*The only real evidence* Ibid., 152.

*"did the defendants"* Ibid., 184–85.

*"systematic violence"* *State*, December 13, 1968.

*The parents of Hammond* Ibid., December 19, 1968.

22  *"But I'm most proud"* Compounding already complicated relations with the Orangeburg community, South Carolina State University has for years faced contentious relations between its board and administration as well as financial difficulties. For more information on recent difficulties facing the college, see Diane Knich, "Issues at State Persist 16 Years Later," *Charleston Post and Courier*, December 26, 2010.

### Chapter 2. The Bystander

31  *"In 1956 there were"* Edgar, *South Carolina*, 545.

32  *But Wannamaker was also* White, "The White Citizens' Council," 271.

*Reading through the FBI investigation* FBI report, August 14–28, 1968.

*Wade Hampton and Willington were poorly funded* For the 2009–10 school year, tuition at Orangeburg Preparatory Schools (OPS) was $3,684 for kindergarten, $5,088 for the first through fourth grades, and $5,220 for the fifth through twelfth grades. Dalton's tuition was $34,100, and Woodberry Forest was $30,750 (plus $10,250 room and board). Hammond School in Columbia, South Carolina, costs $13,990 per year for the ninth through twelfth grades with reduced tuitions for lower grades, but Hammond is not the norm in South Carolina. Many schools belonging to the South Carolina Independent School Association (SCISA) have tuitions on par with OPS. For example Jefferson Davis in Blackville and Robert E. Lee in Bishopville have tuitions in the mid–three thousands. (Information comes from each school's Web site.)

33  *In 2009 Orangeburg-Wilkinson* "Orangeburg-Wilkinson," www.schooldigger.com (accessed June 7, 2010).

*A year earlier Orangeburg Prep*   "Orangeburg Preparatory," ibid.

36  *"encouraged 'every white man in the area'"*   Williams, quoted in Bass and Poole, *The Palmetto State*, 94.

### Chapter 3. Garden City and Palmetto State

42  *"will not be difficult"*   Purry, "Proposals," 137
    *"Some perhaps"*   Ibid.
    *"if a house"*   Ibid.
    *"the Switzers must have"*   Salley, *History of Orangeburg*, 42.

47  *By 1720 there were*   Wood, *Black Majority*, 146.
    *"More than 40 percent"*   Weir, *Colonial South Carolina*, 173.
    *"The first object"*   Equiano, *Interesting Narrative*, 34.
    *"fears"*   Ibid., 34–42.
    *"a scene of horror"*   Ibid., 35.

48  *"Perhaps here"*   Weir, *Colonial South Carolina*, 196.
    *"There lives there"*   Tobler, "Description."
    *"the highest percentage"*   Edgar, *South Carolina*, 311.

49  *"created communities shaped"*   Littlefield, "Slavery," 879.
    *"at that time in the 1890s"*   Atkinson, *Orangeburg*, 11.

50  *"Notice to all whom"*   "Lynched as a Warning," *New York Times*, January 7, 1897.
    *"but thought nothing of it"*   *Orangeburg Times and Democrat*, January 13, 1897.

51  *"Politically and socially"*   Edgar, *South Carolina*, 407. It is important to remember that those who owned much before the war emerged a decade or so later still in fairly good shape (Morris-Crowther, "Economic Study of the Substantial Slaveholders," 313). Economic and political power was still in the hands of a few.
    *"At the turn of the century"*   Ibid., 448.
    *"Physical pain"*   Scarry, *The Body in Pain*, 4.
    *Between 1880 and 1947*   Moore, *Carnival of Blood*, 55.
    *Of these eleven*   Ibid., 205–10.

52  *"On last Wednesday"*   *Orangeburg Times and Democrat*, October 20, 1881.
    *In South Carolina many lynchings*   Moore, *Carnival of Blood*, 1.
    *Popular sentiment*   Ibid., 47.

53  *"The laws in South Carolina"*   *Orangeburg Times and Democrat*, January 24, 1931.

### Chapter 4. Spitting at Jim Crow

Earl Middleton's autobiography, written with Joy Barnes, was invaluable help to me when I was writing and thinking about Jim Crow in Orangeburg. I was fortunate to interview Mary Williams before she passed away on November 29, 2009, and Geraldyne Zimmerman before she passed away on April 10, 2011.

55  *"As I reflected"*  Middleton, *Knowing Who I Am,* 26.
56  *"was terrified"*  Ibid., 27.
*"cultural trauma"*  Eyerman, *Cultural Trauma,* 2.
57  *in 1920, 81 percent of white children*  Green and Fairey, *Orangeburg County,* 56.
59  *"The 'system' was the problem"*  Middleton, *Knowing Who I Am,* 27.
*"We had our church"*  Ibid., 64.
*"She carries forward"*  Ibid., 94.
67  *The South Carolina legislature established*  Edgar, *South Carolina,* 523.
Times and Democrat *published*  Lau, *Democracy Rising,* 215.
*organized a boycott*  Edgar, *South Carolina,* 527.
*Orangeburg white people*  White, "The White Citizens' Council," 261.
*The WCC attacked*  Ibid., 264.
*South Carolina State and Claflin College*  Watters and Rougeau, *Events at Orangeburg,* 31.
68  *Sulton was even able to hire*  White, "The White Citizens' Council," 266.
*In late 1955 several Orangeburg*  Middleton, *Knowing Who I Am,* 91.
69  *At the time Orangeburg County*  Watters and Rougeau, *Events at Orangeburg,* 29–30.

### Chapter 5. Eight Seconds of Holy Hell

75  *"Floyd and black power"*  Livingston, quoted in Watters and Rougeau, *Events at Orangeburg,* 28.
80  *"parleying"*  McLeod, quoted in Bass and Nelson, *The Orangeburg Massacre,* 43.
*This list made it clea*r  Ibid., 40–41.
81  *Eventually campus security*  Sellers, *River of No Return,* 215.
*He told the students he saw*  FBI report, February 15, 1968.
82  *"Someone in the crowd"*  Middleton, *Knowing Who I Am,* 100.
84  *"they could have arrested"*  Nance, quoted in Bass and Nelson, *The Orangeburg Massacre,* 61.
*"spin and crumple"*  Sellers, *River of No Return,* 218.
86  *The seventeen-year-old*  Bass and Nelson, *The Orangeburg Massacre,* 67.
*"A busy life"*  *Chicago Daily Defender,* February 13, 1968.

### Chapter 6. The State's Men

Captain J. C. Pace passed away on November 9, 2009.

93  *On Monday, February 5*  Stokes said they went to Orangeburg during the day. However, this does not correlate well with Stroman and Butler's version of events. Following their version, I would assume that Stokes and Strom went to Orangeburg after the students' first attempt to go in the bowling alley on Monday, February 5. However, there were other attempts by students to

go bowling the week before Stroman's protests. If that was the case, Poston may have been in contact with Strom for some time about what was happening at the bowling alley. Stokes believes this to be the case.

99    *"a central figure"*   Bass and Nelson, *The Orangeburg Massacre*, 27.

100   *"I saw"*   Pendarvis, quoted in the *Charlotte Observer*, February 11, 1968.

     *"insurgent agitator"*   FBI, *Prevention and Control*, 31.

     *"In regular"*   Ibid., 70.

     *If possible, law enforcement*   Ibid., 68.

     *"The old adage"*   Ibid., 82.

101   *"brutal or inhumane"*   Ibid., 87.

     *"The premature"*   Ibid., 82.

     *"1. Unload rifles"*   Ibid., 89.

     *"Prevention and control of civil"*   Ibid., 16.

     *"Any unjust denial"*   Ibid., 17.

     *"key groups"*   Ibid., 36.

     *"bitterness"*   Ibid., 40.

105   *"Lt. Pace of District 7"*   Taylor, quoted in Bass and Nelson, *The Orangeburg Massacre*, 236.

107   *"Unlike Kent State"*   Bass and Poole, *The Palmetto State*, 116.

108   *"exchange of gunfire"*   Bass and Nelson, *The Orangeburg Massacre*, 80; "News Summary," *New York Times*, February 10, 1968.

     *An AP photographer*   Bass and Nelson, *The Orangeburg Massacre*, 82; "2 Killed, 40 Hurt in Carolina Riot," *New York Times*, February 9, 1968.

     *"sparked by black power"*   *New York Times*, February 10, 1968.

     *The governor's representative*   Waters and Rougeau, *Events at Orangeburg*, 18.

     "blast of gunfire"   *New York Times*, February 9, 1968.

     *"several cars"*   *New York Times*, February 7, 1968.

     *"Even if a Klansman"*   *Chicago Daily Defender*, February 13, 1968.

     *"The Orangeburg Massacre"*   Ibid., February 12, 1968.

109   *Brown and SNCC*   Waters and Rougeau, *Events at Orangeburg*, 20.

     "the largest armed"   *Chicago Daily Defender*, February 15, 1968.

     *"paraded in protest"*   *Charlotte Observer*, February 13 and 16, 1968.

     *"extended period"*   *Chronicle of Higher Education*, February 26, 1968.

110   *"white alert teams"*   Ibid., March 11, 1968. The problems that sparked what happened that night were much deeper and more difficult to address than many of those white students imagined. Separate and unequal spheres persisted in the United States and in South Carolina. This fact was underscored a month later in the April 22, 1968, issue of the *Chronicle of Higher Education*, which published statistics on the number of black and white students at colleges and universities throughout the country. In South Carolina black students numbered 3 out of 2,196 at the Citadel; 47 out of 5,704 at Clemson; and 144 out of 11,984 at the University of South Carolina. Conversely only 3 of

1,449 students at State were white, and of the 817 students at Claflin College, only 1 was white.

110 *"James Hoagland was attacked"* *Los Angeles Times,* February 11, 1968.
*The United Klans* *Charlotte Observer,* February 11, 1968.
*"If the governor"* Ibid.
*"There was reckless"* Ibid.

111 *There's no famous tune* The Charleston-based band Soul Driven Train recently released a song called "Orangeburg" (2010). In addition there was a band out of Los Angeles called the Orangeburg Massacre. Their album *Moorea* (2006) includes a description of the 1968 shootings in the liner notes.
*Another image* Bass and Nelson, *The Orangeburg Massacre,* 118.

### Chapter 7. The Struggle

113 *"Negroes were still"* *Charlotte Observer,* March 27, 1968.
*Rev. I. DeQuincey Newman* *Charlotte Observer,* February 12 and 17, 1968.

114 *"go unpunished"* Bass and Nelson, *The Orangeburg Massacre,* 150.
*For example Charles DeFord* Ibid., 145.
*More important, the Department of Justice* Ibid., 151.
*They had previously told* Ibid., 144.
*"lack of enthusiasm"* Ibid., 148.
*"put aside"* McNair, qtd. in ibid., 155.

125 *In April 1969* See *New York Times,* April 29, 1969, and February 23, 1970.

### Chapter 8. "That thing hurt me"

131 *Cleveland Sellers acknowledged at the time* *Jet,* February 22, 1968.
*and in his memoir* Sellers, *River of No Return,* 209.

133 *He believes that his seizures are the result* For recent research on the relationship between traumatic injury and seizures, see Amit Agrawal et al., "Post-Traumatic Epilepsy: An Overview." *Clinical Neurology and Neurosurgery* 108, no. 5 (2006): 433–39; John F. Annegers, and Sharon Pasternak Coan, "The Risks of Epilepsy after Traumatic Brain Injury," *Seizure* 9, no. 7 (2000): 453–57.

134 *"I carry my rage"* Partnoy, "Survivor."

136 *Alfred Shuler* Linda Green, *South Carolina 1860 Agricultural Census;* see also Christine Weaver Shuler, *The History of the Shuler Family,* 42–43.

137 *Shuler also owned* 1860 U.S. Federal Census—Slave Schedules, Charleston County, St. James Goose Creek; Ancestry.com, www.ancestry.com (accessed January 4, 2011).
*In 1860* Orangeburg County's Historical Census Browser, University of Virginia Geospatial and Statistical Data Center, http://mapserver.lib.virginia.edu (accessed January 4, 2011).

*Chapter 9. "A different light than bitterness"*

I am indebted to Johnalee Nelson for sharing with me not only her time but also several binders of materials she has collected from her husband's career. These valuable materials were important for my research. Several discussions with Rev. Don Frampton, pastor St. Charles Avenue Presbyterian Church in New Orleans, helped me tell the story of his father.

144    *"The church is playing"*   Johnalee Nelson, personal records.

145    *"for the purposes"*   Records of the Session, 1964, First Presbyterian Church.
     *"No one shall be excluded"*   Ibid.

146    *"Unrest and violence"*   *New York Times,* February 11, 1968.
     *"We appeal"*   *Charlotte Observer,* February 11, 1968.
     *"it did not approve"*   Ibid., February 14, 1968.

153    *"First Corinthians"*   1 Cor. 13:4–7. In the New International Version verses 4 and 5 read: "Love is patient, love is kind. It does not envy, it does not boast, it is not proud. It does not dishonor others, it is not self-seeking, it is not easily angered, it keeps no record of wrongs."

154    *"W. E. B. Du Bois talks"*   Du Bois, *The Souls of Black Folks,* 10–11.

158    *The 2008 Uniform Crime Report*   These numbers come from the FBI's Uniform Crime Report database, www.fbi.gov/ucr/ucr.htm (accessed May 3, 2011).
     *"There is no way"*   Gilbert and Santaella, "Greyhound to Open New Location in Orangeburg."

*Chapter 10. Editing the Story*

169    *"'Physician, heal thyself'"*   "Orangeburg, Let Us Heal Ourselves," *Orangeburg Times and Democrat,* February 7, 1999.

171    *"traits of a grand"*   Derrida, "On Forgiveness," *On Cosmopolitanism and Forgiveness,* 29.

*Chapter 11. Black, White, and Green*

179    *Jafza initially planned*   McCue, "Orangeburg," 31.
     *One indicator*   "Dubai Sheikh Buys Aiken County Land."

180    *"What helps with test scores"*   Robinson's assertion that economics influences test scores is not off the mark. See Sharon E. Paulson and Gregory J. Marchant, "Background Variables, Levels of Aggregation, and Standardized Test Scores," *Education Policy Analysis Archives* 17, no. 2 (2009): 1–21. The relationship between academic achievement and socioeconomic status has been examined by many education researchers. See Selcuk R. Sirin,"Socioeconomic Status and Academic Achievement: A Meta-Analytic Review of Research," *Review of Educational Research* 75, no.3 (2005): 417–53. There is also some

evidence that a child's educational achievement is related to his or her parent's educational background. See Eric F. Dubow, Paul Boxer, and L. Rowell. "Long-Term Effects of Parents' Education on Children's Educational and Occupational Success," *Merrill-Palmer Quarterly* 55, no.3 (2009): 224–49.

187 *Amnesty International* "United Arab Emirates: Amnesty International Report 2009."
*Human Rights Watch* "Building Towers, Cheating Workers."

Chapter 12. New Narratives

198 *Playwright Calhoun Cornwell* For more on Cornwell and his play, see Healy, "A Time of Darkness Illuminated on the Stage."
199 *"History is a cloudy mirror"* Turner, *Here, Bullet,* 53.
200 *"Yet the river"* Dabbs, *The Southern Heritage,* 21.
*"Language is our common"* Manguel, *The City of Words,* 5.
*"why we are together"* Ibid., 8–9.
*"humanity is caught"* Tutu, *No Future without Forgiveness,* 31.
*"Somewhere deep"* Ibid., 264–65.
205 "beautiful as the sky" Whitman, "Reconciliation," *Poetry and Prose,* 453.

# BIBLIOGRAPHY

*Archives and Government Documents*

Federal Bureau of Investigation. "Orangeburg State College Shooting" files. U.S. Department of Justice, Federal Bureau of Investigation. Washington, D.C.

Orangeburg Historical Society, Orangeburg, South Carolina.

Records of the Session, First Presbyterian Church (USA), Orangeburg, South Carolina.

South Carolina State University Historical Collection and Archives, Miller F. Whittaker Library, South Carolina State University Library, Orangeburg, South Carolina.

South Caroliniana Library, University of South Carolina, Columbia, South Carolina.

*Published Sources*

Ackerman, Hugo S. *A Brief History of Orangeburg.* Columbia, S.C.: Home Federal Savings and Loan Association, 1970?

Aptheker, Herbert. *American Negro Slave Revolts.* 50th anniversary ed. New York: International Publishers, 1993.

Atkinson, Gene. *Orangeburg.* Images of America. Charleston, S.C.: Arcadia, 2001.

Ball, Edward. *Slaves in the Family.* New York: Ballantine, 1999.

Bass, Jack, and Jack Nelson. *The Orangeburg Massacre.* New York: World, 1970. Rev. ed. Macon, Ga.: Mercer University Press, 2002.

Bass, Jack, and W. Scott Poole. *The Palmetto State: The Making of Modern South Carolina.* Columbia: University of South Carolina Press, 2009.

Beacham, Frank. *Whitewash: A Southern Journey through Music, Mayhem, and Murder.* New York: Published by the author, 2002.

Berlin, Ira. *Many Thousands Gone: The First Two Centuries of Slavery in North America.* Cambridge, Mass.: Belknap Press of Harvard University Press, 1998.

*Black Magic.* Directed by Dan Klores. ESPN Films, 2008.

"Building Towers, Cheating Workers: Exploitation of Migrant Workers in the United Arab Emirates." *Human Rights Watch* 18 (November 11, 2006). http://www.hrw.org/en/reports/2006/11/11/building-towers-cheating-workers (accessed April 11, 2011).

Butler, Judith. *Precarious Life: The Powers of Mourning and Violence.* London & New York: Verso, 2004.

Dabbs, James McBride. *The Southern Heritage.* New York: Knopf, 1958.

Derrida, Jacques. *On Cosmopolitanism and Forgiveness.* London & New York: Routledge, 2001.

Du Bois, W. E. B. *The Souls of Black Folks.* New York: Norton, 1999.

"Dubai Sheikh Buys Aiken County Land." *Orangeburg Times and Democrat,* January 13, 2010.

Edgar, Walter. *South Carolina: A History.* Columbia: University of South Carolina Press, 1998.

Equiano, Olaudah. *The Interesting Narrative of the Life of Olaudah Equiano, or Gustavus Vassa the African.* Leeds: James Nichols, 1814. Republished in *The Classic Slave Narratives,* edited by Henry Louis Gates Jr., 1–182. New York: New American Library, 1987.

Eyerman, Ron. *Cultural Trauma: Slavery and the Formation of African American Identity.* Cambridge & New York: Cambridge University Press, 2001.

Federal Bureau of Investigation. *Prevention and Control of Mobs and Riots.* Washington, D.C.: Department of Justice, 1967.

Finnegan, Terence. "Lynching and Political Power in Mississippi and South Carolina." In *Under Sentence of Death: Lynching in the South,* edited by W. Fitzhugh Brundage, 189–218. Chapel Hill: University of North Carolina Press, 1997.

Gilbert, James, and Tony Santaella. "Greyhound to Open New Location in Orangeburg." WLTX Television, May 24, 2010. WLTX.com, May 14, 2010. http://www.wltx.com/news/story.aspx?storyid=87482 (accessed April 11, 2011).

Gobodo-Madikizela, Pumla. *A Human Being Died That Night: A South African Story of Forgiveness.* Boston: Houghton Mifflin, 2003.

Green, J. M., Jr., and W. F. Fairey Jr. *Orangeburg County: Economic and Social.* Columbia: Department of Rural Social Sciences, University of South Carolina, 1923.

Green, Linda L., comp. *South Carolina 1860 Agricultural Census.* Vol. 1. Westminister, Md.: Willow Bend Books, 2006.

Grose, Philip G. *South Carolina at the Brink: Robert McNair and the Politics of Civil Rights.* Columbia: University of South Carolina Press, 2006.

Hackney, Sheldon. "Southern Violence." *American Historical Review* 74 (February 1969): 906–25.

Hadden, Sally E. *Slave Patrols: Law and Violence in Virginia and the Carolinas.* Cambridge, Mass.: Harvard University Press, 2001.

Healy, Patrick. "A Time of Darkness Illuminated on the Stage." *New York Times,* October 20, 2010.

Hine, William C. "Civil Rights and Campus Wrongs: South Carolina State College Students Protest, 1955–1968." *South Carolina Historical Magazine* 97 (October 1996): 310–31.

———. "Orangeburg County." In *The South Carolina Encyclopedia,* edited by Walter Edgar, 686–88. Columbia: University of South Carolina Press, 2006.

Jones, Lewis P. *South Carolina: One of the Fifty States.* Orangeburg, S.C.: Sandlapper Publishing, 1985.

Kraybill, Donald B., Steven M. Nolt, and David L. Weaver-Zercher. *Amish Grace: How Forgiveness Transcended Tragedy.* San Francisco: Jossey-Bass, 2007.

Krog, Antjie. *Country of My Skull: Guilt, Sorrow, and the Limits of Forgiveness in the New South Africa.* New York: Three Rivers Press, 2000.

Lau, Peter F. *Democracy Rising: South Carolina and the Fight for Black Equality since 1865*. Lexington: University Press of Kentucky, 2006.

Littlefield, Daniel C. "Slavery." In *The South Carolina Encyclopedia*, edited by Walter Edgar, 877–80. Columbia: University of South Carolina Press, 2006.

Livingston, Dean B. *Yesteryears: A Newsman's Look Back at the Events and People Who Have Influenced the Histories of Orangeburg and Calhoun Counties*. Orangeburg, S.C.: Trippet Press, 2006.

Mack, Kibibi Voloria C. *Parlor Ladies and Ebony Drudges: African American Women, Class, and Work in a South Carolina Community*. Knoxville: University of Tennessee Press, 1999.

Magarell, Lisa, and Blaz Gutierrez. *Lessons in Truth-Seeking: International Experiences Informing United States Initiatives*. N.p.: International Center for Transitional Justice, 2006. http://www.ictj.org/static//Americas/Greensboro/Greensboro.confreport06 .pdf (accessed April 11, 2011).

Manguel, Alberto. *The City of Words*. Toronto: Anansi, 2007.

McCue, Dan. "Orangeburg: A County That Didn't Give Up." *SC Biz News*, Winter 2007, 30–32.

Middleton, Earl M., with Joy Barnes. *Knowing Who I Am: A Black Entrepreneur's Struggle and Success in the American South*. Columbia: University of South Carolina Press, 2008.

Miller, Adam David. *Ticket to Exile: A Memoir*. Berkeley, Calif.: Heyday Books, 2007.

Moore, John Hammond. *Carnival of Blood: Dueling, Lynching, and Murder in South Carolina, 1880–1920*. Columbia: University of South Carolina Press, 2006.

Moore, Winfred B., Jr., and Orville Vernon Burton, eds. *Toward the Meeting of the Waters: Currents in the Civil Rights Movement of South Carolina during the Twentieth Century*. Columbia: University of South Carolina Press, 2008.

Morris-Crowther, Jayne. "An Economic Study of the Substantial Slaveholders of Orangeburg County, 1860–1880." *South Carolina Historical Magazine* 86, no. 4 (1985): 296–314.

Obama, Barack. "A More Perfect Union." Constitution Center, Philadelphia, March 18, 2008. http://www.npr.org/templates/story/story.php?storyId=88478467 (accessed April 12, 2011).

"Orangeburg County Executive Summary—2009." Orangeburg County Development Commission. http://www.centralsc.org/shared/docs/0/10csca_orangeburg%20 executive%20summary%20updated%202009.pdf (accessed April 12, 2011).

Orwell, George. "Politics and the English Language" (1946). www.orwell.ru/library/ essays (accessed April 12, 2011).

Partnoy, Alicia. "Survivor." Translated by Richard Schaaf, Regina Kreger, and Alicia Partnoy. *Speaking of Faith: Laying the Dead to Rest*. http://speakingoffaith.publicra-dio.org (accessed April 12, 2011).

Purry, Peter [Jean-Pierre]. "Proposals by Mr. Peter Purry of Newfchatel" [written 1731]. In *Historical Collections of South Carolina*, edited by B. R. Carroll, 2:121–23. New York: Harper, 1836.

Rediker, Marcus. *The Slave Ship: A Human History.* New York: Viking, 2007.

Robeson, Elizabeth. "Orangeburg." In *The South Carolina Encyclopedia,* edited by Walter Edgar, 686. Columbia: University of South Carolina Press, 2006.

Roediger, David R. *How Race Survived U.S. History: From Settlement and Slavery to the Obama Phenomenon.* London & New York: Verso, 2008.

Salley, A. S., Jr. *History of Orangeburg County, South Carolina, from Its First Settlement to the Close of the Revolutionary War.* 1898. Reprint, Baltimore: Regional Publishing Company, 1978.

*Scarred Justice.* Directed by Bestor Cram and Judy Richardson. Northern Light Productions, 2009.

Scarry, Elaine. *The Body in Pain: The Making and Unmaking of the World.* New York: Oxford University Press, 1985.

Sellers, Cleveland, with Robert Terrell. *The River of No Return.* Jackson: University Press of Mississippi, 1990.

Shuler, Christine Weaver. *The History of the Shuler Family: A Genealogical Survey.* Savannah: Published by the author, 1974.

Shuler, Jack. *Calling Out Liberty: The Stono Slave Rebellion and the Universal Struggle for Human Rights.* Jackson: University Press of Mississippi, 2009.

"South Carolina Schools." Schooldigger.com. http://schooldigger.com (accessed June 7, 2010).

Tobler, John. "Description of Carolina," 1753. http://ogsgs.org/toblr.htm (accessed April 12, 2011).

Turner, Brian. *Here, Bullet.* Farmington, Maine: Alice James Books, 2005.

Tutu, Desmond. *No Future without Forgiveness.* New York: Doubleday, 1999.

"United Arab Emirates: Amnesty International Report 2009." Amnesty International. http://www.amnesty.org/en/region/uae/report-2009 (accessed April 12, 2011).

Walters, Ronald W. *The Price of Racial Reconciliation.* Ann Arbor: University of Michigan Press, 2008.

Watters, Pat, and Weldon Rougeau. *Events at Orangeburg: A Report Based on Study and Interviews in Orangeburg, South Carolina, in the Aftermath of Tragedy.* Atlanta: Southern Regional Council, 1968.

Weir, Robert M. *Colonial South Carolina: A History.* Columbia: University of South Carolina Press, 1997.

Weyeneth, Robert R. "The Power of Apology and the Process of Historical Reconciliation." *Public Historian* 23 (Summer 2001): 9–38.

*Where Do We Go from Here?* South Carolina Educational Television, 2000.

White, John W. "The White Citizens' Councils of Orangeburg County, South Carolina." In *Toward the Meeting of the Waters: Currents in the Civil Rights Movement of South Carolina during the Twentieth Century,* edited by Winfred B. Moore Jr. and Orville Vernon Burton, 261–73. Columbia: University of South Carolina Press, 2008.

Whitman, Walt. *Poetry and Prose.* New York: Library of America, 1996.

Wilkinson, Jeff. "In Race for Distribution Centers, Midlands Trails Other Regions." *State* (Columbia), February 7, 2010.

Williams, Cecil J. *Freedom & Justice: Four Decades of the Civil Rights Struggle as Seen by a Black Photographer of the Deep South.* Macon, Ga.: Mercer University Press, 1995.

Wood, Peter H. *Black Majority: Negroes in Colonial South Carolina from 1670 through the Stono Rebellion.* New York: Norton, 1975.

Wypijewski, JoAnn. "Black and Bruised." *New York Times Magazine,* February 1, 2004.

# INDEX